First World War

and Army of Occupation

War Diary

France, Belgium and Germany

40 DIVISION
Divisional Troops
Divisional Ammunition Column
8 March 1915 - 31 January 1919

WO95/2599/4

The Naval & Military Press Ltd
www.nmarchive.com
Published in association with The National Archives

Published by

The Naval & Military Press Ltd

Unit 10 Ridgewood Industrial Park,

Uckfield, East Sussex,

TN22 5QE England

Tel: +44 (0) 1825 749494

www.naval-military-press.com

www.nmarchive.com

This diary has been reprinted in facsimile from the original. Any imperfections are inevitably reproduced and the quality may fall short of modern type and cartographic standards.

Contents

Document type	Place/Title	Date From	Date To
Heading	WO95/2599/4		
Heading	40th Division 40th Divl Trench Mortar Btts Jly 1916-Jan 1919		
Miscellaneous	HQ 40th DA	04/08/1916	04/08/1916
War Diary		04/07/1916	20/07/1916
War Diary	Fouquieres	01/07/1916	13/07/1916
War Diary	Le Brebis	03/07/1916	03/07/1916
War Diary	Calonne	04/07/1916	13/07/1916
War Diary	Maroc	21/07/1916	23/07/1916
War Diary	Loos	24/07/1916	31/07/1916
War Diary	Maroc	03/07/1916	31/07/1916
Miscellaneous	Z/40 Trench Mortar Battery		
Miscellaneous			
War Diary	Colonne	13/07/1916	02/08/1916
War Diary	Loos	03/08/1916	03/08/1916
War Diary	Calonne	04/08/1916	05/08/1916
War Diary	Loos & Maroc	06/08/1916	06/08/1916
War Diary	Colonne	07/08/1916	31/08/1916
War Diary		01/08/1916	31/08/1916
War Diary	Loos	06/08/1916	08/08/1916
War Diary	Maroc	08/08/1916	16/08/1916
War Diary	Calonne	17/08/1916	24/08/1916
War Diary	Maroc	01/08/1916	31/08/1916
War Diary		01/08/1916	12/08/1916
War Diary	Colonne	13/08/1916	31/08/1916
War Diary	Maroc	01/09/1916	01/09/1916
War Diary	Loos	01/09/1916	01/09/1916
War Diary	Maroc	02/09/1916	02/09/1916
War Diary	Loos	02/09/1916	03/09/1916
War Diary	Maroc	04/09/1916	04/09/1916
War Diary	Loos	04/09/1916	06/09/1916
War Diary	Maroc	06/09/1916	07/09/1916
War Diary	Loos	07/09/1916	07/09/1916
War Diary	Maroc	08/09/1916	09/09/1916
War Diary	Loos	09/09/1916	10/09/1916
War Diary	Maroc	10/09/1916	11/09/1916
War Diary	Loos	11/09/1916	11/09/1916
War Diary	Maroc	12/09/1916	14/09/1916
War Diary	Loos	14/09/1916	14/09/1916
War Diary	Maroc	15/09/1916	15/09/1916
War Diary	Loos	15/09/1916	15/09/1916
War Diary	Maroc	16/09/1916	16/09/1916
War Diary	Loos	16/09/1916	16/09/1916
War Diary	Maroc	17/09/1916	17/09/1916
War Diary	Loos	17/09/1916	17/09/1916
War Diary	Maroc	18/09/1916	18/09/1916
War Diary	Loos	18/09/1916	18/09/1916
War Diary	Maroc	19/09/1916	19/09/1916
War Diary	Loos	19/09/1916	19/09/1916
War Diary	Maroc	20/09/1916	20/09/1916

War Diary	Loos	21/09/1916	21/09/1916
War Diary	Maroc	21/09/1916	24/09/1916
War Diary	Loos 14 Bis	24/09/1916	24/09/1916
War Diary	Maroc	25/09/1916	25/09/1916
War Diary	Maroc 14 Bis	25/09/1916	25/09/1916
War Diary	Maroc	26/09/1916	26/09/1916
War Diary	Loos 14 Bis	27/09/1916	27/09/1916
War Diary	Maroc		
War Diary	Loos 14 Bis		
War Diary	Maroc	28/09/1916	28/09/1916
War Diary	Loos 14 Bis	28/09/1916	28/09/1916
War Diary	Maroc	29/09/1916	29/09/1916
War Diary	Loos	29/09/1916	30/09/1916
War Diary	Maroc	30/09/1916	30/09/1916
War Diary	Loos 14 Bis	30/09/1916	30/09/1916
War Diary	Maroc	01/09/1916	30/09/1916
War Diary		01/09/1916	23/09/1916
War Diary	Loos	01/09/1916	30/09/1916
War Diary	Maroc	07/09/1916	30/09/1916
War Diary	Calonne	01/09/1916	02/09/1916
War Diary	Maroc	03/09/1916	22/09/1916
War Diary	14 Bis	23/09/1916	30/09/1916
War Diary	Maroc	01/10/1916	01/10/1916
War Diary	Loos 14 Bis	01/10/1916	01/10/1916
War Diary	Maroc	02/10/1916	02/10/1916
War Diary	Loos 14 Bis	02/10/1916	02/10/1916
War Diary	Maroc	03/10/1916	03/10/1916
War Diary	Loos 14 Bis	03/10/1916	03/10/1916
War Diary	Maroc	04/10/1916	04/10/1916
War Diary	Loos 14 Bis	04/10/1916	04/10/1916
War Diary	Maroc	05/10/1916	05/10/1916
War Diary	Loos 14 Bis	05/10/1916	05/10/1916
War Diary	Maroc	06/10/1916	06/10/1916
War Diary	Loos 14 Bis	06/10/1916	06/10/1916
War Diary	Maroc	07/10/1916	07/10/1916
War Diary	Loos 14 Bis	07/10/1916	07/10/1916
War Diary	Maroc	08/10/1916	08/10/1916
War Diary	Loos 14 Bis	08/10/1916	08/10/1916
War Diary	Maroc	09/10/1916	09/10/1916
War Diary	Loos 14 Bis	09/10/1916	12/10/1916
War Diary	Hulluch	12/10/1916	12/10/1916
War Diary	Loos 14 Bis	13/10/1916	13/10/1916
War Diary	Hulluch	13/10/1916	13/10/1916
War Diary	Loos 14 Bis	14/10/1916	14/10/1916
War Diary	Hulluch	14/10/1916	14/10/1916
War Diary	Loos 14 Bis	15/10/1916	15/10/1916
War Diary	Hulluch	15/10/1916	15/10/1916
War Diary	Loos	16/10/1916	16/10/1916
War Diary	Hulluch 14 Bis	16/10/1916	16/10/1916
War Diary	Loos 14 Bis	17/10/1916	17/10/1916
War Diary	Hulluch	17/10/1916	17/10/1916
War Diary	Loos 14 Bis	18/10/1916	18/10/1916
War Diary	Hulluch Loos 14 Bis	17/10/1916	18/10/1916
War Diary	Hulluch Loos	19/10/1916	19/10/1916
War Diary	Hulluch Loos 14 Bis	19/10/1916	19/10/1916
War Diary	Loos 14 Bis Hulluch	20/10/1916	20/10/1916

War Diary	Loos	21/10/1916	21/10/1916
War Diary	14 Bis	21/10/1916	21/10/1916
War Diary	Hulluch Loos	22/10/1916	22/10/1916
War Diary	14 Bis Hulluch Loos	23/10/1916	31/10/1916
War Diary	14 Bis Hulluch	31/10/1916	31/10/1916
War Diary	Maroc	06/10/1916	30/10/1916
War Diary	In The Field	01/10/1916	31/10/1916
War Diary	Loos	01/10/1916	31/10/1916
War Diary	Maroc	01/10/1916	09/10/1916
War Diary	Hulluch	11/10/1916	31/10/1916
War Diary	14 Bis	01/10/1916	31/10/1916
War Diary	Loos Hulluch 14 Bis	01/11/1916	30/11/1916
War Diary	Loos	01/11/1916	26/11/1916
War Diary	Loos	01/11/1916	30/11/1916
War Diary	Hulluch	01/11/1916	30/11/1916
War Diary	14 Bis	01/11/1916	30/11/1916
War Diary	Loos Hulluch 14 Bis	01/12/1916	31/12/1916
War Diary		28/12/1916	28/12/1916
War Diary	Field	01/12/1916	25/12/1916
War Diary	Loos	01/12/1916	09/12/1916
War Diary	Airaines	10/12/1916	31/12/1916
War Diary		04/12/1916	31/12/1916
War Diary	Hulluch	01/12/1916	31/12/1916
Miscellaneous	Z/40 Trench Mortar Battery 40th Division. December 1916		
War Diary	14 Bis	01/12/1916	04/12/1916
War Diary	In The Field	05/12/1916	31/12/1916
War Diary	Airaines	01/01/1917	31/01/1917
War Diary	Airaines	01/01/1917	10/01/1917
War Diary	Camp 21	11/01/1917	25/01/1917
War Diary	Chipilly	28/01/1917	28/01/1917
War Diary	Hurraines	01/01/1917	31/01/1917
Miscellaneous	Z/40 Trench Mortar Battery. 40th Div January 1917		
War Diary	Airaines	01/01/1917	10/01/1917
War Diary	Camp 20	11/01/1917	28/01/1917
War Diary	Chipilly	29/01/1917	09/02/1917
War Diary	Mausepas	09/02/1917	28/02/1917
War Diary	Chipilly	01/02/1917	28/02/1917
War Diary	Chipilly	27/02/1917	27/02/1917
War Diary	Chipilly	01/02/1917	28/02/1917
War Diary	Chipilly	01/02/1917	09/02/1917
War Diary	Maurepas	09/02/1917	10/02/1917
War Diary	Vaux En Amienois	01/02/1917	10/02/1917
War Diary	Maurepas Ravine	11/02/1917	24/02/1917
War Diary	Chipilly	25/02/1917	28/02/1917
War Diary		01/03/1917	31/03/1917
War Diary		29/03/1917	29/03/1917
War Diary	Mauipas (Camp 16.5)	01/03/1917	10/03/1917
War Diary	C Coy	10/03/1917	29/03/1917
War Diary	Field Bouchavesnes Clery	01/03/1917	31/03/1917
War Diary	Chipilly	01/03/1917	04/03/1917
War Diary	Maurepas	04/03/1917	08/03/1917
War Diary	Clery Sector	08/03/1917	09/03/1917
War Diary	In The Field Clory Sector	09/03/1917	13/03/1917
War Diary	Bethune Rd Sector	14/03/1917	18/03/1917
War Diary	Rist Billets Mair Hemwood	19/03/1917	31/03/1917

War Diary	Maurepas	01/03/1917	08/03/1917
War Diary	Hem Wood	08/03/1915	15/03/1915
War Diary	Vaevy	16/03/1917	26/03/1917
War Diary	Hem Wood	26/03/1917	31/03/1917
War Diary		01/04/1917	29/04/1917
War Diary	Hem Wood	01/04/1917	18/04/1917
War Diary	Moistous Fuis	19/04/1917	29/04/1917
War Diary	Caux-En-Aucerno	01/04/1917	09/04/1917
War Diary	Hem Wood	02/04/1917	19/04/1917
War Diary	Moislains Fuis	19/04/1917	19/04/1917
War Diary	Fuis	20/04/1917	30/04/1917
War Diary	Near Hem Wood	01/04/1917	11/04/1917
War Diary	Moislains	19/04/1917	19/04/1917
War Diary	Fins	20/04/1917	27/04/1917
War Diary	Earthworks Hem Wood	01/04/1917	30/04/1917
War Diary		01/05/1917	31/05/1917
War Diary	Fuis	01/05/1917	13/05/1917
War Diary	Gonnelieu	14/05/1917	31/05/1917
War Diary	Fins	01/05/1917	31/05/1917
War Diary		15/05/1917	25/05/1917
War Diary		01/06/1917	30/06/1917
War Diary		24/06/1917	24/06/1917
War Diary	Gonnelieu	01/06/1917	21/06/1917
Miscellaneous			
War Diary	Gonnelieu	26/06/1917	30/06/1917
War Diary	Fins	01/06/1917	30/06/1917
War Diary	Fins	01/06/1917	08/06/1917
War Diary	Vaux-En-Amienois	08/06/1917	20/06/1917
War Diary	Fins	20/06/1917	30/06/1917
War Diary	Fins	01/06/1917	22/06/1917
War Diary	Vaux-En-Amienois	22/06/1917	30/06/1917
War Diary		24/06/1917	24/06/1917
War Diary		01/07/1917	31/07/1917
War Diary	Gonnelieu	01/07/1917	31/07/1917
War Diary	Fins	01/07/1917	14/07/1917
War Diary	Fins	01/07/1917	31/07/1917
War Diary	Fins	23/07/1917	31/07/1917
War Diary	Fins	01/07/1917	31/07/1917
War Diary	Fins	01/07/1917	10/07/1917
War Diary	Villers Plouich	26/07/1917	26/07/1917
War Diary	Fins	01/07/1917	04/07/1917
War Diary		01/08/1917	31/08/1917
War Diary	Gouishried	01/08/1917	31/08/1917
War Diary	Gouishried	01/08/1917	14/08/1917
War Diary	Gonnelieu	01/08/1917	13/08/1917
War Diary	Gonnelieu	08/08/1917	14/08/1917
War Diary	Gonnelieu	17/08/1917	24/08/1917
War Diary	Gouzeaucourt	18/08/1917	22/08/1917
War Diary	Fins	01/08/1917	22/08/1917
War Diary	Welsh Ridge	22/08/1917	31/08/1917
War Diary	Fins	01/08/1917	01/08/1917
War Diary	Gonnelieu	17/08/1917	23/08/1917
War Diary	Villers Plouich	29/08/1917	29/08/1917
War Diary	Fins	01/08/1917	01/08/1917
War Diary	Gonnelieu	17/08/1917	30/09/1917
War Diary		01/09/1917	30/09/1917

War Diary	Gonnelieu	01/09/1917	30/09/1917
War Diary	Welsh Ridge Villers Plovich	01/09/1917	26/09/1917
War Diary	Fins	27/09/1917	27/09/1917
War Diary	Ligny St.	28/09/1917	28/09/1917
War Diary	Flochel	30/09/1917	30/09/1917
War Diary	Fins	01/09/1917	01/09/1917
War Diary	Villers Plouich	01/09/1917	12/09/1917
War Diary	Fins	16/09/1917	16/09/1917
War Diary	Villers Plouich	22/09/1917	24/09/1917
War Diary	Fins	24/09/1917	24/09/1917
War Diary	Gonnelieu	01/09/1917	12/09/1917
War Diary	Gonnelieu	09/09/1917	01/10/1917
War Diary	Fins Etc	13/10/1917	25/10/1917
War Diary	Peronne	26/10/1917	31/10/1917
War Diary	Gonnelieu	01/10/1917	24/10/1917
War Diary	Fuis Peronne	25/10/1917	25/10/1917
War Diary	Peronne	25/10/1917	31/10/1917
War Diary	Ligny St Flochel	01/10/1917	13/10/1917
War Diary	Fins	15/10/1917	16/10/1917
War Diary	Fins & Gonnelieu	17/10/1917	23/10/1917
War Diary	Fins	24/10/1917	25/10/1917
War Diary	Peronne	26/10/1917	31/10/1917
War Diary	Fins	01/10/1917	01/10/1917
War Diary	Villers Plouich	01/10/1917	22/10/1917
War Diary	Fins And Villers Plouich	24/10/1917	24/10/1917
War Diary	Fins	25/10/1917	25/10/1917
War Diary	Flamicourt	25/10/1917	25/10/1917
War Diary	Gonnelieu	01/10/1917	24/10/1917
War Diary	Peronne	25/10/1917	31/10/1917
War Diary	Gouzeaucourt Area	01/11/1917	23/11/1917
War Diary	Peronne Nurlu	01/11/1917	30/11/1917
War Diary	Nurlu	01/11/1917	08/11/1917
War Diary	Gouzeaucourt	08/11/1917	18/11/1917
War Diary	St Emilie	19/11/1917	19/11/1917
War Diary	Sart Farm	19/11/1917	20/11/1917
War Diary	St. Emilie	20/11/1917	21/11/1917
War Diary	Tombois Farm	21/11/1917	23/11/1917
War Diary	St Emilie	28/11/1917	28/11/1917
War Diary	Trescault	24/11/1917	30/11/1917
War Diary	Flamicourt Peronne	01/11/1917	01/11/1917
War Diary	Nurlu	02/11/1917	08/11/1917
War Diary	Gouzeaucourt	09/11/1917	18/11/1917
War Diary	Nurlu	20/11/1917	21/11/1917
War Diary	Haplincourt	22/11/1917	22/11/1917
War Diary	Trescault	23/11/1917	23/11/1917
War Diary	Peronne	01/11/1917	30/11/1917
War Diary	Trescault Neuville Bertincourt Hamlinecourt	01/12/1917	12/12/1917
War Diary	St, Weger	12/12/1917	31/12/1917
War Diary	Trescault	01/12/1917	11/12/1917
War Diary	St. Leger	12/12/1917	31/12/1917
War Diary	Trescault Neuville Bertincourt Hamlinecourt	01/12/1917	12/12/1917
War Diary	St Leger.	17/12/1917	17/12/1917
War Diary	St Leger	12/12/1917	16/12/1917
War Diary	Stray Res No Of	17/12/1917	17/12/1917
War Diary	Bullecourt	18/12/1917	25/12/1917
War Diary	Stray Res	27/12/1917	31/12/1917

War Diary	Bertincourt	01/12/1917	12/12/1917
War Diary	St Leger	13/12/1917	16/12/1917
War Diary	In The Line N of Bullecourt	17/12/1917	31/12/1917
War Diary	Neuville Trescourt Hamlincourt	01/12/1917	11/12/1917
War Diary	St Leger	12/12/1917	31/12/1917
War Diary	St. Leger And N. Of Bullecourt	01/01/1918	31/01/1918
War Diary	St. Leger And Croisilles	01/01/1918	31/01/1918
War Diary	St. Leger	01/01/1918	31/01/1918
War Diary	St. Leger And Croisilles	01/01/1918	31/01/1918
War Diary	Croisilles	01/01/1918	28/02/1918
War Diary	St. Leger		
War Diary	N. Of Bullecourt.		
War Diary	St. Leger	01/02/1918	28/02/1918
War Diary	N. Of Bullecourt	01/02/1918	28/02/1918
War Diary	St. Leger Croisilles	01/02/1918	22/02/1918
War Diary	Fontaine	25/02/1918	25/02/1918
War Diary	Croisilles	28/02/1918	28/02/1918
War Diary	St. Leger N Of Bullecourt	01/03/1918	04/03/1918
War Diary	Souastre	05/03/1918	07/03/1918
War Diary	Boyelles Souastre	08/03/1918	08/03/1918
War Diary	Boyelles Boiry St Martin	09/03/1918	20/03/1918
War Diary	Bucquoy Beaumetz Boisleux-Au-Mont. Monchy-Au-Bois	21/03/1918	27/03/1918
War Diary	Coullemont	27/03/1918	27/03/1918
War Diary	St. Leger	01/03/1918	05/03/1918
War Diary	Sanastre	05/03/1918	08/03/1918
War Diary	Boyelles	09/03/1918	24/03/1918
War Diary	Buegnoy	26/03/1918	26/03/1918
War Diary	Mouchy-Au-Bois Biannach	27/03/1918	29/03/1918
War Diary	St. Leger	01/03/1918	04/03/1918
War Diary	Souastre	05/05/1918	11/05/1918
War Diary	Boiry-St-Martin	12/03/1918	21/03/1918
War Diary	Bugquoy	22/03/1918	24/03/1918
War Diary	Monchy	25/03/1918	26/03/1918
War Diary	Coullemont	27/03/1918	31/05/1918
War Diary	Goullinch	01/04/1918	01/04/1918
War Diary	Suioncourt	02/04/1918	07/04/1918
War Diary	Goucy	08/04/1918	10/04/1918
War Diary	Rebeourche	16/04/1918	16/04/1918
War Diary	Berle-Au-Bois	20/04/1918	30/04/1918
War Diary	Simencourt	01/04/1918	01/04/1918
War Diary	Gouy-En-Artois	05/04/1918	05/04/1918
War Diary	Rebreuviette	11/04/1918	11/04/1918
War Diary	Berles-Au-Bois	16/04/1918	16/04/1918
War Diary	Saulty	26/04/1918	26/04/1918
War Diary	Abbeville	27/04/1918	27/04/1918
War Diary	Val Heureux Near Candas	29/04/1918	30/04/1918
War Diary		01/07/1918	25/07/1918
War Diary		05/07/1918	31/08/1918
War Diary	Wailly	01/09/1918	11/09/1918
War Diary	Qusaich	11/09/1918	28/09/1918
War Diary	Fontaine-Notre Dame	28/09/1918	30/09/1918
War Diary	Proville	01/10/1918	07/10/1918
War Diary	Niergnies	08/10/1918	08/10/1918
War Diary	Awoinot	09/10/1918	09/10/1918
War Diary	Cambrai (Rue De L'ardre)	10/10/1918	13/10/1918

War Diary	Proville	14/10/1918	15/10/1918
War Diary	Morchies	16/10/1918	16/10/1918
War Diary	La Motte	17/10/1918	17/10/1918
War Diary	Armentieres	18/10/1918	25/10/1918
War Diary	Lannoy	26/10/1918	31/10/1918
War Diary	Lannoy	01/11/1918	01/11/1918
War Diary	Warcoing And Pecq	06/11/1918	10/11/1918
War Diary	Warcoing	11/11/1918	14/11/1918
War Diary	Wambrechies	14/11/1918	31/01/1919

40TH DIVISION

40TH DIVL TRENCH MORTAR BTTS

JLY 1916-JAN 1919

DIVISIONAL
Date 4/8/16
No. 317/Bm
ARTILLERY

40th DIV. AMN. COL.
No. 103/47
Date 4/8/16
R. F. A.

~~Oc~~ HQ 40th DA /

Herewith copy of War diary for month of June.

June '16 to Mar '19
4/8/16

[signature]

LT-COLONEL, R.F.A.
COMDG. 40TH DIV. AMN. COL. R.F.A.

General Headquarters
3rd Echelon.

Forwarded

[signature] Lt Col RA

for Brig Genl
4.8.16. Commanding 40th Div Arty

July 1916 to Jan 1919

Instructions regarding War Diaries and Intelligence Summaries are contained in F. S. Regs., Part II. and the Staff Manual respectively. Title pages will be prepared in manuscript.

WAR DIARY
or
INTELLIGENCE SUMMARY.
(Erase heading not required.)

DTMO

40 Div. July

Army Form C. 2118.

D.T.M. officer.

X Y Z. T M Battery

Vol 1

Place	Date	Hour	Summary of Events and Information	Remarks and references to Appendices
	4-7-16		Emplacements left by 1st Div. found to be in a very bad state. One two-inch gun placed in emplacement originally occupied by V1 Trench Mortar Batty. V40 Trench Mortar Batty (late V1) withdrew their guns from Maroc Section & sent it to Calonne.	
	5-7-16		Fired 21 rounds French along enemy's line of trenches in right section. 11 rounds two-inch fired effectively in co-operation with French guns.	
	6-7-16		Two Stokes 4" Smoke Guns taken over from 1st Div. 26 rounds two-inch fired. Much damage done to enemy trenches in right section.	
	7-7-16		53 rounds French fired along enemy's front line trenches in right section. 33 rounds two-inch fired on German Salient in 20.B. Much damage done to houses one completely knocked down.	
	8-7-16		Fired 41 rounds on German Salient causing much damage around haunted house. Fired 15 rounds in left section at triangle and Crassier with good results.	
	9-7-16		In left section we fired 6 two-inch on triangle drawing retaliation.	

T2134. Wt. W708—776. 500000. 4/15. Sir J. C. & S.

Instructions regarding War Diaries and Intelligence Summaries are contained in F. S. Regs., Part II. and the Staff Manual respectively. Title pages will be prepared in manuscript.

WAR DIARY
or
INTELLIGENCE SUMMARY.
(Erase heading not required.)

Army Form C. 2118.

Place	Date	Hour	Summary of Events and Information	Remarks and references to Appendices
	10-7-16		In right Section we fired 52 rounds two-inch, silencing enemy Mortar which has now moved further South. 4 rounds French & 18 rounds two-inch fired in left Section on D. Crassier and triangle drawing heavy artillery retaliation on Support line.	
	11-7-16		In right Sub-section we fired 29 rounds two-inch obtaining several direct hits on supposed M.G. emplacement. 30 rounds fired by French guns around M.G. and T.M. positions. 2 rounds two-inch fired at Saphead on Northern Crassier.	
	12-7-16		On night of 12/13 July a house containing a French 58 M.M. Gun & bomb store was completely blown up - two Gunners - 43978 - J. Shannon, R.G.A., and 59227 - H. Brown, R.G.A., being killed. I visited the scene of the explosion & there was no remaining trace of any material. A crater approx. 60ft in diameter & 25ft deep was made by the explosion.	
	13-7-16		Fired 26 rounds two-inch in retaliation along German line from 4 Guns in right Section. In left Section 30 rounds fired at trenches on Crassier and the triangle. Considerable damage believed to have been caused in triangle.	

T2134. Wt. W708—776. 500000. 4/15. Sir J. C. & S.

Instructions regarding War Diaries and Intelligence Summaries are contained in F. S. Regs., Part II. and the Staff Manual respectively. Title pages will be prepared in manuscript.

WAR DIARY
or
INTELLIGENCE SUMMARY.
(Erase heading not required.)

Army Form C. 2118.

Place	Date	Hour	Summary of Events and Information	Remarks and references to Appendices
	14-7-16		56 rounds two-inch fired at German front line in left section. Firing on triangle drew artillery retaliation. 9 rounds two inch fired at enemy emplacement in right section.	
	15-7-16		Only 5 rounds two-inch fired. These silenced enemy Mortar and one bomb on detonating caused three separate explosions.	
	16-7-16		8 small French bombs fired around M.15.B.6.2. causing explosion in German lines.	
	17-7-16		Two-inch Guns fired on the right section front during the morning - 26 rounds with effect in M.20.B. Small bomb store believed hit.	
	18-7-16		Registering L'pool Street Guns on enemy's trenches south of Double Crassier.	
	19-7-16		40 rounds two-inch fired in left sector - target wire - some wire cut but many shots struck the front trench by mistake.	
	20-7-16		In right sector we fired 70 rounds from 3 two-inch Guns - one large explosion heard behind the enemy's lines. French Guns requested not to fire. 98 rounds fired in left sector from three guns at enemy wire & front line trenches which drew heavy retaliation. - Total rounds fired 168.	

T2134. Wt. W708–776. 500000. 4/15. Sir J. C. & S.

Army Form C. 2118.

Instructions regarding War Diaries and Intelligence Summaries are contained in F. S. Regs., Part II. and the Staff Manual respectively. Title pages will be prepared in manuscript.

WAR DIARY
or
INTELLIGENCE SUMMARY.
(Erase heading not required.)

Place	Date	Hour	Summary of Events and Information	Remarks and references to Appendices
	21-7-16		Y40 T.M. Batty. relieved by X40 Trench Mortar Batty. in the Maroc Section.	
	22-7-16		X40 T.M. Batty. took over emplacements from 16th Div. in Loos Section. Y40 T.M.B. again took over their own emplacements from X40 T.M.B. Headquarters Y40 T.M.B. M.3.C.6½.1.	
	23-7-16		Damaged house covering enemy emplacement. We fired 22 rounds on front line trench south of Double Crassier drawing artillery retaliation. Fired 14 French bombs doing damage to enemy wire in M.15.B.	
	24-7-16		Blew down a house causing very heavy retaliation from Guns & Mortars. Fired 40 rounds on trenches near Harts Crater in retaliation to enemy mortars. Casualties two wounded :- 103585- Gunner Edwards, R.F.A., and Gunner Day, 34193- R.F.A.	
	25-7-16		Our firing in morning caused Artillery & Trench Mortar retaliation. Fired 13 French bombs at wire, cutting it in several places.	
	26-7-16		Did damage to enemy's front line Enemy completely silenced.	
	27-7-16		Fired 15 rounds just South of Double Crassier drawing much retaliation.	
	28-7-16	9.50 am	Orders given that no firing be done by the French Guns until further orders.	
		2.35 pm	Orders given for the two French Guns to be brought out of the trenches at once.	

T2134. Wt. W708—776. 500000. 4/15. Sir J. C. & S.

Instructions regarding War Diaries and Intelligence Summaries are contained in F. S. Regs., Part II. and the Staff Manual respectively. Title pages will be prepared in manuscript.

WAR DIARY
or
INTELLIGENCE SUMMARY.
(Erase heading not required.)

Army Form C. 2118.

Place	Date	Hour	Summary of Events and Information	Remarks and references to Appendices
	28-7-16		New position being made in Boyau 10. 47 rounds fired doing much damage to enemy saps leading towards Seaforth Crater.	
	29-7-16		Fired 46 rounds at target in Cite Cornailles.	
	30-7-16		34 rounds fired silencing enemy Mortar at M.20.B.8844. Bomb recess in Calonne knocked in. Gun position evacuated.	
	31-7-16		41 rounds fired at enemy emplacements & second line trenches in Cite Cornailles doing much damage. Enemy Mortars in Calonne Section using Silencers.	

T2134. Wt. W708—776. 500000. 4/15. Sir J. C. & S.

1/

Instructions regarding War Diaries and Intelligence Summaries are contained in F. S. Regs., Part II. and the Staff Manual respectively. Title pages will be prepared in manuscript.

WAR DIARY
or
INTELLIGENCE SUMMARY
(Erase heading not required.)

V/40 TMB Vol 1

Army Form C. 2118.

V. 40. Trench Mortar Batty. 40th Division

~~Place~~	Date	Hour	Summary of Events and Information	Remarks and references to Appendices
	July		The first four days in July were the batteries last days in the first Division. The batty was then known as V.1, & was commanded by Lt. G. Harrington, the 2nd officer being 2/Lt. McHarland. It consisted of 65 men, which included N.C.O.s. The guns had not yet arrived, 9.45 trench howitzers, which are a copy of the French Heavy Mortar. The batty had previously done a three months course of training at the First Army school of mortars.	
			Until the heavy guns arrived, the batty worked the small 85 mm. French trench mortar. The bombs of these were of two kinds, viz: 90lbs & 40lbs, shaped like torpedoes, with varying charges. There was only one of these guns in action with the batty, & was in position in "Queen's Street" in the "Marne Sector".	
	July 1st		This gun cut the wire on the South side of the triangle, under 2/Lt. Harland, Lt. Harrington being on leave, preparatory to a raid on a large scale, by the K.R.R.'s. In this raid many Germans were captured, but the losses in killed & wounded were enormous on both sides. No firing was done, by the batty for the next three days.	
	July 4th		The 40th Division relieved the First Division, but V. 1. T.M. batty was left behind with the 40th; & took over 4, 85 mm. French T.M.s. in the Calonne Sector. Lt. Harrington returned from leave on that day.	

2353 Wt. W2544/1454 700,000 5/15 D. D. & L. A.D.S.S. Forms/C. 2118.

2./

Instructions regarding War Diaries and Intelligence Summaries are contained in F. S. Regs., Part II. and the Staff Manual respectively. Title pages will be prepared in manuscript.

WAR DIARY

or

INTELLIGENCE SUMMARY.

(*Erase heading not required.*)

Army Form C. 2118.

V. 40. Trench Mortar Batty 40th Div.

Place	Date	Hour	Summary of Events and Information	Remarks and references to Appendices
			One of these four guns was found to be damaged & out of action, & was sent, according to Ordnance. This was replaced by the gun from Queen Street. ~~[illegible]~~	
	July 5th-7th		Lt. Narrington stayed in the line & registered all four guns on points in the enemy's lines.	
	" 7th-8th		2/Lt. Harland relieved Lt. Narrington, the only firing allowed was retaliation for enemy's firing, a matter of from ten to twenty rounds per day.	
	July 9th		Another subaltern joined the battery, by the name of Delahaye a 2nd Lt., & took his place in the line two days later.	
	July 11th		Late in the evening, during a heavy "strafe" by the enemy's T.M.s, a German bomb fell right into the emplacement of No I. gun, & exploded all the ammunition. Nothing was left of the emplacement, house above it, or the two men, Grs. Brown & Shannon, who were the detachment, Gr. Terry of the same detachment had a narrow escape, having left the emplacement a few moments before. He saw the disaster & was himself thrown a distance of about twenty yards. Gunner Donahue of a reserve detachment has since been awarded the "Military Medal", for his courage in searching for the remains.	
	July 12th-17th		No special firing was allowed, except for retaliation.	

3/1

Instructions regarding War Diaries and Intelligence Summaries are contained in F. S. Regs., Part II. and the Staff Manual respectively. Title pages will be prepared in manuscript.

WAR DIARY
or
INTELLIGENCE SUMMARY.
(Erase heading not required.)

Army Form C. 2118.

V.40. Trench Mortar battery. 40th Div.

Place	Date	Hour	Summary of Events and Information	Remarks and references to Appendices
	July 17th.		V.40. battery handed over the guns to a battery of T.M.s formed from the 40th. Division. This battery was commanded by Lt. Henry R.F.A., with Lt. Platt R.F.A. & Lt. Horn 21st Middlesex as 2nd & 3rd. officers. Some difficulty arose as to the names of the two batteries, but was eventually settled by the new battery taking the title of W.40.	
	July 18th.		Major Hill, & Lt Captain Gaden the D.T.M.O.s, reconnoitred a position in Trous 5 Calonne, for the big 9.45 mortar, which had arrived for V.40.	
	July 19th		Lt. Harrington reconnoitered the position in Trous 5. & it was definitely settled that the emplacement should be made in the dynamo house.	
	July 20th.		Lt. Harland took up the working party & the building of the emplacement was started. This work was carried on night & day, by reliefs. A bomb recess was made in the building beside the emplacement & an underground tunnel was discovered which communicated with the men's cellar to the emplacement. This work continued, with the help of the R.E.s until August 6th.	

2353 Wt. W2544/1454 700,000 5/15 D. D. & L. A.D.S.S. Forms/C. 2118.

X. 40. Trench Mortar Battery

July 1916

X/40 TMB

Army Form C. 2118.

Instructions regarding War Diaries and Intelligence Summaries are contained in F. S. Regs., Part II. and the Staff Manual respectively. Title pages will be prepared in manuscript.

WAR DIARY
or
INTELLIGENCE SUMMARY.
(*Erase heading not required.*)

Place	Date	Hour	Summary of Events and Information	Remarks and references to Appendices
Fouquieres	1/7/16 to 3/7/16		Firing practice & gun drill were done. 3/7/16 Personnel left Fouquieres at 12.15 pm by G.S. wagons for Les Brebis taking guns & stores.	
Les Brebis	3/7/16		Arrived at about 1.30 pm dumped stores at mens billet. 5.30 pm personnel together with 4 guns complete, except beds, left for Calonne sector. Lt. H. Jones RGA together with half men of X40 stayed in this sector for instruction, whilst Lt. G A Rhodes and the remainder returned to Les Brebis.	
Calonne	4/7/16	11am	We took over from Y.1.T.M.B. emplacements and 4 beds. We handed over 4 of our beds at Les Brebis, and when they left with their stores they took, without permission, another of our new beds which had a special framing arc attached. The registrations handed over to us for the 4 emplacements were incomplete and of little value, and we had to re-register all the guns. Two of the gun beds handed over to us by the 1st Div were without pins securing howitzer to bed, and we had to take pins from our spare beds at Les Brebis.	

Cont^d

T2134. Wt. W708—776. 500000. 4/15. Sir J. C. & S.

X40. Trench Mortar Battery

Instructions regarding War Diaries and Intelligence Summaries are contained in F. S. Regs., Part II. and the Staff Manual respectively. Title pages will be prepared in manuscript.

WAR DIARY
or
INTELLIGENCE SUMMARY.

(*Erase heading not required.*)

July 1916

Army Form C. 2118.

Place	Date	Hour	Summary of Events and Information	Remarks and references to Appendices
Calonne Contd			The enemy were fairly quiet except that they sent over about a dozen minenwerfer shells near Marble Arch in reply to our registration shots. We did much damage to their front line at M 20 b.	
	5/7/16.		I reported to the O.C. Left Battalion and discussed disposition of emplacements on his front, in consequence, it was arranged to put a gun somewhere in communication Trench 231, this emplacement will have to be strong and have overhead cover as it is a heavily shelled area. From this emplacement we will be able to engage the enemy redoubt in region of M.15. b. 7 3.	
			We fired on communication Trenches leading to suspected enemy emplacement, we also fired on the emplacement M.20 b. 6.4 doing much damage. We also fired on and did much damage to enemy ~~emplacement~~ sap M.15. b. 8. 5½. and his front line at M. 15. b.	
	6/7/16		At 4 am we opened fire from B and C guns on enemy trenches at M. 20 b. and M. 21. a. also registered on a T. M. emplacement at M20. b 8. 6.	
			Contd –	

T2134. Wt. W708—776. 500000. 4/15. Sir J. C. & S.

X.40. Trench Mortar Battery. H1 July 1916.

WAR DIARY
or
INTELLIGENCE SUMMARY.
(Erase heading not required.)

Army Form C. 2118.

Instructions regarding War Diaries and Intelligence Summaries are contained in F. S. Regs., Part II. and the Staff Manual respectively. Title pages will be prepared in manuscript.

Place	Date	Hour	Summary of Events and Information	Remarks and references to Appendices
Calonne cont.	cont. 6/7/16		We got 3 direct hits on enemy earth works at M.20 b.8.6 and blew large gaps in it. We fired at intervals during the day from all guns; at about 10 pm enemy opened shell fire on us in region of B and C guns and the upper portion of howl above B gun was blown in; this did not affect the gun however and we stopped enemy fire after about half an hours engagement. "A" gun fired on house at M.20 b.6.3 which was suspected to be an alternative emplacement for enemy T.M. Lt Rhodes* (came up for instruction) together with remaining men of X.40. *Temporary cover for detachment at "A" gun was started, a party of the Welsh Regt were lent to us. Two Welsh miners also started tunnelling [illegible] at new emplacement at communication trench 231	
	7/7/16		"A" gun registered on "Hamster House" in enemy line, several shots were fired with good effect. Lt Rhodes took over at 11 am. Firing was continued at intervals throughout the day, 33 rounds in all being fired and much damage done to enemy lines at M.20. b and M.15. b.	

X.40 Trench Mortar Battery

WAR DIARY
or
INTELLIGENCE SUMMARY.
(Erase heading not required.)

July. 1916

Army Form C. 2118.

Instructions regarding War Diaries and Intelligence Summaries are contained in F. S. Regs., Part II. and the Staff Manual respectively. Title pages will be prepared in manuscript.

Place	Date	Hour	Summary of Events and Information	Remarks and references to Appendices
Calonne.	8/7/16		41 rounds fired during the day chiefly from "A" "B" and "C" guns at enemy lines at M.20.b. More damage was done to house at M.20 b.6.3. Enemy replied with rum jars around Marble Arch, but our mortars stopped them	
	9/7/16.		Enemy fairly quiet, we fired 20 rounds chiefly for registration purposes, and we cut some wire at M.15.b.	
			Lt Forrest took over from Lt Rhodes at 11.0 am.	
	10/7/16.		Enemy sent over several rum jars near "D" gun, and we replied & stopped them. 52 rounds were fired, all guns being in action, we did much damage at M.20.b to enemy support line, we got 2 direct hits on Enemy T.M emplacement M.20 b.8.6, which had been repaired, and one hit on emplacement at M.20.b.7½.5	
			"A" gun registered on Enemy minenwerfer emplacement at M.20 b.5.2. and got one direct hit on it, doing much damage.	
			The R.E. started work on our new emplacement at Railway Alley (231) and also at "A" gun.	
	11/7/16		Rounds fired 29. Lt. Rhodes took over. Much material damage	
			contd	

T2134. Wt. W708–776. 500000. 4/15. Sir J. C. & S.

X.40 Trench Mortar Battery A.A.

Instructions regarding War Diaries and Intelligence Summaries are contained in F. S. Regs., Part II. and the Staff Manual respectively. Title pages will be prepared in manuscript.

WAR DIARY *or* INTELLIGENCE SUMMARY.

(Erase heading not required.)

July 1916

Army Form C. 2118.

Place	Date	Hour	Summary of Events and Information	Remarks and references to Appendices
Calonne.	cont'd 11/7/16		done to enemy lines and wiring at M.20 b and at M.15.b. We silenced enemy mortars.	
	12/7/16		Rounds fired 24 chiefly in retaliation, much damage was done at M.20 b.	
			Lt Taylor and ½ of Z.40 T.M.B. arrived for instruction at 4.0 pm	
	13/7/16		Lt Taylor took over from ~~Mr~~ Lt Rhodes.	
	13 to 21st		X.40 were in rest billet at Les Brebis. Lectures, physical drill and some gun drill were given to the men.	
Maroc.	21/7/16		Lt Rhodes and ½ of X.40 Bty took over from Y.40 T.M.Bty at the Maroc Sector. Enemy very quiet and no rounds were fired, work proceeding on emplacements.	
	22/7/16		Lt Rhodes and his men from Liverpool St. and Frieze Alley Guns were withdrawn and took over from 16th division at Loos, gun was put in Chalk Quarry and manned, no rounds fired, very quiet	
	23/7/16		Some rounds fired in retaliation only, enemy mortar silenced, work at Queen St "dugout" proceeding well.	

T2134. Wt. W708—776. 500000. 4/15. Sir J. C. & S.

X 40 Trench Mortar Battery WAR DIARY or ~~INTELLIGENCE SUMMARY.~~ July 1916. Army Form C. 2118.

Instructions regarding War Diaries and Intelligence Summaries are contained in F. S. Regs., Part II. and the Staff Manual respectively. Title pages will be prepared in manuscript.

(Erase heading not required.)

Place	Date	Hour	Summary of Events and Information	Remarks and references to Appendices
Loos.	24/7/16		45. rounds fired, chiefly in retaliation, enemy sent over about 15 rum jars in region of South St and Chalk Pit, our fire effectively silenced them.	
	25/7/16		Lt. H. Forrest took over, 40 rounds fired, enemy quiet.	
	26/7/16.		Seaforth Alley Gun dug in and ready for action by 10.30. am Rounds fired 16. 6 of which were for registration, much damage done to enemy lines at M.5.c.	
			Enemy got direct hit on Quarry emplacement with an Aerial Dart and damaged elevating stand, we replaced elevating stand and gun was only out of action for about an hour.	
			"Dug out" at Queen St finished.	
	27/7/16		54 rounds fired, 6 for registration purposes. We did much damage to enemy saps behind Seaforth Crater, they retaliated with rum jars.	
			Enemy sent over some rum jars and Aerial torpedoes at Chalk Pit and South St, our fire silenced them and we did considerable damage to their lines at M.6.d.	
			Contd	

T2134. Wt. W708—776. 500000. 4/15. Sir J. C. & S.

X.40. Trench Mortar Battery

Instructions regarding War Diaries and Intelligence Summaries are contained in F. S. Regs., Part II. and the Staff Manual respectively. Title pages will be prepared in manuscript.

WAR DIARY
or
INTELLIGENCE SUMMARY.

(Erase heading not required.)

July 1916

Army Form C. 2118.

Place	Date	Hour	Summary of Events and Information	Remarks and references to Appendices
Loos.	Cont. 27/7/16		At M.5.c. we badly damaged enemy front line and supports, and cut some wire. Telephone communication established to "Dauntless" H.Qrs and "Duncan".	
	28/7/16		47 rounds fired, we damaged enemy front line at M.6.c – M.6.d and M.5.c, we also did much damage to enemy Saps behind Seaforth Crater. R.E. have started new emplacement at Pall Mall and are also finishing "dugout" at Seaforth Alley.	
	29/7/16		25. rounds fired in retaliation to about 14. rumjars, we did much damage to enemy support lines at M.6.d. and to Saps behind Harts' Crater. Gun bed dug in at Gordon Alley in order to fire on Cameron Crater where enemy are suspected to be mining.	
	30/7/16		Gun mounted at South St. Gordon Alley gun registered on Cameron Crater where we did much damage to enemy Saps. 13 rounds fired. Z Hom. Took over at 4.0 pm.	
	31/7/16		48 rounds fired chiefly in retaliation, much damage done to enemy lines near Harts' Crater and near Seaforth Crater.	

T2134. Wt. W708—776. 500000. 4/15. Sir J. C. & S.

1.

Instructions regarding War Diaries and Intelligence Summaries are contained in F. S. Regs., Part II. and the Staff Manual respectively. Title Pages will be prepared in manuscript.

WAR DIARY
or
INTELLIGENCE SUMMARY
(Erase heading not required.)

Y/40 TMB

Army Form. C. 2118

Y40 T.M.B.
July, 1916

Place	Date	Hour	Summary of Events and Information July.	Remarks and references to Appendices
Maroc	3.7.16.	6pm	Took over line from 1st Division. Two temporary emplacements, Queen Street and Middle Alley, and one emplacement in a fairly good condition at Freeze Alley.	
	4.7.16		No firing owing to bad state of emplacements. Discovered a new and better Trench Mortar emplacement in Queen Street, which was originally occupied by V.1 T.M. Btty.	
	5.7.16.		Commenced making an emplacement at T. Head 16 Off Middle Alley. Riveted sides of emplacement at Freeze Alley, and Middle Alley and continued work on Queen Street emplacement.	
	6.7.16		Moved Gun from emplacement handed over by the 1st Division at Corfax Road to Queen Street and placed bed in position there. (Relieved by right half Battery) at 11.am). At 5 pm commenced registering Freeze Alley Gun. Carried Bombs from Coyka Street to Queen Street emplacement.	
	7.7.16		Continued the work on emplacements and registered Freeze and Middle Alley guns accurately, successfully obtaining four direct hits on the Enemy Front line trench. No Retaliation.	
	8.7.16		Continued improving emplacements. Successfully dislodged a sniper on the slope of the Double Crassier. Obtained successful hits from Freeze Alley Gun, and Registered Queen Street Gun.	
	9.7.16.	9.30am	Successfully ranged Enemy's wire in Northern Crassier causing much damage. (Relieved at noon by Left half Battery.	
		2pm.	Fired 10 successful rounds at enemy's trenches in triangle. Artillery Retaliation.	

2.

Instructions regarding War Diaries and Intelligence Summaries are contained in F. S. Regs., Part II. and the Staff Manual respectively. Title Pages will be prepared in manuscript.

WAR DIARY
or
INTELLIGENCE SUMMARY
(Erase heading not required.)

Army Form. C. 2118

Place	Date	Hour	Summary of Events and Information	Remarks and references to Appendices
Maroc	10-7-16.	10 a.m. 5.15 p.m.	Six effective rounds at Enemy's wire and trenches from Frieze Alley Gun. Fired at suspected M.G. emplacement on Northern Crassier. After firing 4 Shot, three explosions followed. Wood and Debris seen to go high up in the air.	
	11.7.16.		Unable to fire owing to our Infantry having large working parties. Replenished Bomb Stores at Guns.	
	12.7.16	10. am.	Relieved by Right half Battery. Improved and strengthened Middle Alley Dug Out. Fired six Rounds from Frieze Alley Gun. Enemy's Artillery Retaliated heavily. Supervised re-setting of Queen Street Gun.	
	13.7.16		Repaired Frieze Alley emplacement, damage caused by recent firing. (Shock of discharge.) Obtained a direct hit on enemy's sap on Northern Crassier. Planks and boards were thrown into the air. Enemy retaliated with Trench Mortars from the Vicinity of the Triangle.	
	14.7.16.	2 p.m.	Fired 15 rounds from Frieze Alley Gun at Enemy's trench and wire; successfully cutting wire and obtaining four direct hits in trench. In the forenoon enemy heavily shelled our saps and double crassier. Obtained several effective shots from Queen Street Gun at 2.7 pm. Enemy's Artillery Retaliated. Enemy's Field Guns heavily shelled our Trenches between Loos and Double Crassier	

3.

Instructions regarding War Diaries and Intelligence Summaries are contained in F. S. Regs., Part II. and the Staff Manual respectively. Title Pages will be prepared in manuscript.

WAR DIARY
or
INTELLIGENCE SUMMARY

(Erase heading not required.)

Army Form. C. 2118

Place	Date	Hour	Summary of Events and Information	Remarks and references to Appendices
Maroc	15.7.16.	9. am.	Fired of effective rounds from Freize Alley Gun. No Retaliation. Rifle Mechanism of Middle Alley Gun Blown out, tearing threads of Howitzer Gun out of action. Enemy heavily shelled Queen Street. Our Queen St. Gun retaliated on Triangle. (11. am Relieved by left half Battery).	
	~~15.7.16~~	11.30 am.	Found new sight for emplacement in Liverpool Street.	
	16.7.16.		Working Party ~~on~~ Making Liverpool Street emplacement.	
		7.30 pm.	Emplacement completed.	
	17.7.16.		Bed Placed in position at Liverpool Street; ammunition carried to Liverpool Street from Middle Alley. Continued firing from Queen Street and Freize Alley.	
	18.7.16.	10.30 am.	Commenced registering Liverpool Street Gun on Enemys Trenches South of Double Crassier. (Relieved by Right half Battery at 2 pm).	
	19.7.16.	2.0 pm.	Commenced cutting wire for infantry from Liverpool Street and Freize Alley Guns, with very good results. Considerable damage done to Enemys trenches in Triangle by our Queen Street Gun. Heavy retaliation followed.	
	20.7.16.	5.30 pm.	Opened a heavy bombardment on Enemys trenches and wire causing considerable damage, firing in all 98 Rounds from the three Guns.	
		10.30 pm.	Our Artillery opened a heavy Bombardment on the Enemys trenches which lasted until about 1. 3 am. Commenced Laying telephone wire from Freize Alley Gun to new O.P. at 9 am.	

4

Instructions regarding War Diaries and Intelligence Summaries are contained in F. S. Regs., Part II. and the Staff Manual respectively. Title Pages will be prepared in manuscript.

WAR DIARY
or
INTELLIGENCE SUMMARY
(Erase heading not required.)

Army Form. C. 2118

Place	Date	Hour	Summary of Events and Information	Remarks and references to Appendices
Maroc	21.7.16	1.30pm	Relieved by X.40 Battery.	
	22.7.16		Our left half Battery relieved X.40 owing to the inclusion of Loos in the Divisional Front. X 40 Battery proceeded to Loos. Our Queen Street Gun handed over to X.40 Battery and included in the Loos Sector.	
	23.7.16		Removed our Headquarters from Maroc to M.3C 6½.1. O.P. at M.3C 6½.1 Completed and obtained telephone communications with Freize Alley Gun from new O.P. Obtained several direct hits from Freize Alley Gun on Enemys front line. Enemys Artillery retaliated unsuccessfully.	
	24.7.16	7 am.	Relaid Liverpool Street Gun. Obtained very successful firing from Liverpool Street and Freize Alley Guns. Enemy Retaliated. Commenced running wire from Freize Alley to Liverpool Street Gun along Support Trench. Insufficient wire to Complete.	
	25.7.16		Firing done in Morning from Both Guns. Heavy Artillery Retaliation followed on "C" Company, A & S.H. and on our Guns. Called for R.A. Retaliation. Enemy transferred fire more north.	
		2pm.	Relieved by Right Half Battery. Spent remainder of Day replenishing Ammunition supplies at Guns.	

5.

Instructions regarding War Diaries and Intelligence Summaries are contained in F. S. Regs., Part II. and the Staff Manual respectively. Title Pages will be prepared in manuscript.

WAR DIARY
or
INTELLIGENCE SUMMARY
(Erase heading not required.)

Army Form. C. 2118

Place	Date	Hour	Summary of Events and Information	Remarks and references to Appendices
Maroc	26.7.16.	8. am	Continued replenishing Bomb stores. Found large Dump of Ammunition in Dug out in Boyeau 10, and also between Boyeaux 7 and 9. Transferred same to Treize Alley Gun. Continued firing at intervals throughout the day. No Retaliation.	
	27.7.16		Continued firing successfully from Liverpool Street Gun: considerable damage done to enemy's trenches. Enemy retaliated heavily with Mortars and Artillery. Unable to fire from Treize Alley Gun owing to bed having jumped. Continued work throughout day repairing and improving emplacement and made a firm bed for Gun with sandbags and planks.	
		8 pm	Completed repairing emplacement.	
	28.7.16		Continued firing from both Guns inflicting considerable damage on Enemy's Firing and support trenches. Enemy's Artillery and Mortars retaliated heavily.	
	29.7.16		Fired 50 Rounds on Enemy's Trenches from the two Guns obtaining at least 20 Direct hits. Enemy's retaliated with Mortars and Artillery heavily. Took S.T.M.O. to site for new emplacement between Boyeaux 7 and 9. Visited new emplacement at Boyeau 231 ~~where~~ ~~any~~ which Engineers are making	
		11.55 pm.	In co-operation with our R.A., Stokes Guns, and Infantry with Rifle Grenades, we heavily Bombarded the Enemy's trenches South of the Double Crassier for 20 minutes and successfully silenced their Mortars.	

6.

Instructions regarding War Diaries and Intelligence Summaries are contained in F. S. Regs., Part II. and the Staff Manual respectively. Title Pages will be prepared in manuscript.

WAR DIARY
or
INTELLIGENCE SUMMARY
(Erase heading not required.)

Army Form. C. 2118

Place	Date	Hour	Summary of Events and Information	Remarks and references to Appendices
Maroc.	30/7/16	9.30 am	Continued firing from Both Guns. No Retaliation from Enemy Mortars South of Double Crassier after previous nights Bombardment. Rel-	
		pm	Relieved by left half Battery. Remainder of day spent carrying beams wire-netting, sand bags, &c to Guns for overhead cover.	
	31.7.16.		Firing continued ~~from~~ on Enemy's front line and wire. Commenced work on site for new Emplacement between Boyaux 7 and 9. Engineers working on new emplacement in Boyaux 231.	

R. T. Lettsom. 2/Lt.
OC 'Y.40'
T.M.B

Instructions regarding War Diaries and Intelligence Summaries are contained in F. S. Regs., Part II. and the Staff Manual respectively. Title pages will be prepared in manuscript.

WAR DIARY

~~or~~

~~INTELLIGENCE~~ SUMMARY.

(Erase heading not required.)

Army Form C. 2118.

Z/40 TMB

Place	Date	Hour	Summary of Events and Information	Remarks and references to Appendices
			Z/40 Trench Mortar Battery	
			July 1916	
			Oscar P. Taylor Lieut O.C.	

T2134. Wt. W708–776. 500000. 4/15. Sir J. C. & S.

Instructions regarding War Diaries and Intelligence Summaries are contained in F. S. Regs., Part II. and the Staff Manual respectively. Title pages will be prepared in manuscript.

WAR DIARY
or
INTELLIGENCE SUMMARY.
(Erase heading not required.)

Army Form C. 2118.

Place	Date	Hour	Summary of Events and Information	Remarks and references to Appendices
			Officers Lieut C. P. Taylor Genl List (In Command)	
			2nd Lieut R. G. Hammond from 188 Bde R F A (2nd in Comm.)	
			Each half of the battery goes in for four days & comes out for four, starting with No 1 half under Lt Taylor.	

Instructions regarding War Diaries and Intelligence Summaries are contained in F. S. Regs., Part II. and the Staff Manual respectively. Title pages will be prepared in manuscript.

WAR DIARY
or
INTELLIGENCE SUMMARY.
(Erase heading not required.)

Army Form C. 2118.

Place	Date	Hour	Summary of Events and Information	Remarks and references to Appendices
	1916			
Calonne	13 July	2pm	Relieved X-40 Battery in Right Sector. To-day has been spent in making sundry registrations. Hun mortars fairly active, but always cease upon our retaliating	
	14 July	8am	Several 4.2's dropped near A gun. No damage done	
			Visited by Major Dodgson, who went round the gun positions	
			Registered on a Sniper's post at M 20 b 35.35. Blew in back of trench behind it, but did not hit actual plate. Reserve gun arrived at Bomb Store	
	15 July	am 2.30	Moved D gun out & sent back to Le Brebis, also the Reserve gun which had arrived previous evening at orders of DTMO Leaves me with only 3 guns.	
		am 11.30	Observed three explosions in enemy front line at about M 20 b 55.40, ~~that~~ ~~[illegible]~~ from one of our bombs. Must have hit ammunition or grenade store. Sandbags, boards etc flew into the air.	
			To-night, we silenced enemy mortars.	
	16 July		Very quiet day. Bosche mortars quiet, and as a heavy Infantry party is digging a new emplacement at A gun & a Tunnelling Coy of R.E. digging out a mine-shaft near my B & C guns, I am firing only	

T2134. Wt. W708-776. 500000. 4/15. Sir J. C. & S.

Instructions regarding War Diaries and Intelligence Summaries are contained in F. S. Regs., Part II. and the Staff Manual respectively. Title pages will be prepared in manuscript.

WAR DIARY
or
INTELLIGENCE SUMMARY.
(Erase heading not required.)

Army Form C. 2118.

Place	Date	Hour	Summary of Events and Information	Remarks and references to Appendices
			in retaliation at their request	
	17 July	11 am	Arranged a strafe which was not very successful, as it was raining & very misty & hampered Observation of Fire. A gun was slow & as the bed was pumping badly, had to be wholly relaid after each shot & only got 4 off. B was better with 22, & C blew out the rifle mechanism after 2 shots. However, the shooting was excellent. Several dropped right in enemy communication trench from M 20 b 30 32 to M 20 b 48 18, completely filling it up. Also after one of our explosions, ~~there was~~ a number of small explosions occurred in the air over the enemy line, which were probably ~~bombs~~ hand grenades, blown up by our bomb into the air, then to explode.	
		2 pm	No 1 Section relieved by No 2 under 2nd Lieut R G Hammond RFA. Emplacement at A gun to be completed in four more days, at present they have reached the level for the dug-out at both entrances. In the night we retaliated twice, and the enemy mortars ceased firing	

Instructions regarding War Diaries and Intelligence Summaries are contained in F. S. Regs., Part II. and the Staff Manual respectively. Title pages will be prepared in manuscript.

WAR DIARY
or
~~INTELLIGENCE SUMMARY~~.
(Erase heading not required.)

Army Form C. 2118.

Place	Date	Hour	Summary of Events and Information	Remarks and references to Appendices
	July 1916			
Tuesday	18th		This morning we laid wires from B & C guns to the Artillery O.P.	
		4-5pm	C gun fired 15 shots at enemy wire & front line, but had to cease firing owing to dirt falling in & finally stopped when fuze key broke.	
		5-15 – 6.30pm	B gun fired 18 shots on German front line. Several direct hits in trenches were observed. During the night, the usual retaliation took place.	
Wednesday	19th		R.E. Signals connected A gun to O.P. & O.P. to dug-out. We shall thus be in touch with all guns when we have two more telephones. The Artillery O.P. is out of use for several days owing to work going on in strengthening it. In the night we fired from 12.15 to 12.45 in conjunction with the Artillery	
Thursday	20th		This morning, A gun fired 10 shots at a plate put up by a working party yesterday evening. It was found impossible to obtain sufficient right traverse. <u>N.B.</u> The new emplacement here should be made to face more right & C gun should be further left, except when concentrated fire is required. This afternoon, all guns were active in firing at suspected emplacements & houses where working parties have been seen. During the night, we replied vigorously to the enemy, who was unusually active.	

T2134. Wt. W708—776. 500000. 4/15. Sir J. C. & S.

Instructions regarding War Diaries and Intelligence Summaries are contained in F. S. Regs., Part II. and the Staff Manual respectively. Title pages will be prepared in manuscript.

WAR DIARY

~~or~~

~~INTELLIGENCE~~ SUMMARY.

(Erase heading not required.)

Army Form C. 2118.

Place	Date	Hour	Summary of Events and Information	Remarks and references to Appendices
	1916			
Friday	21 July	2pm	No 1 Section took over from No 2.	
		7pm	Was asked by OC Warrior to retaliate on my own guns. Was firing my mortars, when they must have mistaken noise for German ones. Our 4.5 Howitzers also always retaliate when I open fire. They are under the impression that our explosions are Boche ones.	
Saturday	22 July		To-day have been firing on enemy wire. It is in a poor state & they seem to make no effort to repair it. Have removed B gun at orders of DTMO. It has gone to Loos. Have only two guns A & C now	
Sunday	23 July		This morning fired both guns with good effect on support trenches in Cité des Cornailles. Have received a gun, which now makes three.	
Monday	24 July		A gun has been taken out to transfer it to the new emplacement at A. And C gun I have had taken out to dig in the bed again, as it was slanting. So we had a quiet day. The new emplacement and dug-out at A is now nearly finished & is a very strong affair which ought to be proof against anything. This afternoon Gunners	

Army Form C. 2118.

Instructions regarding War Diaries and Intelligence Summaries are contained in F. S. Regs., Part II. and the Staff Manual respectively. Title pages will be prepared in manuscript.

WAR DIARY
or
~~INTELLIGENCE SUMMARY.~~

(*Erase heading not required.*)

Place	Date	Hour	Summary of Events and Information	Remarks and references to Appendices
			Day & Edwards on 'B' gun were wounded by a minenwerfer. They have been evacuated this evening. 'B' gun had been firing and had completely wrecked an enemy house. This must have been an important point, as the enemy immediately retaliated very heavily with minenwerfer, 5.9's & 4.2's. No other damage beyond the wounding of these two men was done.	
Tuesday.	25 July	am 11 – 12.30	Fired 38 rounds. Heavy retaliation ensued. The enemy has been very aggressive for the last few days. His retaliation however did no damage to us, but caused a few casualties in the Infantry.	
			We destroyed one house & severely damaged another at M20b 5.5 & caused much damage to enemy trenches. A gun after 2 shots jumped out of the new wooden lower bed, so I ceased fire on that gun as the shooting was erratic. Rounds fired 38.	
		2pm	No 2 Section relieved No 1.	
Wednesday	26 July	4pm	Fired a few shots from B. & C guns about 4pm & met with a vigorous reply. ~~Fired~~ Upon which, I fired both guns at top speed until	

Instructions regarding War Diaries and Intelligence Summaries are contained in F. S. Regs., Part II. and the Staff Manual respectively. Title pages will be prepared in manuscript.

WAR DIARY
or
~~INTELLIGENCE SUMMARY.~~
(Erase heading not required.)

Army Form C. 2118.

Place	Date	Hour	Summary of Events and Information	Remarks and references to Appendices
			they were too hot to continue, & I observed considerable material damage. A heavy minenwerfer is suspected at M20 b 57 27 & I am moving A gun to fire on this spot. Rounds fired 48.	
Thursday	27 July	am 10-12	B & C fired 12 shots which were replied to, but A gun were still unable to fire on M20 b 57.27. In the afternoon, A was again moved & B & C	
		pm 3.30	registered on points in enemy's support line.	
			Enemy retaliated with rifle grenades to which we replied by an increased rate of fire from our guns, but their retaliation lasted a considerable time	
		pm 6.30	A gun fired on suspected emplacement. Rounds fired 42	
Friday	28 July		B & C guns quiet, as trenches in front required some reconstruction	
		am 11-12	A gun fired 3 shots at T.M. Emplacement at M20 b 57.27.	
		pm 4-5.30	A gun fired 12 more shots at T.M. Emplacement & found line to be ½° L of zero range 390-430 as bed shifted slightly	
		11pm	3 rounds retaliation caused explosion in enemy front line. Rounds fired 32.	

T2134. Wt. W708-776. 500000. 4/15. Sir J. C. & S.

Instructions regarding War Diaries and Intelligence Summaries are contained in F. S. Regs., Part II. and the Staff Manual respectively. Title pages will be prepared in manuscript.

WAR DIARY ~~or~~ ~~INTELLIGENCE SUMMARY.~~

(*Erase heading not required.*)

Army Form C. 2118.

Place	Date	Hour	Summary of Events and Information	Remarks and references to Appendices
	1916			
Saturday	29 July		A gun emplacement completed. B & C retaliation only.	
		am 7-10	A fired 7 shots at enemy T.M.s & 2 were observed to fall specially close to target causing explosions	
		2 pm	No 1 Section relieved No 2.	
		9.30 pm	All guns fired a few rounds to annoy enemy at his "Stand To". Retaliation very heavy, but eventually silenced except for rifle grenades which went on till far into the night. Enemy is using large quantities of rifle grenades lately. Rounds fired 32.	
Sunday	30 July	am 3 30	B gun, ammunition & half the emplacement completely buried by an enemy trench-mortar, which burst at a corner of the house. Fortunately no casualties, though I consider it a miraculous escape for the men. I moved B gun at the earliest opportunity to the old D emplacement in 234, with as much ammunition as I could reach. Shall require fatigue party to dig out remainder.	
			A gun had splendid shooting. Had observed enemy trench mortar firing at M20b 5½.4½ by the trail of blue smoke of the shot. We	

WAR DIARY
or
INTELLIGENCE SUMMARY.
(*Erase heading not required.*)

Army Form C. 2118.

Instructions regarding War Diaries and Intelligence Summaries are contained in F. S. Regs., Part II. and the Staff Manual respectively. Title pages will be prepared in manuscript.

Place	Date	Hour	Summary of Events and Information	Remarks and references to Appendices
	1916		immediately retaliated & got two direct hits on emplacement besides destroying a house & filling in a communication trench near by. An Infantry M.G. Offr is placing a M.G. to command this spot to-night to fire on any enemy working-party who try to repair it.	
			Enemy very active with T.M. & rifle grenades this evening. Our retaliation eventually silenced him. Rounds fired 37.	
Monday	31 July	am 10.30	A gun again fired with good effect at T.M. at M 20 b 5¾. 4½ & also destroyed their O.P. for this gun which was in the chimney of a house at M 20 b 4½. 4¾.	
		11am	6 guns fired on another enemy T.M. I had observed firing at M 21 a 30.25 Partially destroyed house at rear of emplacement. Am giving this spot further treatment.	
		pm 3.30	6 again fired on above spot. Whilst firing, we observed 2 men run out of emplacement to rear of house. We partially blew away earth parapet in front of this position. Little retaliation arrived. Rounds fired 51	

T2134. Wt. W708—776. 500000. 4/15. Sir J. C. & S.

Instructions regarding War Diaries and Intelligence Summaries are contained in F. S. Regs., Part II. and the Staff Manual respectively. Title pages will be prepared in manuscript.

WAR DIARY
or
INTELLIGENCE SUMMARY.
(Erase heading not required.)

DTMO/40

Vol 1

Army Form C. 2118.

D.T.M. Officer

Place	Date	Hour	Summary of Events and Information	Remarks and references to Appendices
Calonne	Aug 1		Enemy shelled Z40 Trench Mortar Battery's position heavily for which we retaliated with 34 rounds.	
"	2		A sap on which the enemy had been working was completely destroyed. The Infantry informed us that they saw men carried away on stretchers.	
Loos	3		X40 T.M.B strafed the whole of the enemy's front line near Loos.	
Calonne	4		Z40 T M B - - - - - - - throughout the day.	
"	5		" " " enemy houses & Support line, expending 46 rounds.	
Loos & Maroc	6		X & Y Batteries wire cutting throughout the day.	
Calonne	7		Z Batty. strafed enemy saps.	
	8		22 rounds expended by X Batty. strafing craters - M.6.b. Y16 T.M.B attached to 40th Div. T.M. Batteries.	
	9		X40 expended 40 rounds strafing "Triangle" & cutting wire.	
	10		Z40 wire cutting throughout the day with very successful results South of the Sap at M.15.d.4.	
	11		120th Infantry Brigade relieved by the 121st Infantry Brigade in the Maroc Section. W, X, & Z Trench Mortar Batteries continued wire cutting throughout the day - X & Z expending 106 rounds.	

2353 Wt. W2544/1454 700,000 5/15 D. D. & L. A.D.S.S. Forms/C. 2118.

Instructions regarding War Diaries and Intelligence Summaries are contained in F. S. Regs., Part II. and the Staff Manual respectively. Title pages will be prepared in manuscript.

WAR DIARY
or
INTELLIGENCE SUMMARY.
(Erase heading not required.)

Army Form C. 2118.

Place	Date	Hour	Summary of Events and Information	Remarks and references to Appendices
	Aug 12		Z40 Batty. Successfully strafed houses and enemy front line trenches at M.20.b. and M.15.a. expending 54 rounds W40 Battery expended 28 rounds French - strafing. Owing to the Infantry being relieved, X40's fire at M.10.a. was limited on this day.	
	13		Strafe on suspected emplacements in houses at Cornailles - 29 rounds expended. Much debris was thrown into the air. Much wire cutting done at M.10.a. and M.5.d.	
	14		Z40 T.M.B. in conjunction with W40 successfully bombarded a sap just north of junction of railway with G.F.L. at M.15.b.	
	15		Z40 strafed houses & trenches in Cornailles expending 62 rounds. 119th Inf. Bde. relieved by the 120th Bde. in the Calonne Section.	
	16		X40 wire cutting, expending 20 rounds. No other firing today on account of T.M. and also Infantry reliefs.	
	17		Y40 wire cutting & bombarding enemy front line trenches successfully, expending 45 rounds.	
	18		X40 relieved Z40 in the right section today therefore advisable postpone	

Instructions regarding War Diaries and Intelligence Summaries are contained in F. S. Regs., Part II. and the Staff Manual respectively. Title pages will be prepared in manuscript.

WAR DIARY
or
INTELLIGENCE SUMMARY.
(Erase heading not required.)

Army Form C. 2118.

Place	Date	Hour	Summary of Events and Information	Remarks and references to Appendices
			the proposed Trench Mortar Concentration at M.20.b. 4739 tomorrow until Friday, as they will scarcely know sufficient about their front by tomorrow for an organised concentration.	
	Aug. 18		During the early hours of the morning Carfax Rd. & Queen St. were heavily shelled by enemy. Y40 retaliated on enemy trenches from all guns. Carfax Rd., Queen St, & King St. shelled heavily with 4.2's at night. Successfully bombarded trenches & houses, Cornailles, covered by Artillery fire.	
	19		Y40 blew in enemy communication trench at M.10.a. 6.6. & shelled enemy trenches South of the Double Crassier.	
	20		14th H.L.I. moved into right subsection in place of 13th E. Surrey Regt., which moved into Bde. Support. The 14th A. & S. H. moved into the left subsection in place of the 11th R. Lanc. Regt., which moved into Bde. Reserve. W.X. & Y40 Batteries were cutting.	
	21		Enemy wire cut at M.4.c. 7553	
	22		" " " . Good results obtained, also on saps.	
	23		Wire cutting & strafe on saps.	

2353 Wt. W2544/1454 700,000 5/15 D. D. & L. A.D.S.S. Forms/C. 2118.

Army Form C. 2118.

WAR DIARY
or
INTELLIGENCE SUMMARY.
(Erase heading not required.)

Instructions regarding War Diaries and Intelligence Summaries are contained in F. S. Regs., Part II. and the Staff Manual respectively. Title pages will be prepared in manuscript.

Place	Date	Hour	Summary of Events and Information	Remarks and references to Appendices
	Aug 24		Hostile T. Mortar silenced at M.20.b. 4228. Suspected emplacement hit at M.20.b.4541.	
	25		Concentrated bombardment - M.20.b. - by X40 - Excellent results obtained on enemy front line trenches.	
	26		Wire cutting at "Triangle" - Good results obtained.	
	27		Enemy trenches in & around Cornailles strafed.	
	28		Wire cutting at "Triangle". Wire cutting around Saps at H.31.b	
	29		Y40 wire cutting & strafing enemy M.G., which drew heavy retaliation. Also silenced enemy aerial torpedo Gun.	
	30		Wire cutting. Y40 fired 22 rounds at enemy support and communication trenches, drawing slight retaliation.	
	31		Slight damage done to house near Dutchman's Barn. Y cut two big gaps in enemy wire at M.4.c.73. & M.4.c.6½.2½.	

2353 Wt. W2544/1454 700,000 5/15 D. D. & L. A.D.S.S. Forms/C 2118.

W/40 TMB Vol 1

W/40 T. M. B.
2/9/16

Army Form C. 2118.

WAR DIARY
or
~~INTELLIGENCE SUMMARY.~~
(Erase heading not required.)

Instructions regarding War Diaries and Intelligence Summaries are contained in F. S. Regs., Part II. and the Staff Manual respectively. Title pages will be prepared in manuscript.

Place	Date	Hour	Summary of Events and Information	Remarks and references to Appendices
	Aug 1st		Three 58mm French Guns in Action, ordinary retaliation work until the 18th inst.	
	14th		Joined with other Mortars in concentration attack on German positions.	
	14th-15th		Ordinary retaliation work.	
	16th		Engaged on wire cutting.	
	17th		Ordinary retaliation work.	
	18th		Joined with other Mortars in concentration attack on German positions.	
	18-25		Ordinary retaliation work.	
	25		Joined with other Mortars in concentrated attack on Bûte de Carnelles, One gun put out of action, but repaired, & in action again the same day.	
	25th-31st		Ordinary retaliation work.	
	31st		Handed over all three guns to V63 T. M. Bty, sent ten men on Medium T. M. Course to 1st Army School, & remainder of Battery went into reserve.	

W. Henty 2nd Lt R F A
C.O. W/40 T.M.B.

X 40. Trench Mortar Battery

Instructions regarding War Diaries and Intelligence Summaries are contained in F. S. Regs., Part II. and the Staff Manual respectively. Title pages will be prepared in manuscript.

WAR DIARY
or
INTELLIGENCE SUMMARY.
(Erase heading not required.)

August 1916

Army Form C. 2118.

X/40 TMB Vol 2

I

Place	Date	Hour	Summary of Events and Information	Remarks and references to Appendices
Loos.	6/8/16.		Rounds fired 39 (3 Guns) In Hand 112. Great difficulty in securing fatigue parties. Aboukir never answered request for party. No 1 gun left with only 16 bombs. Arranged for all guns to cut wire No 1 gun at M5 c 2½ - 7½ d 3.7 No 2 gun. M.6.c. 2½ - 6 d 3½ 6. No 3 gun M6.c - 9½ . 8. d M6.a ½ - 8½ No 4 gun M6.c. 78.45 d 88.45. Just had order to fire No 1. on Triangle from 7.45 to 8.45 PM, but only have 16 bombs left owing to Aboukir (H.Q. K.O.R.L.) not answering my note for fatigue party. Spent hours during the night endeavouring to find Capt Freeland 173rd Tunnelling Coy R.E. in King + Queen St, during a heavy bombardment by Rum Jars, Rifle Grenades Etc, without success. Rounds fired 39 In Hand 112.	
	7/8/16		Runner found Capt R.E at 6/30 AM in Carfax Road, re enemy mine under Queen St gun. Capt. Freeland not turned up, Orders for Nos 2.3 & 4 guns to be moved to Moroc. No 1 & detachment to remain where it is, move on 8th inst. To night 2 alternate beds at Quarry & Gordon Alley to be moved to Moroc. Found two bomb stores near Queen St containing one 30 & the other about 100 bombs, some fuzed. No 4 Gun cutting wire, also No 3, though 1 & 3 are short of bombs + No 2 is out of action, owing to R.E. working on emplacement, very heavy T.M & grenade fire from Enemy daily.	

(Continued)

2353 Wt. W2544/1454 700,000 5/15 D. D. & L. A.D.S.S. Forms/C. 2118.

X 40. Trench Mortar Battery.

WAR DIARY
or
INTELLIGENCE SUMMARY.
(*Erase heading not required.*)

Army Form C. 2118.

Instructions regarding War Diaries and Intelligence Summaries are contained in F. S. Regs., Part II. and the Staff Manual respectively. Title pages will be prepared in manuscript.

August 1916

II

Place	Date	Hour	Summary of Events and Information	Remarks and references to Appendices
Loos (Continued)	Aug 7th		cannot adequately reply owing to shortage of bombs. Infantry bad at supplying fatigue parties, except East Surreys + sometimes A & S.H. Frantic appeals for retaliation by H.L.I. & A&S.H. Latter have no T.M or Stokes in their front. Nearly all emplacements bad. Chalk pit Gun almost inaccessable, owing to hostile T.M's + rifle grenades incessantly falling in Quarry. No 4. Gun has no bomb dug-out (blown in) + have to use men's dug-out for bombs. Men sleep in Supports. Rounds fired 55, In hand 100 Nos 3 + 4 fired 10 rounds apiece at Enemy's wire. Out of 5 successive shots by No 3 gun with No. 31^a time fuze 3 were "duds"	
	8/8/16		Handed over to 16th Division at 2 P.M. Guns at South St. Quarry & Seaforth alley. We retain Queen St position, South St bed taken to Queen St position. Everything else removed to Bomb store Moroc by A + S.H. fatigue party. Bombs handed over:- South St. Gun 5. Quarry Gun 38. Seaforth alley Gun 59. - Total 102. In T.M Bomb-store 62 bombs, 22 boxes tails, No componant parts. In Brigade Bomb-Store 109 bombs 15 boxes of tails, 36 boxes of componant parts.	
Moroc	8/8/16		Took over Freize Alley + Liverpool St Guns from Y 40, with bombs. Freize Alley 37	

(Continued)

X 40 Trench Mortar Battery

Instructions regarding War Diaries and Intelligence Summaries are contained in F. S. Regs., Part II. and the Staff Manual respectively. Title pages will be prepared in manuscript.

WAR DIARY
or
INTELLIGENCE SUMMARY.
(Erase heading not required.)

August 1916

Army Form C. 2118.

III

Place	Date	Hour	Summary of Events and Information	Remarks and references to Appendices
Moroc Continued	8/8/16		Liverpool St 44. Treize Alley fired 3 rounds at 500^y at Enemy's communication & front line junction. 1st dropped 10^y short, the next two in the middle of no-mans land, obviosly faulty charges tho' new boxes.	
"	9/8/16.		Treize alley gun fired accurately, Registered all guns & gave them angles ranges & targets. Nos 1 & 2 very bad emplacements & dug outs particularly the latter, quite useless for proctection & very cramped. Went down to Carfax Road in the morning, found Capt Freeland's dug-out, but could not find him, am going again @ 9 P.M. Received receipt & 2 boxes of T. tubes from 16th Div Loos. Puit 16 shelled by 9.2's, much quieter sector than Loos. Bombs fired 40. In hand 108 No 3 heard an explosion after firing a bomb into Sap at 5° Right. Capt Freeland R.E, says the idea that there is an Enemy mine shaft under our Queen St Gun is absurd, it would have had to pass right through our defensive tunnels	
Moroc	10/8/16.		Took over from 2nd Lieut Reid. Fired a few rounds in retaliation to various rum jars	
"	11/8/16		Firing to-day chiefly in retaliation, set up telephone communication with Liverpool Street Gun. The wire is continually being cut by aerial torpedos.	

Continued

X 40 Trench Mortar Battery

Army Form C. 2118.

WAR DIARY
or
INTELLIGENCE SUMMARY.
(Erase heading not required.)

August 1916

IV

Instructions regarding War Diaries and Intelligence Summaries are contained in F. S. Regs., Part II. and the Staff Manual respectively. Title pages will be prepared in manuscript.

Place	Date	Hour	Summary of Events and Information	Remarks and references to Appendices
Moroc (Continued)	12/8/16		Took the bearing of the Liverpool St Gun & also registered it on enemys wire, support & communication trenches. Not much firing to-day on account of Infantry changing	
	13/8/16		Registered Liverpool St & Treize Alley guns Took the initiative as regards firing. The enemy retaliated on the Gun with artillery fire, & knocked the trench in near the Gun.	
	14/8/16		Registered Liverpool St & Treize Alley Guns. Enemy again retaliated with artillery fire doing no damage. Queen St emplacement knocked in, doing no harm to the Gun.	
	14/8/16		Took over from 2/Lt G.A. Horn. Arranged to connect By. H.Q. with Liverpool St telephone wire near Boyau 13 New bomb store No 71 Liverpool St. Gun rifle mechanism out of action. also Queen St, the latter damaged by shrapnel. Artillery fatigue party say it is impossible to remove French Bombs from King St. they are heavy, awkward & trenches slippery. Rounds Fired 40, in hand 125.	
	Aug 15th		General Reid visited H.Q.s & guns at 9. AM, seemed quite satisfied, established telephone communication between By H.Q. Boyau 13 & wire to Liverpool St Gun.	

(Continued).

2353 Wt. W2544/1454 700,000 5/15 D. D. & L. A.D.S.S./Forms/C. 2118.

X 40 Trench Mortar Battery

WAR DIARY
or
INTELLIGENCE SUMMARY.
(*Erase heading not required.*)

August 1916

Army Form C. 2118.

V

Instructions regarding War Diaries and Intelligence Summaries are contained in F. S. Regs., Part II. and the Staff Manual respectively. Title pages will be prepared in manuscript.

Place	Date	Hour	Summary of Events and Information	Remarks and references to Appendices
Maroc (Continued)	15/8/16		Mended latter wire in 4 places & line between TM H.Q & Treize Alley gun in 3 places at 4 PM, communication between Coy H.Q & Liverpool St again broken 4-15 PM. Fired 3 rounds at Enemys wire from Treize Alley Gun at Zero. First range 480^Y in this side of hostile wire, second shot at 490^Y on edge of parapet & wire, 3rd shot 485^Y in junction of communication & front line. 3° too much to the left & 20^Y too far. Guns very irregular particularly in range. Firing returned up to 20 pipsqueaks on our Reserve & Treize Alley corner. Bed of Queen St gun cracked right across. Alternative bed also semi-unservicable, another bed found 3 bays further in.	
		5/15 PM	Fired 6 more shots at enemys front trench 490^Y went over & 480 in trench. Enemy retaliation with 4-5° in their own wire. Engineers doing no work in Treize Alley emplacement or dug-out. Have started two entrances to dug-out in Liverpool St. Latter Gun out of action 6-7 PM. in order to shift bed to obtain arc of fire reaching side of double crassier. New bed sent to Queen St 30 bombs & 6 boxes componant parts removed from house No 115 to No 71. 20 bombs & 4 boxes componant parts sent to Treize Alley gun. Message re bombs King St received 3 hours to late for action. {Bombs in advance bomb store Maroc} {111 bombs 22 boxes componant parts} House no 71 = 61 " 6 " " "	
			(Continued)	

2353 Wt. W2544/1454 700,000 5/15 D. D. & L. A.D.S.S. Forms/C. 2118.

X 40 Trench Mortar Battery **WAR DIARY** *or* **INTELLIGENCE SUMMARY.** August 1916. Army Form C. 2118.

Instructions regarding War Diaries and Intelligence Summaries are contained in F. S. Regs., Part II. and the Staff Manual respectively. Title pages will be prepared in manuscript.

(Erase heading not required.)

VI

Place	Date	Hour	Summary of Events and Information	Remarks and references to Appendices
Moroc Continued.	16/8/16.		Fired several rounds from Treize Alley & Liverpool St guns [struck out] both at trenches & wire. Relieved by Y 40 at 11-30 AM proceeded to Calonne to relieve Z 40 at 1. PM. Took over 4 guns, no firing on account of Infantry reliefs.	
Calonne	17/8/16		General Reid visited A B & C guns snipers post etc at 9-AM. Registered C gun by periscope from front line, observations difficult. B gun completed near A. Registered A B & C from Artillery O.P in cinema. C cannot quite reach objective, started rum jar retaliation. C gun were left no book by Z 40. A & C both firing with 'T' Tubes. Rounds fired 27 Rounds in hand 127. Took up & relaid 'B' bed.	
	18/8/16		Registered B gun at 9 AM & saw head cover over emplacement completed by Pioneers. Strafe at 5.10 very successful. A gun fired in strafe 24. B gun 20 & C. 21 rounds. Total 65. D gun fired 10 rounds at 4 PM. Rounds fired at each gun during day & including ~~Total~~ those fired in strafe. A 26. B 22. C 26 & D 31. Grand Total 105. Bombs in hand 51. A. rifle mechanism broken while men were round the corner, Completely smashed & bent. Whole strafe excellent. Heavies, Stokes, Rifle Grenades & T. M's. Several houses levelled, very short of ammunition	

(Continued)

2353 Wt. W2544/1454 700,000 5/15 D. D. & L. A.D.S.S. Forms/C. 2118.

X 40 Trench Mortar Battery

WAR DIARY
or
INTELLIGENCE SUMMARY.
(Erase heading not required.)

August 1916

Army Form C. 2118.

Instructions regarding War Diaries and Intelligence Summaries are contained in F. S. Regs., Part II. and the Staff Manual respectively. Title pages will be prepared in manuscript.

VII

Place	Date	Hour	Summary of Events and Information	Remarks and references to Appendices
Calonne (Contd)	18/8/16		Out of 10 rounds by D at 4 P.M. 7. were "duds" No 31[A] Time Fuze.	
	19/8/16.		Handed over to 2 Lt Horn at 3 P.M. A & B Guns 40 bombs C gun 37 + D gun 45 bombs. In bombstore 134 bombs + tails + 26 Boxes of componant parts. 150 T Tubes + 1 box of detonator cartridges.	
Calonne	"	3.P.M	Took over from Lt Reid	
	20/8/16.		Registered D gun on enemys wire + front trenches. Work being carried on by the Engineers at 231 and by the Pioneers in Chaptel Alley. A.B. + C guns fired on Enemys front line + wire doing considerable damage.	
	21/8/16		Registered C Gun on Enemy's sap. Premature in D gun which blew in the pit. The gun was not damaged, but no more firing will be possible for some days. The Engineers are repairing the damage.	
	22/8/16		Registered C gun on enemy M.G and strafed this point from 5 PM untill 8 P.M. Result M.G disappears. Engaged enemys T.M.s with A + B guns	
	23/8/16		Reset C Gun to bearing 220°. Did not do much firing to-day.	
	24/8/16.		Connected all the guns by Telephone + strafed enemys T.M.s with A B + C guns + got a direct hit. Handed over to Lt Taylor, but remained with my Nos I. for forthcoming strafe.	

2353 Wt. W2544/1454 700,000 5/15 D. D. & L. A.D.S.S. Forms/C. 2118.

"Y.40" T.M.B. **WAR DIARY** *or* **INTELLIGENCE SUMMARY** *(Erase heading not required.)*

Y/40 TMB August Vol 2

Army Form. C. 2118

Instructions regarding War Diaries and Intelligence Summaries are contained in F. S. Regs., Part II. and the Staff Manual respectively. Title Pages will be prepared in manuscript.

August 1916

Place	Date	Hour	Summary of Events and Information	Remarks and references to Appendices
Maroc.	1-8-16	9am	Visited new emplacement under construction in Boyau 231. We fired at enemies front and support trenches at M.5.c and M.4.c, with good effect. Very heavy retaliation on our support and reserve trenches. Our Artillery very quiet. Head cover completed on our Liverpool & Queen Street emplacements. Enemy far more active in this sector than formerly, this being very noticeable. Spare ammunition recess in Boyau 12 blown up by 4.2 HE, this recess was empty at the time.	
	2nd		Enemy distributed heavy fire all along the sector. Our T.M.s retaliated on his support & front lines. At dusk [illegible] in co-operation with our artillery we fired a number of rounds at the enemies front & communication trenches.	
	3rd	9am	We bombarded the enemies trenches. No retaliation.	
		3pm	We continued firing at enemies front & support lines, very slight retaliation.	
	4th		Enemy very inactive. No 1 gun out of action owing to bed having jumped. Now No 1 gun in action again. Whilst	

Army Form. C. 2118

WAR DIARY
or
INTELLIGENCE SUMMARY

(Erase heading not required.)

Instructions regarding War Diaries and Intelligence Summaries are contained in F. S. Regs., Part II. and the Staff Manual respectively. Title Pages will be prepared in manuscript.

Place	Date	Hour	Summary of Events and Information	Remarks and references to Appendices
[illegible]	4 (cont)		laying wire to our No 2 gun, we suffered the foll: casualties — 1 man killed 1 severely wounded 1 slightly wounded.	
	5th		We fired 20 rounds at enemies wire at M.10.a.5½.9½ and M.4.c.9.4 cutting two large gaps.	
	6th		Fired 37 rounds at enemies wire. Batteries of enemy artillery retaliated heavily on both our guns. Called for artillery support. Engineers deepened both trenches leading to guns.	
	7th		Continued cutting enemies wire. Heavy artillery retaliation.	
	8th	10am	Fired 15 rounds at enemies front line. Enemy retaliated with aerial darts and [illegible] artillery. Noticeable increase of enemies aerial darts.	
	[illegible]	1pm	Handed over line to "X.40" T.M.B.	
	16th	11am	Took over from X Battery. Quarter strength gun - split bed, placed [illegible] in position. Cut wire at M.4.c.1½.3½ M.5.c.2½.3½ M.10.a.1½.5½ [illegible] Trench at M.10.a.6½.6½. Enemy retaliated heavily. [illegible] gun damaged by enemy artillery.	

3

Instructions regarding War Diaries and Intelligence Summaries are contained in F. S. Regs., Part II. and the Staff Manual respectively. Title Pages will be prepared in manuscript.

WAR DIARY
or
INTELLIGENCE SUMMARY
(Erase heading not required.)

Army Form. C. 2118

Place	Date	Hour	Summary of Events and Information	Remarks and references to Appendices
Maroc	17th	4pm	Fired 20 rounds at enemies front & support line in A 7b. Retaliation – not owing to [illegible] of [illegible]. 10 am [illegible] at M.4.c.7½.3½ and left [illegible] gun. Heavy retaliation in the form of 4.2's and aerial darts on each of our guns.	
	18th		During the early hours Fairfax Rd and Queen St. heavily shelled.	
		9pm	We retaliated on enemies trenches from all our guns. Removed French Aerial Torpedoes from Kings Road, these were left by the 1st Division. Fairfax Rd, Queen St & King St shelled heavily by 4.2 at night.	
	19th		We fired on enemies communication trench at M.10.a.6.6 and junction at M.10.a.7.3, and shelled enemies trenches S. of Double Crassier and in A 7b.	
	20th		Fired 50 rounds from Nos 1 & No 3 gun, paying particular attention to enemies support trenches in A 7b & 8 [illegible] [illegible], obtaining several direct hits. Established telephone communication with No 3 gun.	

Army Form. C. 2118

Instructions regarding War Diaries and Intelligence Summaries are contained in F. S. Regs., Part II. and the Staff Manual respectively. Title Pages will be prepared in manuscript.

WAR DIARY
or
INTELLIGENCE SUMMARY
(Erase heading not required.)

Place	Date	Hour	Summary of Events and Information	Remarks and references to Appendices
Maroc	21st		Fired 41 rounds at enemies front line from M.5.c.2.8½ to M.5.c.3.5 in retaliation. Hostile retaliation about 2 hours later very severe.	
	22nd		Fired 55 rounds at suspected O.P's, M.G's and T.M's in M.4.c and M.5.c. Hostile retaliation – in afternoon – very heavy. We retaliated later ~~with~~ in cooperation with our heavier 9.2"s (Artillery) and effectively silenced enemy for the remainder of the day	
	23rd		We cut wire at M.5.c.2½.0 and M.4.c.7½.3½. We cleared bombs from Boyau 28, which was on the emplacement occupied by 11th Division.	
	24th		Fired 30 rounds at enemies support line from M.5.c.0.7½ to M.5.c.1½.5½ and cut wire at M.5.c.3.5. Enemy retaliated with 77 mm guns and heavy T.M's. Our Artillery effectively silenced same.	
	25th		Fired chiefly at their wire around 9pm. and cut same in several places. We also fired at enemies Trench at M.4.d.9.6 and rifles with fixed bayonets were seen to fly into the air.	

5/

Instructions regarding War Diaries and Intelligence Summaries are contained in F. S. Regs., Part II. and the Staff Manual respectively. Title Pages will be prepared in manuscript.

WAR DIARY
or
INTELLIGENCE SUMMARY
(Erase heading not required.)

Army Form. C. 2118

Place	Date	Hour	Summary of Events and Information	Remarks and references to Appendices
March	26th		Queens Street gun out of action in morning. The sand bags of the emplacement being blown in on top of gun by 77mm guns. Our No 1 gun blew up a listening post at M.10.a.6.5½. No 2 gun swept enemy support line M.4.c.9.2 drawing heavy retaliation.	
	27th		Kings Street & Cooper Rd heavily shelled. Our 2 Ins retaliated on enemies trenches (support) in the aftn, and silenced enemies T.M's. No 2 Gun out of action owing to mechanism trouble. Trench boards left in Kings Street by 1st Division.	
	28th		Mechanism trouble with No 1 & 2 guns. Found both guns in action again, and fired at enemies support lines in aftn. Enemy moderately quiet.	
	29th		We fired 45 rounds at enemy points and emplacements in M.4.c and M.5.c. And silenced enemy aerial torpedo gun. This torpedo gun has not fired since.	

Instructions regarding War Diaries and Intelligence Summaries are contained in F. S. Regs., Part II. and the Staff Manual respectively. Title Pages will be prepared in manuscript.

Army Form. C. 2118

WAR DIARY
or
INTELLIGENCE SUMMARY
(Erase heading not required.)

Place	Date	Hour	Summary of Events and Information	Remarks and references to Appendices
Marœ.	30th		No 1 gun fired 11 rounds at enemies support lines and M.G. and T.M. emplacements. No 2 gun fired 32 at enemies support and communication trenches in M.4.c. Slight retaliation.	
	31st	4.50am	No 3 gun in co-operation with our artillery fired for five minutes at enemies front line from M.5.c.2.8½ to M.5.c.3.5, and about that time we exploded a mine. We continued firing from No 3 gun, at intervals throughout the day, at enemies communication & support trenches. No 2 gun cut two big gaps in enemies wire at M.4.c.1/3 and M.4.c.4½.3½.	
			R. J. Williams (Lieut) OC. Y.40. T.M.B.	

Instructions regarding War Diaries and Intelligence Summaries are contained in F. S. Regs., Part II. and the Staff Manual respectively. Title pages will be prepared in manuscript.

WAR DIARY or ~~INTELLIGENCE SUMMARY.~~

(Erase heading not required.)

Z 40 T.M.B.

Army Form C. 2118.

Vol 2

Place	Date	Hour	Summary of Events and Information	Remarks and references to Appendices
	1916			
Tuesday	1 Aug		An inspection of enemy line shows we have done enormous damage. We have fired nearly all day, damaging trenches & playing upon & around known enemy T.M. emplacements.	
		pm 6.15 -6.45	The damage we have done to enemy was confirmed by the fact that for half an hour his artillery subjected our 'A' position to a heavy bombardment of Whiz-Bang 4E + 4.2's. They rained around A gun but not the slightest damage was done & we sent over 2 or 3 after it had finished to show we were still alive. Rounds fired 46.	
Wednesday	2 Aug		Two days ago, an Infantry Offr showed us a sap at M21a½7. which we said was always occupied at night by a heavy enemy party working there whom our M.G's could not touch. We have gradually registered this spot, one shot every 8 hours for the last 2 days to hide our intention from the enemy. At 3.30. yesterday afternoon this target was registered & the gun laid on it. At 1.30am this morning we fired 15 rounds into it & daylight revealed the damage we had done. The sap was completely wrecked & sandbags & boards	

T2134. Wt. W708–776. 500000. 4/15. Sir J. C. & S.

Instructions regarding War Diaries and Intelligence Summaries are contained in F. S. Regs., Part II. and the Staff Manual respectively. Title pages will be prepared in manuscript.

WAR DIARY

~~or~~

~~INTELLIGENCE SUMMARY.~~

(*Erase heading not required.*)

Army Form C. 2118.

Place	Date	Hour	Summary of Events and Information	Remarks and references to Appendices
			lying broken outside it. The enemy were observed moving away casualties on stretchers.	
			As retaliation for this, the enemy again subjected our gun positions to-day to a violent artillery bombardment from 9.10 am – 9.30 & from 12.0 to 12.40. Not the slightest damage was done to us & we fired back in each case at the end of his demonstration.	
			'D' gun has fired 10 in retaliation to aerial darts, which were immediately silenced	
			All guns were heavily engaged & we have to-day fired 101 rounds. No enemy light mortar has fired for over 2 days.	
		2pm	No 1 Section relieved by No 2.	
		7pm	D retaliated on aerial darts. Again silenced after 2 shots.	
Thursday	3 Aug	3am	All guns fired 3 rounds to annoy the Boche.	
		10.15 -11.15	A fired at old German emplacement which seems to have another gun in it	

T2134. Wt. W708—776. 500000. 4/15. Sir J. C. & S.

Instructions regarding War Diaries and Intelligence Summaries are contained in F. S. Regs., Part II. and the Staff Manual respectively. Title pages will be prepared in manuscript.

WAR DIARY
or
INTELLIGENCE SUMMARY.
(Erase heading not required.)

Army Form C. 2118.

Place	Date	Hour	Summary of Events and Information	Remarks and references to Appendices
		pm 12.15	A gun O.P. hit by shell, & badly damaged. Snipers bruised, not seriously hurt	
		10–12.30	C fired 12 shots on German TM's in Cité des Cornailles.	
		5pm	All guns fired a few rounds to show we were alive	
		7pm	Showed C gun to RE & they hope to strengthen it on Saturday.	
			Rounds fired 41. Retaliation – moderate mostly Whiz Bangs.	

T2134. Wt. W708—776. 500000. 4/15. Sir J. C. & S.

Instructions regarding War Diaries and Intelligence Summaries are contained in F. S. Regs., Part II. and the Staff Manual respectively. Title pages will be prepared in manuscript.

WAR DIARY
or
~~INTELLIGENCE~~ SUMMARY.
(Erase heading not required.)

Army Form C. 2118.

Place	Date	Hour	Summary of Events and Information	Remarks and references to Appendices
Thursday	3rd		[illegible] a great deal from A gun which was shelled with 5.9s and several smaller shells. This gun's position is excellent & any number of rounds can be fired in safety.	
Friday	4th	11.30 a.m.	A shot from A gun caused an explosion in CORNAILLES but unfortunately was not observed.	
		2pm	All guns fired 10 shots but drew little retaliation except aerial darts from the neighbourhood of Port [illegible].	
		[illegible] pm	Removing wood from vault of church.	
Saturday	5th		A new position had been found for us in a church altar [illegible] ROAD. This has been filled with wood by the infantry.	
		10 a.m.–2	We spent two hours removing this wood & digging away clay from the inside of the gun position.	

T2134. Wt. W708–776. 500000. 4/15. Sir J. C. & S.

Instructions regarding War Diaries and Intelligence Summaries are contained in F. S. Regs., Part II. and the Staff Manual respectively. Title pages will be prepared in manuscript.

WAR DIARY
~~or~~
~~INTELLIGENCE SUMMARY.~~
(*Erase heading not required.*)

Army Form C. 2118.

Place	Date	Hour	Summary of Events and Information	Remarks and references to Appendices
	1916 August			
Sunday	6	2pm	No 2 Section relieved by No 1.	
			We are pretty well wholly engaged in cutting wire round 3 saps, as Infantry are raiding by one of them in a weeks time	
			Have installed a gun in old emplacement under ruined church to fire at wire at sap opposite. Had great deal of trouble with this position	
			To-night we have dug out the emplacement sufficient for gun to fire. 2 of Other guns carried on cutting wire. A gun fired at trenches.	
Monday	7		Fired new gun, but not sufficient clearance on top of emplacement to get lower ranges. Ceased fire & commenced to remove brick wall in front to push gun further forward.	
			Installed telephone from new gun to convenient O.P.	
			2 gun cut wire very successfully, also C gun. A gun got direct hit on bomb recess.	
			No enemy light mortars have fired here for over a week. We have silenced them, having destroyed their position.	

Instructions regarding War Diaries and Intelligence Summaries are contained in F. S. Regs., Part II. and the Staff Manual respectively. Title pages will be prepared in manuscript.

WAR DIARY

~~or~~

~~INTELLIGENCE SUMMARY.~~

(Erase heading not required.)

Army Form C. 2118.

Place	Date	Hour	Summary of Events and Information	Remarks and references to Appendices
August	1916			
Tuesday	8	11am	Fired 31 rounds at wire from new gun. Gun not very steady.	
		3pm	Again fired new gun, but enemy retaliated heavily with 77mm H.E. getting 5 direct hits on emplacement. Obliged to cease fire as emplacement filled with dirt. Afraid enemy have exact range of church which is a well known old TM emplacement to them.	
			Other guns have carried on cutting wire successfully at other pts.	
Wednesday	9		This morning have relaid bed of new gun, as left of target was not covered before. Our fire again met with heavy retaliation. Gun was filled with earth. Obliged to cease fire & dismount gun to remove same. We are experiencing several cases of damp cordite at present, giving miss-fires.	
			Other guns fired at wire, enemy trenches & caused considerable damage. Enemy wire is much cut about.	
Thursday	10		Our new gun again fired at wire, until a trench mortar was put in our position, as the emplacement is better suited for a French gun	

Instructions regarding War Diaries and Intelligence Summaries are contained in F. S. Regs., Part II. and the Staff Manual respectively. Title pages will be prepared in manuscript.

WAR DIARY
or
INTELLIGENCE SUMMARY.
(Erase heading not required.)

Army Form C. 2118.

Place	Date	Hour	Summary of Events and Information	Remarks and references to Appendices
	10th (contd).		This emplacement has only been a temporary affair & was not a good position for a 2-inch gun.	
			A gun has met with heavy artillery retaliation, but neither gun or emplacement damaged. Suspect we have caused great damage as enemy always retaliate heavily on us with artillery.	
			1 Rifle Mechanism damaged at C gun.	
			Gunner McEwen evacuated, wounded by 77mm at D gun.	
		3pm	No 2 Section relieved No 1	
Friday	11th	9am	A Gun retaliated on the enemy trenches in S3ob to the aerial darts fired by them from Point 16 Bis.	
			The rest of the day was fairly quiet as the artillery were cutting wire in front of most of the enemy saps.	
Saturday	12th		During the morning we worked hard to get gun at RAILWAY ALLEY ready for action	
		7pm	This gun carried out a combined strafe with the French 58mm mortars in HORTON ROAD against the enemy front line trenches opposite.	

T2134. Wt. W708—776. 500000. 4/15. Sir J. C. & S.

Instructions regarding War Diaries and Intelligence Summaries are contained in F. S. Regs., Part II. and the Staff Manual respectively. Title pages will be prepared in manuscript.

WAR DIARY
or
~~INTELLIGENCE SUMMARY~~.
(Erase heading not required.)

Army Form C. 2118.

Place	Date	Hour	Summary of Events and Information	Remarks and references to Appendices
CALONNE	Aug 13	11.30 am	A gun fired 8 shots at chimney (suspected O.P.) in CORNAILLES	
		12.15 pm	A & C gun fired 6 shots each retaliation into enemy's front line in T.12.a.	
			In the afternoon we moved D gun from BOYAU 234 to an alternative position beside A gun.	
		7.0 pm	In the evening RAILWAY ALLEY fired 12 shots on suspected german T.M. but the light was getting bad for observation.	
Monday	14th		With the help of the Pioneers we built head cover for the second gun at A position.	
			A position was chosen in CHAPTEL ALLEY for a new emplacement to be built for us by the pioneers.	
			The trench leading to this will be very bad in winter for parties carrying bombs to use.	
Tuesday	15th		A & C guns ranged on 1.20.b 47-39.	
			The second gun at A could not reach this spot and had to be dug up and re planted.	
			C gun cannot fire so far right but is firing as near to it as possible	

T2134. Wt. W708—776. 500000. 4/15. Sir J. C. & S.

Instructions regarding War Diaries and Intelligence Summaries are contained in F. S. Regs., Part II. and the Staff Manual respectively. Title pages will be prepared in manuscript.

WAR DIARY

or

~~INTELLIGENCE SUMMARY.~~

(Erase heading not required.)

Army Form C. 2118.

Place	Date	Hour	Summary of Events and Information	Remarks and references to Appendices
Wednesday	16th	11am	B gun (2nd gun at A position) ranged on 1920t 47-39 There appears to be nothing at this spot but the guns are registered on an old ruin very near. Relieved by X 20 Battery at 3 p.m.	

T2134. Wt. W708—776. 500000. 4/15. Sir J. C. & S.

Army Form C. 2118.

Instructions regarding War Diaries and Intelligence Summaries are contained in F. S. Regs., Part II. and the Staff Manual respectively. Title pages will be prepared in manuscript.

WAR DIARY

or

~~INTELLIGENCE SUMMARY.~~

(Erase heading not required.)

Place	Date	Hour	Summary of Events and Information	Remarks and references to Appendices
	1916			
Thursday	Aug 24	noon	Joined X Battery at Calonne X Officer & Nos 1 are staying till tomorrow morning, as there is a concentrated T.M. demonstration at 5 am.	
		4pm	Registered A, B, C guns on enemy TM emplacement at M20b 5.4	
Friday	Aug 25	5am	Fired 3 guns in conjunction with Stokes, French, Heavy & Artillery. Shots were concentrated around and at M 20 b 5.4 at which point are two enemy T.M. emplacements. Day was just breaking, but shots were observed to do great damage	
		7am	Heavy enemy retaliation.	
		3pm	Successfully bombarded enemy emplacement at M. 20 b. 6.4 with 2 guns	
			Rounds fired to day 89.	
			C emplacement requires much work, as earth is falling in under shock of discharge. It will take 2 or 3 days.	
Saturday	Aug 26	am 10.30	Bombarded enemy trenches in M 20 b with A & B guns. Rained heavily, somewhat interfering with Obsn.	
		pm 3-5	Bombarded enemy wire & front line in M 20 b. Destroyed a house.	
		4pm	C gun again in action. Registered on M 20 b front line	

Instructions regarding War Diaries and Intelligence Summaries are contained in F. S. Regs., Part II. and the Staff Manual respectively. Title pages will be prepared in manuscript.

WAR DIARY
or
INTELLIGENCE SUMMARY.
(Erase heading not required.)

Army Form C. 2118.

Place	Date	Hour	Summary of Events and Information	Remarks and references to Appendices
Sunday	Aug 27	10 am	Yesterday observed enemy TM firing continually. This morning registered on emplacement at extreme range. Ready to retaliate if it fires. A gun.	
		am-pm 10-7	~~C gun~~ B & C guns bombarded enemy support trench in M30 a 0 b	
		3pm	Gunner Rhodes accidentally wounded (No 1 at C gun). Detonator exploded in his hand. He was in action. D gun now in action. Registered on enemy TM. Have now 4 guns in action.	
Monday	Aug 28	6am	Retaliated on enemy TM, silencing it after 3 rounds. Spent morning & afternoon in conducting DTMO of relieving Division through Sector. Inspected new emplacements being constructed in Chapel Alley	
		2/pm	No 2 Section relieved No 1	

T2134. Wt. W708—776. 500000. 4/15. Sir J. C. & S.

Instructions regarding War Diaries and Intelligence Summaries are contained in F. S. Regs., Part II. and the Staff Manual respectively. Title pages will be prepared in manuscript.

WAR DIARY

or

~~INTELLIGENCE SUMMARY.~~

(Erase heading not required.)

Army Form C. 2118.

Place	Date	Hour	Summary of Events and Information	Remarks and references to Appendices
Tuesday 29th			Retaliation firing only.	
			The day was exceptionally quiet; the enemy rarely fires unless we fire first.	
		11a.m.	The O.C. X/63 arrived to take over this sector.	
		2pm	I shewed him round the entire front.	
		3pm	We retaliated (30 rounds) on the CORNER OF CORN ALLEY [illegible] aerial dart on HIXON RD & DURHAM QUAD.	
Wednesday 30th			Rain all day & trenches in a fearful state particularly CHAPTEL ALLEY.	
		7.30am	Only 10 rounds fired all day when the heavy T.M. fired 4 shots.	
			No fatigue parties obtainable.	
Thursday 31st		11am	The second officer of X/63 arrived. I shewed him the sector. His men relieved mine. We brought away every thing except three double frames which would not have fitted any other emplacements. These they signed a receipt for.	
		10.30pm	Relief complete.	

Instructions regarding War Diaries and Intelligence Summaries are contained in F. S. Regs., Part II, and the Staff Manual respectively. Title pages will be prepared in manuscript.

WAR DIARY
or
INTELLIGENCE SUMMARY.
(Erase heading not required.)

DTMO 40 Di

From 40TH DIVL. T. M. OFFICER.

September, 1916.

Vol 3

Army Form C. 2118.

Place	Date	Hour	Summary of Events and Information	Remarks and references to Appendices
Maroc	1		Enemy front line bombarded by our T.M's.	
Loos	1		Owing to the activity of Hostile T.M's, ours retaliated with good effect.	
Maroc	2		Our T.M's. fired on enemy trenches in M.10.c. and M.5.c. One shell caused	
"			a fire which lasted a considerable time.	
Loos	2		Hostile T.M's. very active on Loos Crassier - they were silenced by our Mortars.	
"	3		" " " " to which ours retaliated.	
Maroc	4		Our T.M's. bombarded enemy front line trenches.	
Loos	4		" " " " " "	
"	5	10/30a	In morning, enemy T.M. bombarded our trenches near Seaforth Crater	
"			very vigorously. Our Mortars and Artillery retaliated and	
"			Silenced the enemy.	
"	6		Our T.M's. were wirecutting.	
Maroc	6		" " " "	
"	7		Y40 T.M.B. bombarded enemy wire from 2 till 4 p.m., and from 5 till 7 p.m.	
"			expending 21 rounds in first bombardment, and 46 in Second.	
Loos	7		X40 T.M.B. fired 30 rounds in retaliation to enemy Mortars.	

2353 Wt. W2544/1454 700,000 5/15 D. D. & L. A.D.S.S. Forms/C 2118.

Army Form C. 2118.

Instructions regarding War Diaries and Intelligence Summaries are contained in F. S. Regs., Part II. and the Staff Manual respectively. Title pages will be prepared in manuscript.

WAR DIARY
or
INTELLIGENCE SUMMARY.
(Erase heading not required.)

Place	Date	Hour	Summary of Events and Information	Remarks and references to Appendices
Maroc	8		Z40 bombarded enemy trenches and wire, expending 101 rounds, which	
〃			were observed to be very effective. This drew retaliation from enemy	
〃			Artillery.	
〃	9		Our Mortars bombarded enemy trenches from M.4.d.8.5 to M.4.d.87.60,	
〃			doing considerable damage.	
Loos	9		Hostile T.M's. more active than usual all through the day, but	
〃			were silenced by our Mortars.	
〃	10		Our T.M's. continued wire cutting.	
Maroc	10		〃 〃 〃 〃 〃	
〃	11		〃 〃 cut large gaps in enemy wire opposite Fosse 16, and also did	
〃			very much damage to enemy wire S. of the Double Crassier. Enemy	
			retaliation was very feeble.	
Loos	11		58 rounds were expended by X40 firing in retaliation to enemy Mortars.	
Maroc	12		Our T.M's. bombarded ~~#~~ enemy communications near Northern Crassier,	
〃			and also cut wire. Enemy Artillery retaliated to which our artillery replied.	
〃			Gunners Campbell and Donohue, (V40), and Gr. Johnson, (Z40) went to 1st Army Rest	
			Camp at Equihen, near Boulogne.	

2353 Wt. W2544/1454 700,000 5/15 D. D. & L. A.D.S.S. Forms/C. 2118.

Instructions regarding War Diaries and Intelligence Summaries are contained in F. S. Regs., Part II. and the Staff Manual respectively. Title pages will be prepared in manuscript.

WAR DIARY
or
INTELLIGENCE SUMMARY.
(Erase heading not required.)

Army Form C. 2118.

Place	Date	Hour	Summary of Events and Information	Remarks and references to Appendices
Maroc	13		Our T.M's. continued wire cutting.	
"	14		" " " " "	
Loos			" " bombarded hostile trenches on the whole front, in reply to which the Germans sent over a few rifle grenades.	
Maroc	15		Wire cutting continued.	
Loos			Our Mortars bombarded enemy trenches and cut much wire, to which there was no retaliation. We silenced enemy T. Mortar and aerial torpedo fire. During the afternoon our Mortars blew up two enemy ammunition dumps.	
Maroc	16		Our T.M's. continued their wirecutting.	
Loos	16		" " active all day - cutting wire and bombarding enemy trenches.	
Maroc	17		At Fosse 16 our Mortars made many clear gaps in enemy wire.	
Loos	17		Our T.M's. bombarded enemy trenches and emplacements round Harrison's and Seaforth Craters.	
Maroc	18		120th Inf. Bde. relieved by the 119th Inf. Bde. Our T.M's. continued wire cutting but weather conditions made it difficult to observe.	

Instructions regarding War Diaries and Intelligence Summaries are contained in F. S. Regs., Part II. and the Staff Manual respectively. Title pages will be prepared in manuscript.

WAR DIARY
or
INTELLIGENCE SUMMARY.
(Erase heading not required.)

Army Form C. 2118.

Place	Date	Hour	Summary of Events and Information	Remarks and references to Appendices
Loos	18		Our Mortars continued their wirecutting, but weather conditions	
"			made it difficult to observe.	
Maroc	19		Wire cutting continued.	
Loos			" " "	
Maroc	20		Y40 expended 172 rounds in cutting wire and bombarding enemy	
"			trenches in retaliation to Minenwerfer fire which was very	
"			heavy on Neuf Alley and Support Line	
Loos	21		X40 bombarded Seaforth and Hart's Craters with 65 rounds.	
Maroc			V40 Heavy T.M.B. fired 5 rounds, and Y40 fired 165 rounds in	
"			strafe on enemy trenches - very effective bombardment -	
"			The last shot from the Heavy Trench Mortar appeared to blow	
"			up a dugout.	
~~Loos~~	22		On night of 22/23 W40 relieved Z40 in Maroc, and Z40 relieved	
			a medium Mortar Battery of the 3rd Division in the 14 bis	
			Section on night of 23/24. Z40 handed over 3 guns to W40	
			in Maroc, and Z40 took over 4 Guns from the 3rd Divl. T.M.B. which	
			they relieved in the 14 bis Section. On night of 22/23 the 120th Inf. Bde.	
			relieved the 76th Inf. Bde. in the 14 bis Section.	

Instructions regarding War Diaries and Intelligence Summaries are contained in F. S. Regs., Part II. and the Staff Manual respectively. Title pages will be prepared in manuscript.

WAR DIARY
or
INTELLIGENCE SUMMARY.
(Erase heading not required.)

Army Form C. 2118.

Place	Date	Hour	Summary of Events and Information	Remarks and references to Appendices
Maroc	22		Y40 bombarded enemy wire and trenches with 106 rounds - one of the bombs started a fire which lasted for 30 minutes. Enemy Mortars near Fosse 16 were silenced by our T.M. fire.	
"	23		Y40 bombarded enemy trenches with good effect. A Minenwerfer emplacement at M.10.C. 35.50., and two O.P's. were also fired on. Puits 16 Tower knocked down by Y40 T.M. Battery - During the day 80 rounds were expended by this battery.	
"	24		Y40 fired on gaps into which large coils of wire had been thrown by the enemy - this was cleared away by us with 43 rounds.	
Loos			X40 bombarded enemy trenches with 46 rounds.	
14 Bis			Today we took over the 14 bis Section - Z40 T.M. Battery registering various points in enemy's line with 21 rounds.	
Maroc	25		Y40 fired 26 rounds on enemy trenches in M.10.c. - Infantry raiding party reported that the trenches were much damaged. W40 fired 16 rounds on enemy wire and trenches - one bomb throwing a great deal of material into the air.	

2353 Wt. W2544/1454 700,000 5/15 D. D. & L. A.D.S.S. Forms/C 2118.

Instructions regarding War Diaries and Intelligence Summaries are contained in F. S. Regs., Part II. and the Staff Manual respectively. Title pages will be prepared in manuscript.

WAR DIARY
or
INTELLIGENCE SUMMARY.
(Erase heading not required.)

Army Form C. 2118.

Place	Date	Hour	Summary of Events and Information	Remarks and references to Appendices
Maroc 14 Bis	25		V40 fired 2 rounds 9.45" - both fell short - in "No Man's Land".	
			Z40 fired 46 rounds on trenches in H.25.d.	
Maroc	26		Y40 fired 30 rounds on gaps in wire and enemy trenches in M.10.c.	
Loos 14 bis			X fired 48 rounds on trenches in M.6.c.	
			Z fired 15 on trenches in H.25.d.	
	27		Grs Donohue (V40) and Johnson (Z40) returned from 1st Army Rest Camp at Equihen, near Boulogne - Gr. Campbell (V40) did not return from the Camp, having reported sick there 26/9/1916.	
Maroc			Y40 fired 40 rounds on enemy support line in M.10.c.	
Loos			X40 bombarded enemy trenches with 60 rounds.	
14 Bis			Z40 fired 11 on enemy trenches in H.25.d.	
Maroc	28		Y fired 45 rounds on enemy trenches. W fired 30 on enemy trenches North and South of the Double Crassier. V fired 5 rounds 9.45" between 11.5 a.m. and 11.40 a.m., and 6 between 3.10 p.m. and 3.40 p.m. on enemy trenches in M.10.c. - effective shooting and much damage done to enemy trenches - 2 rounds fell short in "No Man's Land".	

2353 Wt. W2544/1454 700,000 5/15 D. D. & L. A.D.S.S. Forms/C. 2118.

Instructions regarding War Diaries and Intelligence Summaries are contained in F. S. Regs., Part II. and the Staff Manual respectively. Title pages will be prepared in manuscript.

WAR DIARY
or
INTELLIGENCE SUMMARY.
(Erase heading not required.)

Army Form C. 2118.

Place	Date	Hour	Summary of Events and Information	Remarks and references to Appendices
Loos 14 Bis	28		X fired 91 rounds on enemy front line trenches - Very effective shooting.	
			Z fired 66 rounds on trenches in H.25.d.	
Maroc	29		In the afternoon Y fired 145 rounds, doing very much damage to enemy trenches - Material observed flying in all directions.	
–			V fired 9 rounds 9.45" on enemy trenches.	
Loos			X bombarded trenches with 113 rounds.	
	30		Capt. Norrington, R.G.A. Trench Mortar Staff Officer for Loos, transferred to the R.F.C. - Capt. Killingback, 121st Inf. Bde., took over Capt. Norrington's duties (pro-tem.)	
Maroc			V fired 4 rounds 9.45" at trench in M.10.c. - all fell short of the target, one falling in our own support line near Neuf Alley.	
"			W fired 30 rounds on front line trenches and wire in M.4.c. and M.5.c.	
"			Y fired 45 – – – – – – – M.10.c.	
Loos 14 Bis			X – 21 – trenches in M.6.c. and N.1.a.	
			Z – 18 – – – H.25.d.	

2353 Wt. W2544/1454 700,000 5/15 D. D. & L. A.D.S.S. Forms/C. 2118.

Army Form C. 2118.

WAR DIARY
or
INTELLIGENCE SUMMARY.
(Erase heading not required.)

V/40 TMB

Instructions regarding War Diaries and Intelligence Summaries are contained in F. S. Regs., Part II. and the Staff Manual respectively. Title pages will be prepared in manuscript.

V.40. T.M. battery — September 1916.

Place	Date	~~Hour~~	Summary of Events and Information	Remarks and references to Appendices
Maroc.	Sept. 1st–5.		On the first of this month the battery took over a new position in S. Maroc. The R. Es had been building a new emplacement, bomb store & dug-out. This was completed on the 5th.	
	5–6th		On the nights of the fifth & sixth the gun & ammunition were put into position in the new emplacement, & were got ready for action.	
	8th.		Received orders to get the gun out of action, & leave ammunition with a guard over it, both guns, one in Les Brebis, were packed up ready to move & the detachments chosen. They were to go, with the officers, to another division for five days.	
	10th.		Orders received on 8th were cancelled & the gun was put back into action the same night.	
	11th–15th		No firing was done, several improvements were made in emplacement & dug-outs, by R. E. s.	
	16th.		Five rounds were fired, D.T.M.O. observed. Fairly satisfactory shooting, but gun did not fire to map range.	
	21st.		Lt Henry of W.40, who was in charge during B.C's absence on leave, fired three rounds into enemy's trenches, all rounds went over into enemy's trenches, but did not reach targets. Gun again did not fire to map range.	
	22nd.		Lt. Henry again fired 5 rounds with the same result, the bed shifted & had to be relaid.	
	28th.		Lt. Delahaye fired three rounds which fell into the enemy's wire.	

2353 Wt. W2544/1454 700,000 5/15 D. D. & L. A.D.S.S. Forms/C. 2118.

Instructions regarding War Diaries and Intelligence Summaries are contained in F. S. Regs., Part II. and the Staff Manual respectively. Title pages will be prepared in manuscript.

WAR DIARY
or
INTELLIGENCE SUMMARY.
(Erase heading not required.)

Army Form C. 2118.

V. 40. T. M. Batty. September 1916.

Place	Date	Hour	Summary of Events and Information	Remarks and references to Appendices
Maroc.	Sept. 24th–25th		This time was spent in making a firm bed for the gun.	
	28th.		Lt Harland fired six rounds, these were all much too short. Firing by map range the rounds ought to have gone over into the support line. The majority fell into the wire just in front of the German front line.	
	29th.		Again fired, nine rounds. This was not such erratic shooting as before. The gun fired very steadily as regards line. Two rounds fell behind the German support line & brought up a large quantity of debris. However there were still a number of shorts into the enemy's wire & "No man's land".	
	30th.		Again fired, 4 rounds. Very bad shooting indeed. The first round fell into the enemy's wire. The second fell only ten yards in front of our own support line. The crater made by this round was examined, & was very much smaller than expected. Two more rounds were fired which fell in the middle of "No man's land".	
			A report was made on the ammunition & it has been condemned. A new charge of greater strength is being issued in place of the 16½ ozs.	

2353 Wt. W2544/1454 700,000 5/15 D. D. & L. A.D.S.S. Forms/C. 2118.

Instructions regarding War Diaries and Intelligence Summaries are contained in F. S. Regs., Part II. and the Staff Manual respectively. Title pages will be prepared in manuscript.

WAR DIARY
or
~~INTELLIGENCE SUMMARY.~~
(Erase heading not required.)

W/40 TMB
Sept 1916.

Army Form C. 2118.

Place	Date	Hour	Summary of Events and Information	Remarks and references to Appendices
	Sept 1.		This battery in billets. Ten men sent on medium T.M. course.	
			Ten men sent on heavy T.M. course. Eight men attached to R.E.s	
			at Loos for making 2" medium emplacements.	
	12.		Men returned from T.M. courses.	
	13		Ten men transferred to V/40 Heavy Trench Mortar Battery.	
	14		Eight men attached to Y/40 and Z/40 for further instructions in the line	
	22		Battery went into action at Maroc relieving Z/40 and taking over	
			their guns and stores and bombarded enemy	
	23.		Trenches and T.M. emplacements until the end of the month.	

W. Henry 2Lt R.F.A.
OC/X/40 T.M.B.

2353 Wt. W2544/1454 700,000 5/15 D. D. & L. A.D.S.S./Forms/C. 2118.

1.   X. 40. T. M. B.

Instructions regarding War Diaries and Intelligence Summaries are contained in F. S. Regs., Part II. and the Staff Manual respectively. Title pages will be prepared in manuscript.

WAR DIARY
or
INTELLIGENCE SUMMARY.
(Erase heading not required.)

Army Form C. 2118.

X/40 TMB

Place	Date	Hour	Summary of Events and Information	Remarks and references to Appendices
Loos.	1/9/16.	11.A.M.	Took over from Y. 30. T. M. B. 3 emplacements & guns complete. No. 1 at the junction of South St. & Pall Mall, No. 2. in the Chalk Pit, & No. 3 in Seaforth Alley. Two of the guns were in a neglected condition. The guns at South St. & Seaforth Alley were out of action, the former owing to faulty thread would not permit a rifle mechanism to be screwed in. The latter had a smashed bed, it having given way under the cross head & prevented any traverse being obtained. Both pits were also bent. C. U. South Wales Borderers wished wire cut each side of northern Sunken Road.	Firing in retaliation only on account of work being done on emplacements
		1.30 P.M.	Gnr Patterson was wounded in the right shoulder by a hostile T.M. while in the Chalk Pit. Not bad. Taken to Advanced Dressing Station & sent away.	
		6 P.M.	New bed & gun arrived. All guns in action again.	
		7 P.M.	Artillery fatigue only consisted of 11 men without any N.C.O. No means of communication with guns except by runners. Cannot find an O.P. where one can see more than the German front line, hence great difficulty in registering the guns accurately. Rounds fired in ½ day. 6. On hand 127.	

T2134. Wt. W708—776. 500000. 4/15. Sir J. C. & S.

2.

Instructions regarding War Diaries and Intelligence Summaries are contained in F. S. Regs., Part II. and the Staff Manual respectively. Title pages will be prepared in manuscript.

WAR DIARY
or
INTELLIGENCE SUMMARY.
(Erase heading not required.)

Army Form C. 2118.

Place	Date	Hour	Summary of Events and Information	Remarks and references to Appendices
Loos.	2/9/16		Rifle mechanism at Seaforth Alley & Chalk Pit blown out & broken. Replaced in few hours. Raid off, but am continuing wire cutting to left of Sunken Road. Heavy fire by Minnenwerfer both sides of Crassier. Artillery Fatigue only 7 men & 1 N.C.O. Fired 23. 2nd hand 129.	Firing in retaliation only
	3/9/16.		Observing Seaforth Alley gun from house on reserve line. Chalk Pit & Smith St. from Loos Crassier & saps. Seaforth Alley also from Sap on end of Crassier. Gun Corporal reported ill - bad feet. Remaining at guns.	on account of work being done on emplacements
		5.P.M.	Bombardment by Enemy with all sorts of projectiles South of Crassier. Again at 8.P.M. Minnenwerfer coming from end of Crassier. Fired 27 2nd hand 137.	
		8.P.M.	Enemy blew Camouflet at Seaforth Crater at 8 P.M.	
	4/9/16.		Chalk Pit gun out of action action owing to thread for rifle mech: being worn smooth. Seaforth Alley mechanism broken. Chalk Pit ~~bomb~~ store blown in.	
		6.30 P.M.	New & 2 rifle mech: arrive. All guns in action again. Altered Seaforth Alley bed 5° more right & registered 3 targets before dark. Fired 22. 2nd hand 118.	
	5/9/16.	7 A.M.	Registered Seaforth Alley, Chalk Pit & Smith St: drawing heavy retaliation in each case. Enemy shots invariably fell in open ground. Enemy T.M. very active round Hart's Crater.	

T2134. Wt. W708—776. 500000. 4/15. Sir J. C. & S.

3.

Instructions regarding War Diaries and Intelligence Summaries are contained in F. S. Regs., Part II. and the Staff Manual respectively. Title pages will be prepared in manuscript.

WAR DIARY
or
INTELLIGENCE SUMMARY.
(Erase heading not required.)

Army Form C. 2118.

Place	Date	Hour	Summary of Events and Information	Remarks and references to Appendices
Loos.	6/9/16.		Fired Chalk Pit & South St: on enemy front line & wire drawing heavy retaliation. New guns put in at South St:	
	7/9/16.		Seaforth Alley guns cutting wire. Chalk Pit & South St: firing in retaliation only.	
	8/9/16.		Met G.O.C. 119th Bde. & took him to see South St: guns. Enemy T.M. very quiet. Seaforth Alley guns continued wire cutting.	
	9/9/16.		Registered 6 targets for Seaforth Alley & 7 for Chalk Pit, drawing practically no retaliation.	
		9. P.M.	Enemy mine (small) blown at Harrison's Crater. Fired 21. 2nd hand 115.	
	10/9/16.	10. A.M.	Fired South St: & Chalk Pit guns on enemy wire & trenches, drawing slight retaliation.	
		2.30 P.M.	Fired Seaforth Alley on trenches & wire. Fired 58. 2nd hand 98. Work continuing slowly on South St: & Seaforth Alley emplacements. Collected 1 mile of old telephone wire in Piccadilly. Have sent it to D.T.M.O. to be exchanged. Also collected 200 yards of good wire. Rumours of spy about asking for T.M. emplacements. Have warned detachments.	
	11/9/16.	7.30 A.M.	Registered Seaforth Alley guns on more targets. New fuze No. 105. B. arrived. Gives good detonation.	
		9 A.M.	Fired South St: guns on front line & wire. Also Chalk Pit guns. Slight	

A.

Instructions regarding War Diaries and Intelligence Summaries are contained in F. S. Regs., Part II. and the Staff Manual respectively. Title pages will be prepared in manuscript.

WAR DIARY
or
INTELLIGENCE SUMMARY.
(Erase heading not required.)

Army Form C. 2118.

Place	Date	Hour	Summary of Events and Information	Remarks and references to Appendices
Loos.	11/9/16 (Cont.)		retaliation with rifle grenades. Fired 30. In hand 99.	
	12/9/16		Registered some more targets for Smith St: gun, drawing 2. aerial darts in retaliation. Chalk Pit emplacement is suffering from senile decay, & needs attention. Very quiet day. Work on Smith St: & Seaforth Alley emplacements hinders firing. Fired 31. In hand 116.	
	13/9/16.		Registered 2 more targets for Smith St: gun. Fairly quiet day.	
	14/9/16.	11 A.M.	Enemy bombarded heavily. We retaliated heavily.	
	15/9/16.		Heavy hostile T.M. activity. We retaliated until ammunition was exhausted.	
	16/9/16.		Fired 54 rounds in morning from Smith St: & Chalk Pit guns. Registered 3 more targets for Seaforth Alley gun.	
	17/9/16.	11 A.M.	Fired 12 rounds from Smith St: gun, one bomb which dropped in enemy front line at M.6.c.¼-5. caused 2 explosions besides that of the bomb. Fired 35. In hand 118.	
	18/9/16.		Rain & wind all day. At 9 A.M. fired 8 rounds from Smith St: gun, 6 of which failed to explode owing to heavy wind causing them to fall on their sides. Consequently little firing was done under such conditions. The abolition	

T2134. Wt. W708–776. 500000. 4/15. Sir J. C. & S.

Instructions regarding War Diaries and Intelligence Summaries are contained in F. S. Regs., Part II. and the Staff Manual respectively. Title pages will be prepared in manuscript.

WAR DIARY
or
INTELLIGENCE SUMMARY.
(Erase heading not required.)

Army Form C. 2118.

Place	Date	Hour	Summary of Events and Information	Remarks and references to Appendices
	Cont.			
Loos.	18/9/16.		of No 31. A & B Time fuzes has cut down the percentage of 'duds' enormously. Not more than 1 in 100 are duds when using Newton & 105. B fuzes. Altered Seaforth Alley gun 10° more right to enable it to cut wire easily each side of Northern Sunken Rd. registered on wire & front line. Fired 24. 2nd hand 138.	
	19/9/16.		Raining. Chalk Pit gun fired a good deal during the night. Very little firing possible to-day owing to infantry relief taking place. Telephone communication between H. Quarters & Smith St. & Chalk Pit guns by tapping into Company wires at Enclosure avenue & Hay Hill, & annexing old Company wires in Smith St. Unfortunately there was only a couple of hundred yards of wire available, & only two telephones. Fired 43. 2nd hand 132. Lot of mis-fires with black cartridges.	
	20/9/16.	10 A.M.	Established night lines for all guns. Fired 20 rounds from Chalk Pit & Smith St. at 10 A.M. 1 failed to explode. One round from Chalk Pit fell 150 yards short. Raining off & on. Cut wire with Seaforth gun just to left of Sunken road. M.6 b 8-5. Also from Smith St. gun at M. 6. c 1/4-5. Fairly gusty wind, making accurate firing difficult. 2" T.M's very unreliable. Two rounds at ranges varying 50 yards will sometimes drop in the same spot, tho' the gun is carefully laid by reliable N.C.O's. Fired 57 2nd hand 116.	

T2134. Wt. W708—776. 500000. 4/15. Sir J. C. & S.

6.

Instructions regarding War Diaries and Intelligence Summaries are contained in F. S. Regs., Part II. and the Staff Manual respectively. Title pages will be prepared in manuscript.

WAR DIARY
or
INTELLIGENCE SUMMARY.
(Erase heading not required.)

Army Form C. 2118.

Place	Date	Hour	Summary of Events and Information	Remarks and references to Appendices
Loos.	21/9/16.		As ordered Chalk Pit & South St. Guns fired at regular intervals from 3 P.M. till 5.30. P.M. Aerial dart & Field artillery retaliation.	
	22/9/16.		Registered more targets for Seaforth Alley guns & altered 2. Telephone communication established between our H.Q's & Hatchetts. Hostile T.M's active round Seaforth & Harrison's Craters. We retaliated heavily until he ceased.	
	23/9/16.		Cut wire at M.6.b.8-5. Heavy retaliation with T.M's.	
		5 P.M.	Bombarded hostile front & support trenches to right of Hart's and Harrison's Crater. Practically no retaliation.	
	24/9/16.	1.45 A.M.	Chalk Pit & South St. guns were supposed to open fire & keep going for half an hour. Owing to a misunderstanding between the Infantry & the gunners, the Chalk Pit guns did not fire at all. South St. guns fired from 1.45 to 2.15 A.M. All guns cutting wire on points previously specified.	
	25/9/16.		South St. guns fired from 1.35 A.M. to 2.30 A.M. in conjunction with artillery & Stokes.	
		2 P.M.	We sent off a mine just to right of Seaforth Crater. Seaforth Alley guns joined in Artillery barrage, firing 18 rounds. Fired 40. In hand 59. In bomb store 319.	

T2134. Wt. W708—776. 500000. 4/15. Sir J. C. & S.

7.

Instructions regarding War Diaries and Intelligence Summaries are contained in F. S. Regs., Part II. and the Staff Manual respectively. Title pages will be prepared in manuscript.

WAR DIARY
or
INTELLIGENCE SUMMARY.
(Erase heading not required.)

Army Form C. 2118.

Place	Date	Hour	Summary of Events and Information	Remarks and references to Appendices
Loos.	26/9/16.	2.30 P.M.	Fired 30 rounds from Chalk Pit & South St. on Enemy front line first, then lifting onto supports & communication trenches. Enemy 4.2 shrapnel over Regent St.	
		3 P.M.	to which Chalk Pit gun retaliated, no artillery retaliation forthcoming. Excellent O.P's for all guns discovered in Puit on Loos Crassier. Telephone wire & telephones badly needed. Very laborious & unsatisfactory registering guns with the aid of runner from building on Loos Crassier. South St. gun continued wire-cutting at M.6.c.1/4-5. There appears to be a gap at this spot. Fired 48. On hand 136. Artillery carrying parties now satisfactory, tho' they require careful watching.	
	27/9/16.		Infantry relief taking place, hence little firing.	
		3 P.M.	Fired 15 rounds each from South St. & Chalk Pit guns on all targets, lifting from front line onto supports. 6 Heavy T.M's on Haymarket in retaliation. Silenced by South St. gun.	2 small fires in Enemy support lines caused by South St. gun. Lasted only 5 mins.
		6 P.M.	Fired 60 from Seaforth Alley gun on various targets. Showed Capt. Rennington [?] S.O. new O.P. in Puit on Crassier. Fired 60. On hand 119. Store 268.	
	28/9/16.		Very misty. Observation impossible.	
		12.30 P.M.	Fired 10 rounds from each gun. 5 Heavy T.M's on Haymarket in retaliation.	

8.

Instructions regarding War Diaries and Intelligence Summaries are contained in F. S. Regs., Part II. and the Staff Manual respectively. Title pages will be prepared in manuscript.

WAR DIARY
or
INTELLIGENCE SUMMARY.
(Erase heading not required.)

Army Form C. 2118.

Place	Date	Hour	Summary of Events and Information	Remarks and references to Appendices
	Cont.			
Loos.	28/9/16.		1 round from Chalk Pit gun fell 150 yards short just missing sap cup to left of Hart's Crater.	
		3 P.M.	Fired 10 rounds from each gun. Same retaliation as in the morning. Silenced by Smith St. gun. Hostile artillery active throughout the day, especially with 4·2's on billets off Enclosure Avenue. Fired 91. 2nd hand 123. 2nd stone 242.	
	29/9/16.	9.30 A.M.	Fired 10 rounds each from Chalk Pit & Smith St. Heavy T.M. retaliation on Haymarket & Hay Hill, & light T.M's on Regent St. One round from Chalk Pit failed to explode.	
		5 P.M.	As ordered all 3 guns fired at rate of 1 every 2 minutes till 6 P.M.	
	30/9/16.		Very quiet day. Seaforth Alley gun continued wire cutting.	
			Norman Reid 2/Lt. R.F.A.	
			for O. C. X. 40. T.M.B.	
			1. 10. 16.	

Page 1

Instructions regarding War Diaries and Intelligence Summaries are contained in F. S. Regs., Part II. and the Staff Manual respectively. Title Pages will be prepared in manuscript.

WAR DIARY
or
INTELLIGENCE SUMMARY
(Erase heading not required.)

Army Form. C. 2118

Y/40 TMB

September 1916

Place	Date	Hour	Summary of Events and Information	Remarks and references to Appendices
Haron.	3/9/16.		Took over four new emplacements. Ran wire to same and took Guns down to Emplacements. Unable to place Guns in, owing to Engineers working on Emplacements.	
	4/9/16.		Placed all Guns in position by 11.0 am.	
		2 pm.	Commenced Registering all Guns and cut considerable amount of wire from M.10.c.3.9½ to M.10.c.2.8.	
	5/9/16.		Fired 205 Rounds and cut large Gaps in the enemy's wire in M.10.c and M.9.d.	
	6/9/16.		Continued cutting wire fired 67 Rounds. Most effective shooting. Requested to cease firing owing to Infantry Relieving.	
	7/9/16.		No firing owing to Engineers working on emplacements.	
	8/9/16.		Continued cutting wire Rounds fired 198. Gaps cut at M.9.d.9.3 and M.9.d.9.35. Obtained a direct hit on Enemy working party at M.10.c.4.6. Enemy's heavy Artillery Retaliated on our Guns. Our Artillery silenced same.	

2.

Instructions regarding War Diaries and Intelligence Summaries are contained in F. S. Regs., Part II. and the Staff Manual respectively. Title Pages will be prepared in manuscript.

WAR DIARY
or
INTELLIGENCE SUMMARY
(Erase heading not required.)

Army Form. C. 2118

Place	Date	Hour	Summary of Events and Information	Remarks and references to Appendices
Hearoc.	13/9/16		Rounds fired 160. Enemys Artillery Retaliated. but large Gaps in Enemys Wire at M.10.c 15.75. M.10.c.15.65. M.10.c. 10.60. M.10.c. 10.50. M.9.d 95.35. and M.9.d 93.30.	
	14/9/16		Rounds fired 146. Gaps kept open & enlarged at M10c 15.75, M10c 15.165, M10c 10.50 & M9d 93.30	
	~~-/-/-~~		~~[illegible]~~. Heavy minenwerfer retaliated to our fire, sweeping support line but was eventually silenced by artillery. Wirecutting continued.	
	15/9/16		Rounds fired 207. Fire noted for 20 minutes in enemy front line M9d 92.32. No retaliation to our fire.	
	16/9/16		Rounds fired 247. Combined operations were carried out between the Artillery, Heavy, Medium, & Stokes Trench Mortars. Excellent effect was noticed on the enemy wire especially at M10c 10.50 which is the centre of a large open piece of ground quite stripped of wire. Enemy T.M's fired 4 rounds.	

3.

Instructions regarding War Diaries and Intelligence Summaries are contained in F. S. Regs., Part II. and the Staff Manual respectively. Title Pages will be prepared in manuscript.

WAR DIARY
or
INTELLIGENCE SUMMARY
(Erase heading not required.)

Army Form. C. 2118

Place	Date	Hour	Summary of Events and Information	Remarks and references to Appendices
Havre	17/7/16		Rounds fired 103. Enlarged gaps in Enemy's wire and shelled strong points in enemy's trenches.	
	18/7/16		Rounds fired 30. Unable to observe owing to fog and Rain. Unable to recommence firing in afternoon owing to large Infantry Working parties repairing damage done to trenches by Rain.	
	19/7/16		Round fired 80. Unable to continue firing owing to Infantry Relief considerable damage done to enemy wire.	
	20/7/16		Rounds fired 172. Enemy retaliated heavily with Hummer weapons, doing considerable damage to our support line. We Retaliated heavily along [illegible] front and support trenches	
	21/7/16		Rounds fired 165. In co-operation with our heavy T.M. and Stokes Guns and artillery we bombarded heavily the enemy's trenches at the following points. [illegible] 7½ ... 15.10.c. 12.5½. 21.10.c 12.5 and 14.9.d 9.3¾ in Retaliation.	

4

Instructions regarding War Diaries and Intelligence Summaries are contained in F. S. Regs., Part II. and the Staff Manual respectively. Title Pages will be prepared in manuscript.

WAR DIARY
or
INTELLIGENCE SUMMARY
(Erase heading not required.)

Army Form. C. 2118

Place	Date	Hour	Summary of Events and Information	Remarks and references to Appendices
Maroc	22/9/16		Rounds fired 106. Rounds fired chiefly in retaliation on enemy's front line. Fire caused in Front line M10c 1·5½. During previous night a machine gun in Puits 16 was effectively silenced by one of our bombs. Minenwerfer activity gave way to slight enemy artillery activity.	
	23/9/16		Rounds fired 80. Intermittent firing at enemy wire and front line. No 2 gun, at the second shot of a series against Puits 16 buildings, hit the tower at its base, bringing it down. Rounds fired at suspected minenwerfer and the strong point known as the "beehive". Minenwerfer much quieter owing to our 6" howitzer.	
	24/9/16		Rounds fired 43. Gap in enemy wire kept open from M10c 1·4½ to M10c 1·5¼ and at M10c 1·5¾. Front line also shelled at different points during the day. Unable to fire more owing to shortage of ammunition on guns.	
	25/9/16		Rounds fired 25. No more ammunition available on guns. Infantry report enemy wire in very bad state and there trenches filled in & unrecognisable at certain points.	

5

Instructions regarding War Diaries and Intelligence Summaries are contained in F. S. Regs., Part II. and the Staff Manual respectively. Title pages will be prepared in manuscript.

WAR DIARY
or
INTELLIGENCE SUMMARY.

(Erase heading not required.)

Army Form C. 2118.

Place	Date	Hour	Summary of Events and Information	Remarks and references to Appendices
[illegible]	26/9/16		Rounds fired 30. Unable to fire more owing to shortage of Ammunition on Guns. We shelled Enemy's front line and communication trenches, obtaining many direct hits and doing considerable damage.	
	27/9/16		Rounds fired 40. We distributed our fire along Enemy's support line [illegible]. Owing to Infantry Relief we were unable to fire more.	
	28/9/16		Rounds fired 45. We shelled enemy's support trench and strong points in [illegible]. Enemy Minenwerfer fired seven rounds in Retaliation four of which were duds.	
	29/9/16		Rounds fired 145. In conjunction with our Heavy T.M. and Stokes Guns, we effectively shelled Enemy's trenches in M.10 c. and M.9.d, obtaining at least 80 direct hits.	
	30/9/16		Rounds fired 48. No 4 moved & fired from Treize Alley at wire M10a 5¾·3½. No Two moved to No One emplacement. Premature at 3 during the afternoon; framework of shaft in emplacement destroyed; other damage negligible. 3 gun immediately moved to no 2 emplacement.	

R. T. [illegible] Lieut
[illegible] 40 TMB.

2353 Wt. W2541/1454 700,000 5/15 D. D. & L. A.D.S.S./Forms/C. 2118.

Instructions regarding War Diaries and Intelligence Summaries are contained in F. S. Regs., Part II. and the Staff Manual respectively. Title pages will be prepared in manuscript.

WAR DIARY
or
~~INTELLIGENCE SUMMARY.~~
(Erase heading not required.)

Army Form C. 2118.

Z 40
TMB

Place	Date	Hour	Summary of Events and Information	Remarks and references to Appendices
CALONNE				
	September			
Friday	1/9/16		The 40th Division is to give up this sector and we are being relieved by the 33rd Division. Their officers came over yesterday and the battery and the infantry today. We are leaving five beds here and have taken five good beds from them. The second half battery came up at night and we took down the guns etc. The day after tomorrow we are to go up to [illegible] to relieve Y/40. The relief passed off successfully and was completed by 8 p.m. We have not fired for two days as we expected the relief yesterday and so took our guns out of action to be ready. However all has gone well.	
Saturday	2/9/16		Battery in rest. Three guns (complete) were cleaned up by us this morning and handed over to X 40 Trench Mortar Battery.	

T2134. Wt. W708—776. 500000. 4/15. Sir J. C. & S.

Instructions regarding War Diaries and Intelligence Summaries are contained in F. S. Regs., Part II. and the Staff Manual respectively. Title pages will be prepared in manuscript.

WAR DIARY

or

~~INTELLIGENCE~~ SUMMARY.

(Erase heading not required.)

Army Form C. 2118.

Place	Date	Hour	Summary of Events and Information	Remarks and references to Appendices
MAROC				
Sunday	3/9/16		2/40 took over the northern half of the CAMBRAI sector from 1/40. There are only two guns in action in QUEEN STREET and LIVERPOOL STREET. We are to go into rest in eight days from now when Y battery have completed theirs. The relief was completed by 5 p.m. I spent last night up here to learn the sector.	
Monday	4/9/16		Have had a good look round sector. O.P. for QUEEN STREET is in SOUTH STREET near ST JAMES. O.P. for LIVERPOOL STREET is a disused art. O.P. in TRIANGLE ALLEY	
Tuesday	5/9/16		The emplacements are both very old and are very difficult to keep clean, especially in this rainy weather that we are having now, but — we have to put up with things	
Wednesday	6/9/16		QUEEN STREET emplacement still very unsafe. The headcover such as it is behind the gun is very rickety owing to the bombardment of this part of the line just before we came in. It has been patched up but will probably shake down whenever we fire many shots as it rests on the bed.	
Thursday	7/9/16		Relief of 1st half by second half. The new officer's name is WARD. He has taken over second half battery. Little firing owing to rain which made observation extremely difficult, indeed almost impossible.	

T2134. Wt. W708–776. 500000. 4/15. Sir J. C. & S.

Instructions regarding War Diaries and Intelligence Summaries are contained in F. S. Regs., Part II. and the Staff Manual respectively. Title pages will be prepared in manuscript.

WAR DIARY
or
~~INTELLIGENCE~~ SUMMARY.
(Erase heading not required.)

Army Form C. 2118.

Place	Date	Hour	Summary of Events and Information	Remarks and references to Appendices
MAROC				
Friday	8/9/16		The O.P. in SOUTH STREET is not too good. South of here O'HAGAN & I explored the St. Crassier, but the view from here is not sufficiently good to warrant the laying of a new telephone wire. Other means of communication	
Saturday	9/9/16		Laid one from LIVERPOOL STREET up the S. CRASSIER and along to the sap at the end. This makes an excellent [illegible] for the trenches to the South.	
Sunday	10/9/16		Visited the new emplacements in SERRAY STREET & CORDIALE AVENUE. Both are much too small and will have to be much altered. Both guns in action fired intermittently throughout the day.	
Monday	11/9/16		The ~~QUEEN~~ STREET gun drew the fire of two enemy T.Ms from the triangle. This is too much for one gun to take on. Another gun (CORDIALE AVENUE) is to cover this and is very necessary. Relief complete 4.30 p.m.	
Tuesday	12/9/16		Again fired on the triangle supported by 4.5 Howitzers (Major HALL's battery). We soon silenced one of the enemy T.Ms. I suspect the enemy of having many alternative emplacements in his line and of only using each one for 24–72 hours & then shifting. This only when one or other has been discovered.	

Instructions regarding War Diaries and Intelligence Summaries are contained in F. S. Regs., Part II. and the Staff Manual respectively. Title pages will be prepared in manuscript.

WAR DIARY
or
~~INTELLIGENCE SUMMARY~~.
(Erase heading not required.)

Army Form C. 2118.

Place	Date	Hour	Summary of Events and Information	Remarks and references to Appendices
MARC Wednesday	13/9/16		In the morning fired LIVERPOOL STREET on trenches S of the CRASSIER. In the afternoon we fired from QUEEN STREET all along the triangle's southern side.	The Queen Street gun was badly shelled this evening fairly late, but I saw it retaliating.
Thursday	14/9/16		From the S. CRASSIER we observed shots falling on trench junction at M. This trench can be overlooked now by the S. CRASSIER and the snipers are to watch this tonight. Working parties are suspected to leave trenches here.	
Friday	15/9/16		Relieved by 2nd half battery. The wire to QUEEN STREET has been relaid from the junction [illegible] JERMYN STREET and not up CARFAX ROAD as before. This will prevent many breakages.	
Saturday	16/9/16		Emplacement at QUEEN STREET showed signs of falling in. The headcover has been rebuilt but it is still none too secure. LIVERPOOL STREET gun is very dirty but the difficulties of keeping this clean are very great. SUMP AT dug in corner seems to be useless	
Sunday	17/9/16	8 a.m.	Bombarded position whence enemy's T.M. has been observed to fire across the CRASSIERS. 12 bombs fell on or around emplacement but it was impossible to see the damage	
Monday	18/9/16		Shifted our billet to 607 from 630 as the latter is in a battalion area. The new billet is too small but is better than the one given us before. LIVERPOOL STREET shelled and the trench blocked between gun and SEVENTH AVENUE. Gunmen unhurt.	

T2134. Wt. W708–776. 500000. 4/15. Sir J. C. & S.

Instructions regarding War Diaries and Intelligence Summaries are contained in F. S. Regs., Part II. and the Staff Manual respectively. Title pages will be prepared in manuscript.

WAR DIARY
or
~~INTELLIGENCE SUMMARY.~~
(Erase heading not required.)

Army Form C. 2118.

Place	Date	Hour	Summary of Events and Information	Remarks and references to Appendices
MAROC Tuesday	19/9/16		Relieved 2nd half battery. relief complete by 4.30pm. Our wire on the CRASSIER is cut to pieces and the wire to CORDCARR AVENUE has not yet been begun.	
Wednesday	20/9/16		Generals (ART, CORPS & ARMY) came to inspect emplacements. Missed them at each place but emplacements are beautifully clean.	
Thursday	21/9/16		The new emplacement in CORDCARR AVENUE has begun firing. We are still trying to complete the wire between this gun & the O.P. in SOUTH STREET in order to control the fire (which should be very useful), but our wire does not look like being sufficient. The battery is to go to the 14 Bis SECTOR, up north of LOOS.	
Friday	22/9/16		2nd half battery relieved in MAROC by W/140. Two of their men who had been attached have been left behind, one at QUEEN STREET & one at LIVERPOOL STREET. This seems a good arrangement for W/140. but we are a bit short of men.	
14 Bis Saturday	23/9/16		Relieved V/B in 14 Bis Sector. The sector is very quiet unless stirred up by us. The state of the trenches is appalling & the gun positions are bad (except CHALK PIT). In the evening the support line was heavily shelled in retaliation for the morning strafe of V/B.	
Sunday	24/9/16		Spent the day in looking at the emplacements and trying to find O.Ps. Laying is only possible by compass & is best corrected from front line although little is seen here.	

Instructions regarding War Diaries and Intelligence Summaries are contained in F. S. Regs., Part II. and the Staff Manual respectively. Title pages will be prepared in manuscript.

WAR DIARY
or
~~INTELLIGENCE SUMMARY~~.
(Erase heading not required.)

Army Form C. 2118.

Place	Date	Hour	Summary of Events and Information	Remarks and references to Appendices
14 Bis. Monday	25/9/16		We spent the morning removing ammunition from the disused emplacements in HULL LANE to the guns in action. All the four disused emplacements are in a very bad state and look as if they were fired from before completed. Rounds fired 26.	
Tuesday	26/9/16		Infantry reliefs caused little firing in the morning. In the afternoon we bombarded the supposed position of a 'minenwerfer' which fires on POSEN ALLEY.	
Wednesday	27/9/16		Little to report. Our positions were shelled in the evening with 4.2s but most of these fell behind the support line and to our right.	
Thursday	28/9/16		With the gun in CHALK PIT ALLEY we replied vigorously to an aerial dart battery (2 guns). We could not reach it, but did infinitely more damage to the enemy trenches than they did to ours. This hun battery seems to be on an allowance, as it has never retaliated with more than 12 darts per day.	
Friday	29/9/16		Enemy quiet all day. In the morning we fired CHALK PIT gun in the extreme right position. It reaches the Point at 480. This gun has a triple bed & so far had not been fired in this direction.	
Saturday	30/9/16		Little firing owing to battalion reliefs. A few shots were fired into enemy's wire and a patrol was able to creep through in the night.	

T2134. Wt. W708—776. 500000. 4/15. Sir J. C. & S.

40

Vol 4

Army Form C. 2118.

WAR DIARY
or
INTELLIGENCE SUMMARY.
(*Erase heading not required.*)

Instructions regarding War Diaries and Intelligence Summaries are contained in F. S. Regs., Part II. and the Staff Manual respectively. Title pages will be prepared in manuscript.

October, 1916.

D. T. M. Office, 40th Division.

Place	Date	Hour	Summary of Events and Information	Remarks and references to Appendices
	Oct 1916			
Maroc	1		W Batty. fired 36 rounds on enemy trenches.	
			Y " " 147 " bombarding enemy trenches and wire, and the buildings of Puits 16 were fired on between 8.55 pm and 9.30 pm in support of Infantry raid.	
Loos			X fired 45 rounds on trenches - enemy replied with Trench Mortars on our front & support line.	
14 bis			Z fired 51 on trenches doing much damage.	
Maroc	2		W fired 21 and Y 38 on enemy trenches.	
Loos			X fired 34 on enemy trenches.	
14 bis			Z fired 63 on enemy trenches - enemy retaliated with T.M's on our trenches, between 2.30 pm & 4.45 pm. - Our artillery retaliated.	
Maroc	3		W fired 61 on the Triangle - enemy Mortars retaliated and they were engaged by 8" Hows (1st Corps H.A.) Y Batty bombarded enemy trenches with 126 rounds.	
Loos			X fired 40 bombarding enemy trenches - enemy retaliated weakly with T.M's. Our artillery shelled the active hostile T. Mortars	

2353 Wt. W2544/1454 700,000 5/15 D. D. & L. A.D.S.S. Forms/C. 2118.

Army Form C. 2118.

Instructions regarding War Diaries and Intelligence Summaries are contained in F. S. Regs., Part II. and the Staff Manual respectively. Title pages will be prepared in manuscript.

WAR DIARY
or
INTELLIGENCE SUMMARY.
(Erase heading not required.)

Place	Date	Hour	Summary of Events and Information	Remarks and references to Appendices
	Oct. 1916.			
14 bis	3		Z heavily bombarded Puits 14 bis and trenches in the vicinity.	
Maroc	4		V fired 4 rounds 9.45" - two hits on trenches were obtained and two on enemy wire.	
			W fired 49 rounds bombarding enemy trenches - no retaliation.	
			Y " 40 " " " " "	
Loos			X bombarded enemy trenches with 82 rounds.	
14 bis			Z ~ ~ ~ ~ 27 ~ . Sec Lt R.H. Walker, from King's Own Royal Lancasters, attached to W40 T.M.B.	
Maroc	5		W fired 35 registering various points on enemy trenches.	
			Y ~ 103 on trenches and the Beehive.	
Loos			X ~ 31 ~ ~ .	
14 bis			Z ~ 24 ~ ~ round Puits 14 bis, doing much damage.	
Maroc	6		V ~ 9 rounds 9.45" - 6 direct hits on enemy trenches, doing much damage - one round fell short into No-Man's-Land. W fired 25 on enemy trenches and Y 72 on enemy trenches.	
Loos			X fired 41 bombarding trenches - enemy retaliated heavily on our trenches with Medium Trench Mortars.	

2353 Wt. W2544/1454 700,000 5/15 D. D. & L. A.D.S.S. Forms/C. 2118.

Army Form C. 2118.

Instructions regarding War Diaries and Intelligence Summaries are contained in F. S. Regs., Part II. and the Staff Manual respectively. Title pages will be prepared in manuscript.

WAR DIARY
or
INTELLIGENCE SUMMARY.

(*Erase heading not required.*)

Place	Date	Hour	Summary of Events and Information	Remarks and references to Appendices
	Oct 1916			
14 bis	6		Z bombarded enemy trenches with 114 rounds	
Maroc	7		W and Y " " " " 37 and 84 rounds respectively	
Loos			X fired 4 rounds - enemy replied with a few T. Mortar rounds.	
14 bis			Z fired 16 rounds on enemy trenches - This Battery had a premature at their No. 3 Gun in the Quarry - 121524 Gr. C. Duerden, R.F.A. was killed, & 20293 Gr. J.H. Walton, R.F.A. & 34049 Gr. J. McCarthy, R.F.A. ~~& Gr. J. G. ...~~ were wounded.	
Maroc	8		W fired 30 and Y 97 bombarding trenches, doing much damage	
Loos			X fired 50 bombarding trenches - there was no retaliation.	
14 bis			Z fired 46 " " - enemy replied with 77 m.m. on our trenches from direction of Benifontaine - our artillery replied by shelling his support & communication trenches.	
		5/30 a.m.	W had a premature at one of their guns this morning - Sec. Lt. W. Henry, R.F.A., 29466 Bdr. W.L. Evans, R.F.A., 42253 Gr. W. Melvin, R.F.A., 34313 Gr. W. Smith, R.F.A., and 127729 Gr. S. Taylor, R.F.A., being killed and totally buried.	

2353 Wt. W2544/1454 700,000 5/15 D. D. & L. A.D.S.S. Forms/C. 2118.

Instructions regarding War Diaries and Intelligence Summaries are contained in F. S. Regs., Part II. and the Staff Manual respectively. Title pages will be prepared in manuscript.

WAR DIARY
or
INTELLIGENCE SUMMARY.
(Erase heading not required.)

Army Form C. 2118.

Place	Date	Hour	Summary of Events and Information	Remarks and references to Appendices
	Oct. 1916			
Maroc	9		Gave up the Maroc Section to the 37th Divn. Our Heavy T.M. in Maroc was given up, also the Medium T.M. positions Nos. 1 to 8 inc., we taking over an equivalent from the 8th Divn. On leaving the Maroc Section we went to the Hulluch Section.	
Loos			X fired 32 on enemy trenches.	
14 bis			Z fired 29 on enemy trenches.	
Loos	10		X fired 23 on enemy trenches.	
14 bis			Z fired 21 on enemy trenches.	
Loos	11		X fired 20 on enemy trenches.	
14 bis			Z fired 43 on enemy trenches.	
Loos	12		X fired 95 on enemy trenches.	
14 bis			Z fired 19 on enemy trenches.	
Hulluch			Y fired 10 registering targets in the new Section.	
Loos	13		X fired 102 bombarding enemy trenches doing a great deal of damage.	
14 bis			Z fired 37 bombarding enemy trenches to which enemy did not reply.	
Hulluch			Y fired 92 bombarding enemy trenches.	

Army Form C. 2118.

Instructions regarding War Diaries and Intelligence Summaries are contained in F. S. Regs., Part II. and the Staff Manual respectively. Title pages will be prepared in manuscript.

WAR DIARY
or
INTELLIGENCE SUMMARY.

(Erase heading not required.)

Place	Date	Hour	Summary of Events and Information	Remarks and references to Appendices
	Oct 1916			
14 bis	14		Z bombarded enemy trenches with 34 rounds to which there was no reply.	
Loos			X " " " " 70 rounds. Hostile T.M. fired on our trenches in retaliation.	
Hulluch			Hostile T.M's very active today on Hulluch Crater. Our T.M's & artillery retaliated - Y Battery firing 34 rounds.	
Loos	15		X fired 11 on enemy trenches - no retaliation.	
14 bis			Z " 12 " " " " "	
Hulluch			Y " 21 " " " - enemy replied with a few T.M's. - Our Artillery retaliated immediately & the hostile T.M's ceased fire.	
Loos	16		X fired 61 bombarding Hart's & Harrison's Craters.	
Hulluch			Y " 25 " enemy front & support line.	
14 bis			Z " 59 cutting wire in front of Puits 14 bis & shelling enemy support line.	
Loos	17		X fired 47 retaliating against hostile Mortar fire & bombarding enemy trenches.	
14 bis			Z fired 31 bombarding enemy trenches.	

2353 Wt. W2544/1454 700,000 5/15 D. D. & L. A.D.S.S. Forms/C. 2118.

Instructions regarding War Diaries and Intelligence Summaries are contained in F. S. Regs., Part II. and the Staff Manual respectively. Title pages will be prepared in manuscript.

WAR DIARY
or
INTELLIGENCE SUMMARY.
(Erase heading not required.)

Army Form C. 2118.

Place	Date	Hour	Summary of Events and Information	Remarks and references to Appendices
	Oct. 1916			
Hulluch	17		Y bombarded enemy trenches with 31 rounds.	
Loos	18		X fired 12 rounds on Harrison's Crater.	
14 bis			Y bombarded enemy trenches with 60 rounds, starting a fire in one trench which lasted for ½ an hour.	
Hulluch			Z bombarded enemy trenches with 52 rounds.	
Loos	19		X fired 21 in reply to which, hostile Mortars fired a few rounds at lengthy intervals on our trenches.	
Hulluch			Y bombarded enemy trenches with 28 rounds.	
14 bis			Z fired 51 on enemy trenches - wood & iron girders thrown into the air.	
Loos	20		X bombarded enemy support line with 37 rounds.	
14 bis			Z " " trenches with 58 rounds.	
Hulluch			Y " " " " 75 rounds - a lot of woodwork was thrown into the air.	
Loos	21		X fired 51 rounds in bombardment of enemy trenches. Today this Batty. also fired 1 round French 58 m.m.	

2353 Wt. W2544/1454 700,000 5/15 D. D. & L. A.D.S.S. Forms/C. 2118.

Army Form C. 2118.

Instructions regarding War Diaries and Intelligence Summaries are contained in F. S. Regs., Part II. and the Staff Manual respectively. Title pages will be prepared in manuscript.

WAR DIARY
or
INTELLIGENCE SUMMARY.

(Erase heading not required.)

Place	Date	Hour	Summary of Events and Information	Remarks and references to Appendices
	Oct. 1916.			
14 bis	21		Z fired 40 on enemy trenches - enemy T.M's. unusually active on our trenches.	
Hulluch			Y fired 32 in bombardment of enemy trenches.	
Loos	22		X " 64 " " " " - behind Harrison's and Hart's Craters.	
14 bis			Z bombarded enemy trenches with 76 rounds.	
Hulluch			Y " " " " 109 " . Little retaliation.	
Loos	23		X " " " " 30 " .	
14 bis			Z " " " " 40 " .	
Hulluch			Y " " " " 30 " .	
Loos	24		X fired 8 rounds on Harrison's Crater.	
14 bis			Z bombarded enemy trenches with 69 rounds	
Hulluch			Y " " " " 60 "	
Loos	25		X bombarded enemy trenches with 91 rounds. This Batty. also fired 37 rds. French 58 m.m.	
14 bis			Z " " " " 82 " .	
Hulluch			Y " " " " 62 " .	

Instructions regarding War Diaries and Intelligence Summaries are contained in F. S. Regs., Part II. and the Staff Manual respectively. Title pages will be prepared in manuscript.

WAR DIARY
or
INTELLIGENCE SUMMARY.
(Erase heading not required.)

Army Form C. 2118.

Place	Date	Hour	Summary of Events and Information	Remarks and references to Appendices
	Oct. 1916			
Loos	26		X bombarded enemy trenches with 37 rounds.	
14 bis			Z " " " " 69 " .	
Hulluch			Y " " " " 48 " .	
Loos	27		X " " " " 74 " .	
14 bis			Z " " " " 21 " .	
Hulluch			Y " " " " 58 " .	
Loos	28		X " " " " 20 " .	
14 bis			Z " " " " 38 " .	
Hulluch			Y " " " " 63 " .	
Loos	29		X " " " " 31 " .	
14 bis			Z " " " " 47 " .	
Hulluch			Y " " " " 12 " .	
Loos	30		X fired 141 rounds in strafe on Triangle - the enemy retaliated heavily with Trench Mortars.	
14 bis			Z bombarded enemy trenches with 34 rounds.	
Hulluch			Y " " " " 78 " - enemy replied with aerial darts.	

2353 Wt. W2544/1454 700,000 5/15 D. D. & L. A.D.S.S. Forms/C 2118.

Instructions regarding War Diaries and Intelligence Summaries are contained in F. S. Regs., Part II. and the Staff Manual respectively. Title pages will be prepared in manuscript.

WAR DIARY
or
INTELLIGENCE SUMMARY,
(Erase heading not required.)

Army Form C. 2118.

Place	Date	Hour	Summary of Events and Information	Remarks and references to Appendices
Loos	Oct. 1916 31		X. fired 24 rounds on enemy trenches.	
14 bis			Z " 52 " " " "	
Hulluch			Y " 30 " " " "	

O.G. Gaden Capt.
Divl. T. M. Officer.
40th Division.

2353 Wt. W2544/1454 700,000 5/15 D. D. & L. A.D.S.S. Forms/C. 2118.

Instructions regarding War Diaries and Intelligence Summaries are contained in F. S. Regs., Part II. and the Staff Manual respectively. Title pages will be prepared in manuscript.

WAR DIARY
or
INTELLIGENCE SUMMARY.
(Erase heading not required.)

V/40 TMB Army Form C. 2118.

V/40 Trench Mortar Battery.

Place	Date	~~Hour~~	Summary of Events and Information	Remarks and references to Appendices
Maroc.	Oct:		At the beginning of the month the battery was still in action in Maroc, firing on the enemy's trenches in front of Puits 16. The whole time in action from in that position great trouble was caused through bad charges, & it was the greatest difficulty to get the rounds over the German front line, the majority fell in "No man's" land.	
	1.X.16.		No firing done.	
	2.X.16.		A very quiet day, heavy rain, no firing done.	
	3.X.16.		Rained all the morning but cleared up towards noon, heavy strafe by Medium T.Ms & others, to which the ~~Ge~~ German heavy mortar retaliated. H.T.M did not fire as repairs were being done to passage leading from gun-pit to dug-out.	
	4.X.16.		Rained most of the day. Fired four rounds on trenches in M.10.c, two of which fell short in "No-man's land".	
	5.X.16.		No firing done.	
	6.X.16.		A German was seen in front line inspecting gap in wire in M.10.c.1.5, in front of which was a crater made by the H.T.M. Fired nine rounds, two of which fell in enemy's front line, & three others, in	

2353 Wt. W2544/1454 700,000 5/15 D. D. & L. A.D.S.S. Forms/C 2118.

Army Form C. 2118.

Instructions regarding War Diaries and Intelligence Summaries are contained in F. S. Regs., Part II. and the Staff Manual respectively. Title pages will be prepared in manuscript.

WAR DIARY
or
INTELLIGENCE SUMMARY.
(Erase heading not required.)

Place	Date	Hour	Summary of Events and Information	Remarks and references to Appendices
			succession fell into enemy's support line, two fell in our own wire & one in the enemy's. The last round was extremely bad. It was fired at the same range as the three which fell into the support line, but dropped short & destroyed our own front line in M.9.D. 6.9. This was an exceptionally large crater, about 20 ft. deep & 60 in diameter.	
			The passage leading to the gunpit was badly shaken. These were the last rounds the battery fired from that position.	
	7.X.16.		Fine day but windy, German aeroplane flew over but bolted on being hotly engaged by one of our B.E. planes.	
	8.X.16.		Lt Henry of W.40. was killed in Queen Street, being blown up with his gun. Engineers started work on emplacement.	
	11.X.16.		Handed over the gun & emplacement complete to the relieving division.	
	12.X.16.		Took over gun & emplacement from the 3rd. Div at Hulluch. This emplacement was very bad, having little or no cover & no flash screen, & very poor shelter for the detachment.	
	12th to 30th X.16.		This time was spent in building a new emplacement at Hulluch & finishing the one started at Loos.	

[illegible] Capt.
O.C. V/40 T.M. Batty.

2353 Wt. W2544/1454 700,000 5/15 D. D. & L. A.D.S.S. Forms/C. 2118.

Instructions regarding War Diaries and Intelligence Summaries are contained in F. S. Regs., Part II. and the Staff Manual respectively. Title pages will be prepared in manuscript.

WAR DIARY

~~or~~

~~INTELLIGENCE SUMMARY.~~

(Erase heading not required.) October, 1916.

Army Form C. 2118.

W40 Trench Mortar Battery, 40th Division.

Place	Date	Hour	Summary of Events and Information	Remarks and references to Appendices
In the Field	1.10.16	—	At the commencement of the month the Battery was in action in the Left Subsection, Maroc Section, with three guns in action. The Battery was in two detachments, the detachment under 2/Lieut. Henry being in the line; the other detachment was resting at Les Brébis.	
do.	2.10.16	3 p.m.	The detachment under Lieut. Stanford relieved the detachment under 2/Lieut. Henry in the line.	
do.	6.10.16	3 p.m.	The detachment under 2/Lieut. Henry relieved the detachment under Lieut. Stanford in the line. 2/Lieut. Walker, 11th Bn., King's Own Royal Lancaster Regiment, having been attached to the Battery, was attached to 2/Lieut. Henry's detachment for instruction.	
do.	8.10.16	5.30 a.m.	A premature explosion in the gun-pit at Jermyn Street (Left Maroc) caused the ammunition store, containing some thirty or forty rounds, to blow up. The emplacement, bomb store, dug-out and trench were completely destroyed; and 2/Lieut. Henry, 1 Bombardier, and 3 Gunners, who were in the emplacement at the time, were killed and totally buried. 2/Lieut. Walker took over command of the detachment, and Lieut. Stanford took over command of the Battery from this date.	
do.	9.10.16	12 noon	The 37th Division relieved the 40th Division in the Right Sub-section, Maroc Section; and this Battery handed over three emplacements to the right of the Double Crassier to X 37 Trench Mortar Battery.	
do.	10.10.16	12 noon	Owing to the decision to convert this Battery from a Medium to a Heavy Battery, this Battery	

2353 Wt. W2544/1454 700,000 5/15 D. D. & L. A.D.S.S./Forms/C. 2118.

(contd.)

Instructions regarding War Diaries and Intelligence Summaries are contained in F. S. Regs., Part II. and the Staff Manual respectively. Title pages will be prepared in manuscript.

WAR DIARY
or
INTELLIGENCE SUMMARY.

(Erase heading not required.) October, 1916 (contd)

Army Form C. 2118.

W40 Trench Mortar Battery, 40th Division

Place	Date	Hour	Summary of Events and Information	Remarks and references to Appendices
			was withdrawn from the line, handing over one gun in action to X40 Trench Mortar Battery, which was occupying the Loos Section. The whole Battery came into billets at Les Brébis. Two Sergeants were posted to the Battery from the W8 Trench Mortar Battery, 8th Division.	
In the Field.	12.10.16	—	Seven men joined the Battery from the 40th D.A.C.	
do.	14.10.16	—	Eight men were attached to Y40 Trench Mortar Battery to assist in the construction of emplacements and dugouts in the Hulluch Section.	
do.	22.10.16	—	One corporal, one bombardier and 27 gunners were posted to the Battery from the various units of the 40th Divisional Artillery.	
do.	24.10.16	—	The eight men attached to Y40 Battery were relieved, and replaced by twenty-four men.	
do.	29.10.16	—	Six men were attached to Z40 Battery for work on emplacements.	
do.	31.10.16	—	The Battery was still in billets at Les Brébis, but with 30 men attached to other Batteries in the trenches. The total strength had now risen to 3 officers, 57 other ranks.	

Mark Stanford Lieut.
O.C. W40 T.M. Bty.

2353 Wt. W2544/1454 700,000 5/15 D. D. & L. A.D.S.S./Forms/C. 2118.

1/ X. 40. Trench Mortar Battery. October.

WAR DIARY
or
INTELLIGENCE SUMMARY.
(Erase heading not required.)

Army Form C. 2118.

Instructions regarding War Diaries and Intelligence Summaries are contained in F. S. Regs., Part II. and the Staff Manual respectively. Title pages will be prepared in manuscript.

X40 TMB

Place	Date	Hour	Summary of Events and Information	Remarks and references to Appendices
Loos.	1.10.16.		During the morning registered Seaforth Alley gun on various 20ft spots on the front line. Work continuing slowly on two new emplacements in Seaforth Alley. Fired Chalk Pit gun heavily on spot behind Hart's crater from which aerial darts were reported to come. Heavy retaliation. Fired 21. At guns 110.	
	2.10.16.		Registered Seaforth alley gun on sap behind Shoreditch crater. At 6.40 P.m. we bombarded this sap while Stokes guns put up a barrage on the German Supports to enable the Suffolks to make a raid.	
		8.30.P.m.	Chalk Pit & South St: guns retaliated to a heavy bombardment by enemy. They immediately ceased. Fired 45. At guns 103.	
	3.10.16.	3.30.P.m.	All guns commenced firing at 2 min: intervals in conjunction with the Stokes. After firing only 8 rounds the washers broke at Seaforth Alley, & after two further attempts which fell in dangerous proximity to our front line, the gun ceased fire. There was heavy minenwerfer retaliation near South St: Rounds fired in bombardment 76 (South St. 30. Chalk Pit 36. Seaforth Alley 10)	
	4.10.16.		Rounds fired 82. In hand 109. Made 4 efforts personally to fire Seaforth Alley gun trying new washers & fresh boxes of charges, & not fuzing the bombs for safety of our infantry. At extreme range they just reached the Seaforth Crater. Gun out of action. Raining all day.	

2353 Wt. W2544/1454 700,000 5/15 D. D. & L. A.D.S.S. Forms/C. 2118.

2/

X. 40. Trench Mortar Battery.

Instructions regarding War Diaries and Intelligence Summaries are contained in F. S. Regs., Part II. and the Staff Manual respectively. Title pages will be prepared in manuscript.

WAR DIARY
or
INTELLIGENCE SUMMARY.
(Erase heading not required.)

Army Form C. 2118.

Place	Date	Hour	Summary of Events and Information	Remarks and references to Appendices
Loos.	Cont. 4.10.16.	4.P.M.	Fired 15 rounds from Chalk Pit & 7 from South St.	
		9.30P.M.	7.11 P.M. Chalk Pit gun 5 rounds to assist infantry in a raid.	
	5.10.16.		Fired 43. In hand 91. Again raining. Am ordered to shift Seaforth Alley bed so as to fire on N.1.a. 40-80. Subsequently cancelled.	
		3.P.M.	Fired 6 rounds from South St. & 10 from Chalk Pit. Shortage of bombs prohibits further expenditure. All appeals for infantry carrying parties are fruitless. Fairly quiet day. Only rifle grenade activity. Artillery fatigue 4 men short. No officer.	
	6.10.16.	Noon	Fired 31. Guns. 94. Store 316. Fired 15 from Chalk Pit & South St. guns registering some more targets to replace old ones. Artillery fatigue again only 16 men. Frantic appeals for infantry fatigue party are still without success. Put in new gun at Seaforth Alley. Fired at 500 yards range. Bombs first reached German front line. Complaints re a bomb from South St. gun falling in Dead Man's Sap wounding 3 men. Went up at once & found very small hole in parapet, & after 30 mins searching & digging all I could find was a piece of a German Aluminium Time Fuze. Quite possible a bad charge did cause bomb to fall short, but it is very doubtful if it was a 2" bomb which fell there. Using battery having 2 telephones & practically no wire at all (the quantity being so small as to be negligible)	

3/

X. 40. T. M. B.

Instructions regarding War Diaries and Intelligence Summaries are contained in F. S. Regs., Part II. and the Staff Manual respectively. Title pages will be prepared in manuscript.

WAR DIARY
or
INTELLIGENCE SUMMARY.

(Erase heading not required.)

Army Form C. 2118.

Place	Date	Hour	Summary of Events and Information	Remarks and references to Appendices
Loos	Cont. 6.10.16		Great difficulty is experienced in registering the guns as the only spot from which anything can be seen is the top of the Puit in Loos Crassier. With the assistance of a runner one can fire about 1 shot per hour.	
	7.10.16.	10 A.M.	Fired 41. 2nd hand at guns 87. Store 332. Fired 10 each from South St. & Chalk Pit guns. During the day fired 26. At guns 133.	
	8.10.16.		Heavy enemy mortaring on Regent St. South St. retaliated. Seaforth alley bed sunk while firing necessitating relaying	
	9.10.16.		Heavy hostile trench mortars round Harrisons crater. South St. guns retaliated heavily. Fired on several 20ft spots on enemy front line in the course of the day with all guns	
	10.10.16.		Fired 39. At guns 142. Handed over Seaforth Alley gun to Z. 40. T. M. B. & took over Cordiale avenue from W. 40. T. M. B. The latter has neither rifle mechanism nor T vent. Chalk Pit gun out of action in afternoon owing to plug filling T vent hole blowing out.	
	11.10.16.		Guns at Cordiale Avenue & Chalk Pit out of action. Fired 83. At guns 148	
		3.20.	Fired 10 rounds from South St on trench at M. 6. c. 1-48. from which spot aerial darts were supposed to come. Obtained 6 direct hits in trench. New barrel for Chalk Pit	

2353 Wt. W2544/1454 700,000 5/15 D. D. & L. A.D.S.S. Forms/C. 2118.

4

X. 40 T.M.B.

Instructions regarding War Diaries and Intelligence Summaries are contained in F. S. Regs., Part II. and the Staff Manual respectively. Title pages will be prepared in manuscript.

WAR DIARY
or
INTELLIGENCE SUMMARY.
(Erase heading not required.)

Army Form C. 2118.

Place	Date	Hour	Summary of Events and Information	Remarks and references to Appendices
Loos.	11.10.16		Arrived at 7 P.M. Guns in action at 8. P.M. Good emplacement at Cordrale Avenue, but no registration or targets whatever handed over. Owing to peculiar bed frame, it is only possible to obtain a traverse of 9° either way.	
	12.10.16		Fired 20. At guns 147. Store 342. Component parts 60 complete + 10 without cartridges.	
		10 A.M.	Fired 10 each from Smith St. & Chalk Pit guns on various targets, the first 5 from each on the front line, the last 5 on the supports.	
		12.30 P.M.	Fired 5 from Smith St.	
		2 P.M.	Fired 10 each from Smith St. & Chalk Pit.	
		4 P.M.	Fired another 10 from each.	
		4 P.M.	Cordrale Avenue gun in action again. Fired 10 rounds in registration. Rather uncertain as gun was firing very erratically. There was minenwerfer retaliation on Regent St. & on Engineers dump against Double Crassier. Artillery fatigue only 14 men. Cordrale Avenue emplacement bending beam supporting head cover, needs 2 more supports at least. Chalk Pit emplacement collapsing from senile decay, the falling chalk greatly hindering firing.	
	13.10.16	9 A.M.	Fired 95. At guns 98. Store 338. Fired 10 rounds registering Cordrale Avenue gun.	
		2 P.M.	Fired 10 rounds each from Chalk Pit, Smith St. & Cordrale Avenue guns causing T.M. retaliation	

2353 Wt. W2544/1454 700,000 5/15 D. D. & L. A.D.S.S. Forms/C. 2118.

5

X. 40. T.M.B.

Instructions regarding War Diaries and Intelligence Summaries are contained in F. S. Regs., Part II. and the Staff Manual respectively. Title pages will be prepared in manuscript.

WAR DIARY
or
INTELLIGENCE SUMMARY.
(Erase heading not required.)

Army Form C. 2118.

Place	Date	Hour	Summary of Events and Information	Remarks and references to Appendices
	Cont:			
Loos	13.10.16		A new Minenwerfer fired from behind Harts Crater onto Piccadilly & Loos Crassier. 99% of the rounds fall harmlessly into field between front & supports.	
		3.30 P.M.	Fired 10 rounds from each gun. Heavy Minenwerfer retaliation on Piccadilly, Regent St & Haymarket. Small T.M's dropping as far as Enclosure Avenue.	
		4.30.	Fired 5 rounds from each gun.	
			Fired 102. At guns 88. Store 291.	
	14.10.16.	10 A.M.	Fired 10 from Cordrale Avenue. Slight retaliation.	
		2.30 P.M.	Fired 10 from each gun. Eliciting Minenwerfer retaliation. 3 duds from South St.	
		5 P.M.	At 5 P.M. bolt of Chalk Pit rifle mechanism became bent. Carried on with bolt of a rifle.	
		6 P.M.	Chalk Pit bed broke, & emplacement collapsed. Started building new temporary emplacement in open. Work of our renovating old Queen St emplacement not yet commenced. Found live box in dug-out. Artillery fatigue had two men wounded (1 very slight) by machine gun fire near 2" Bomb Store. R.E. Officer says Cordrale Avenue emplacement unfit to fire out of. The percentage of blinds is very small, averaging about 2 in every 100 rounds fired. No more 105.B fuzes are being sent. They gave an excellent detonation.	
	15.10.16.		Fired 70. At guns 78. In store 247.	

6.

X. 40. T.M.B.

Instructions regarding War Diaries and Intelligence Summaries are contained in F. S. Regs., Part II. and the Staff Manual respectively. Title pages will be prepared in manuscript.

WAR DIARY
or
INTELLIGENCE SUMMARY.
(Erase heading not required.)

Army Form C. 2118.

Place	Date	Hour	Summary of Events and Information	Remarks and references to Appendices
Loos.	Cont. 15.10.16.		Work being done on Old Chalk Pit emplacement. Aerial dart into Pit wounded a Sapper working on Emplacement. Very quiet day on the whole.	
	16.10.16		Fired 11. At guns 115. Owing to infantry relief taking place, not much firing was possible.	
		4.58 P.M.	Received Test S.O.S. in which Enemy was supposed to be attacking round Harrisons Crater. South St gun fired exactly 13 mins. after message reached the Battery Headquarters. Rifle mechanism blew out of Cordiale this evening.	
	17th 10.16		Fired 61. At guns 207.	
		7. A.M.	Very heavy of firing of all sorts by Enemy lasting from 7. A.M. to 12. noon. Chalk Pit emplacement knocked about, & Entrance to Cordiale Avenue guns' dug-out blown in. South St. Gun retaliated.	
	18.10.16		Fired 47. At guns 186. In store 140. only 4 complete boxes of component parts, 12 boxes without cartridges. Very quiet day. Bombs from South St. falling short	
	19.10.16		Fired 12. At guns 218. Cordiale Avenue will be out of action for a week at least, Chalk Pit for another 4 or 5 days. Fired rounds at odd intervals on Enemy Saps.	
	20.10.16		Fired 24. At guns 199. No firing before mid-day on account of infantry relief. Queen St. Emplacement will not be ready for a week. ditto new South St Emplacement.	

2353 Wt. W2544/1454 700,000 5/15 D. D. & L. A.D.S.S. Forms/C. 2118.

7

X. 40. T.M.B

Instructions regarding War Diaries and Intelligence Summaries are contained in F. S. Regs., Part II. and the Staff Manual respectively. Title pages will be prepared in manuscript.

WAR DIARY
or
INTELLIGENCE SUMMARY.
(Erase heading not required.)

Army Form C. 2118.

Place	Date	Hour	Summary of Events and Information	Remarks and references to Appendices
Loos.	Cont. 20.10.16.	2 P.M.	Gun in action in open position in Quarry registered	
	21.10.16.		Fired 37. At guns 223. Store 225. 38 boxes of Com. parts complete & 14 without cartridges. Quarry open gun firing to left of Harts Crater thereby covering new ground. Zero line crosses enemy front line at M.6.d. 1/2 - 8 1/2. Covered position zero line was at M.6.c. 7-6. Caused 3 small explosions at M.6.d. 1-7. Registered some new targets for Chalk Pit open position. Fired in bursts from South St. No retaliation whatever.	
		8 P.M.	Got into shaft at Cordiale Avenue gun as tunnel to gun & approach trench were still blocked up. Found gun intact & 1 bomb in emplacement which was fired. One bomb from South St gun fell into Huns trenches at exact spot from which smoke was issuing at M.6.c.15-32. Tins & pieces of board were seen to fly in the air. Smoke ceased. All types of cartridges are bad. Many missfire & also get jammed in the rifle-mechanism. Those painted all black are very bad. All are made by the Birmingham Metal Coy. South St. gun dropped one in our lines	
	22.10.16.		Fired 51. At Guns 237.	
		10 A.M.	Chalk Pit gun caused another double explosion at M.6.d.1-7. South St gun at the 6th shot again dropped one behind our front line. Replaced washers which were bent & mechanism, & continued. Next 5 were alright.	

8

Instructions regarding War Diaries and Intelligence Summaries are contained in F. S. Regs., Part II. and the Staff Manual respectively. Title pages will be prepared in manuscript.

WAR DIARY
or
INTELLIGENCE SUMMARY.

(Erase heading not required.)

Army Form C. 2118.

Place	Date	Hour	Summary of Events and Information	Remarks and references to Appendices
Loos	Cont. 22.10.16	6-30 P.M.	Again climbed into Cordiale Avenue shaft. Took two bombs in & fired them at saddle gap in Double Crassier from which machine guns & snipers were covering the guns & approaches. At 2nd shot rifle mechanism blew out putting the gun out of action. Trench guns cleared & levelled by my 2 gunners. R.E. would not do it. Tunnel to guns still impassable.	
	23.10.16		Fired 64. At guns 231. Wire being laid from these H.Q to Smith St gun instead of tapping into Coy. wires. Fired on various targets on enemy front & support trenches. Coy Commanders always ask us not to fire at night because of work in trenches. It would be almost impossible anyway owing to lack of candles & torches. The allowance is 6 candles per day for 4 gun dug-outs & a H.Q's. Impossible to lay guns & fuze bombs by matches.	
	24.10.16		Fired 39. In hand on guns 350. Only guns in action are Smith St. & the open position in the Chalk Pit. Chalk Pit gun had to be taken up & relaid. Telephone wire completed to Smith St gun. Old Chalk Pit emplacement rebuilt & gun in action in it. Telephone wire laid from O.P. in Smith St. between St. James & Carfax Rd, down Carfax Rd to Queen St gun with a branch to Cordiale Avenue gun.	
	25.10.16		Arranged a strafe from noon until 4 P.M. after 8 rounds Chalk Pit bed broke. Smith	

2353 Wt. W2544/1454 700,000 5/15 D. D. & L. A.D.S.S. Forms/C. 2118.

9. X. 40. T.M.B

Instructions regarding War Diaries and Intelligence Summaries are contained in F. S. Regs., Part II. and the Staff Manual respectively. Title pages will be prepared in manuscript.

WAR DIARY
or
INTELLIGENCE SUMMARY.
(Erase heading not required.)

Army Form C. 2118.

Place	Date	Hour	Summary of Events and Information	Remarks and references to Appendices
Loos	cont 25.10.16		St: fired 83. & French gun in Queen St 37.	
	26.10.16		Fired 128. At guns –	
			Fired on various registered targets during the day. Very slight retaliation	
	27.10.16		Fired 27. At guns 238.	
			French gun at Queen St. replaced by 2". Cordrale Avenue is in action for retaliation only as engineers are working there. Registered Chalk Pit gun on M. 6. c. 8.4 to assist in raid at 11 P.M. Started firing at 9.35 & continued until 10.55. with great difficulty on account of every cartridge jamming necessitating removing rifle mechanism after every round, knocking cartridge out with a nail & replacing. Fired 22. On enquiring at Coy. H.Q. in Chalk Pit× ~~at~~ 11.30 P.M. was informed raid was cancelled. No one had informed me. South St. new emplacement quite useless. It is far too deep necessitating an enormous shaft which has a tarpaulin loosely slung over the top which no one can reach. Facing slope starts 2 ft 6 in high instead of on ground level. Could only fire at certain ranges. Took South St gun 15 cartridges to fire 4 rounds. One went only 30 yards & dropped in Regent St. a 'dud'. It was recovered and fired. Two duds in 4 rounds from Chalk Pit. Telephone wires now laid from H.Q. at M.c.a. 35-99. to Hatchetts & to South St gun. Also from O.P in South St. to Queen St & Cordrale Avenue guns.	× 10 yards away
			Cordrale gun out of action. Range indicator broken & pins securing missing. 2 rifle mechs. broken during day	

10. X 90. T.M.B.

Instructions regarding War Diaries and Intelligence Summaries are contained in F. S. Regs., Part II. and the Staff Manual respectively. Title pages will be prepared in manuscript.

WAR DIARY
or
INTELLIGENCE SUMMARY.
(Erase heading not required.)

Army Form C. 2118.

Place	Date	Hour	Summary of Events and Information	Remarks and references to Appendices
Loos	28.10.16		Fired 84. At guns 301. Divn store 30. No component parts with cartridges. Cartridges jamming at all guns. A day of disasters. Quarry bed had to be relaid. Ditto Smith St: Cordrale being out of action but pins drawing to Queen St. also range indicator. Telephone wires in Queen St. were broken by aerial darts as soon as mended, & communication could not be obtained between O.P. & guns for more than 1 or 2 rounds at a time. Registration very slow. No rations received last night. Arrived 4. P.M. to-day. Quarry bed relaid 5° more left.	
	29.10.16		Fired 20. At guns 383 Store 30 bombs. No. Com: parts. Tragedies continue. 6 new Rifle Mechanisms arrived at this night from D.T.M.O. Bad ones. One was burred & would not screw in 2 broke in 6 rounds. Had none left at 6 P.M. Rc	
		10.A.M.	Registered targets for Queen St. causing a series of explosions (small) at M.4.d.92.55. & clouds of white-blue smoke. Impossible to keep telephone communication between O.P. & Queen St. again cut after 4 rounds. Smith St. bed broken. New bed in action at 4. P.M. Infantry relief taking place prevents firing. I was not & never am informed when reliefs are about to take place	
		4.P.M.	Registered a few targets for Quarry guns.	
	30.10.16		Fired. 31 At Guns. 368 Store 13 bombs & no component parts at all. Raining	
		9 A.M.	Spent an hour mending telephone wires between Queen St. guns & junction of Carfax Rd. No time or wire to mend gaps along Cordrale Avenue. Registered Queen St. & Cordrale Avenue guns. Latter dropped 2 short & former 1 short & had 3 duds. Fired 25 rds from Chalk Pit & Smith St. chiefly in retaliation for	

11.

X. 40. T.M.B.

Instructions regarding War Diaries and Intelligence Summaries are contained in F. S. Regs., Part II. and the Staff Manual respectively. Title pages will be prepared in manuscript.

WAR DIARY
or
INTELLIGENCE SUMMARY.
(Erase heading not required.)

Army Form C. 2118.

Place	Date	Hour	Summary of Events and Information	Remarks and references to Appendices
Loos.	cont 30.10.16		Minenwerfer dropping on R.E. Chalk Dump in Regent St. from the direction of the rear of Harrison's crater.	
		3.P.M.	Fired 10 rounds from each gun firing first on the enemy front line, & then lifting onto the supports & communication trenches.	
		6.P.M.	Note from infantry saying where & when patrols would be out during the night. An excellent thing which the 40th Div: infantry now do.	
	31.10.16.		Fired 141. At guns 364. In Loos store 230 bombs & component parts for 200. Chalk Pit mechanism woodwork smashed & bent. Out of action.	
		10.A.M.	Fired 10 rounds from Smith St.	
		3.P.M.	Fired 15 rounds from Smith St. & 10 from Queen St & Cardiac Avenue.	

Norman Reid 2/Lieut. R.F.A.
O.C. X.40. T.M.B.

T2134. Wt. W708–776. 500000. 4/15. Sir J. C. & S.

Instructions regarding War Diaries and Intelligence Summaries are contained in F. S. Regs., Part II. and the Staff Manual respectively. Title pages will be prepared in manuscript.

WAR DIARY
or
INTELLIGENCE SUMMARY.
(Erase heading not required.)

Army Form C. 2118.

Y40 T. M. B.

Place	Date	Hour	Summary of Events and Information	Remarks and references to Appendices
Maroc	1/10/16		Rounds fired 147. We occupied the old Emplacement at Treize Alley and effectively cut wire at M. 10. a 60.35. During the raid at night Nos 2 and 4 Guns bombarded Point 16 to keep down Machine Gun Fire. After the Raiding Party had returned, these Guns with the assistance of No. 1 bombarded Enemy's front and Support Lines. Enemy heavy T.M. Retaliation on our front line.	
"	2/10/16		Rounds fired 38 at Enemys trenches in M. 10. c. 11. 50 Bad weather hindered operations.	
"	3/10/16		Rounds fired 107. Enemys front and Support trenches bombarded from M. 10. c and M. 9. d. Dugout blown in and set on fire.	
"	4/10/16		Rounds fired 50. We continued bombarding Enemys front line and Support trenches. No Retaliation	
"	5/10/16		Rounds fired 103. Doing considerable damage to Enemy's front line and causing two fires. We obtained several direct hits on the "Beehive" and removed a considerable number of bricks from same.	

2/

Instructions regarding War Diaries and Intelligence Summaries are contained in F. S. Regs., Part II. and the Staff Manual respectively. Title pages will be prepared in manuscript.

WAR DIARY
or
INTELLIGENCE SUMMARY.
(Erase heading not required.)

Army Form C. 2118.

Place	Date	Hour	Summary of Events and Information	Remarks and references to Appendices
Maroc.	6/10/16.		Rounds fired 72. We swept Enemy's front and support lines in M.11.c and M.9.d. Trench boards seen to fly up in several places, and obtained a few more direct hits on [illegible]. We established telephone communication to No. I Gun over the open owing to the bad state of the Support trench. No Retaliation to our firing.	
	7/10/16.		Rounds fired 84. We continued Bombarding Enemy's trenches paying particular attention to his communication trench junctions. Very Effective Shooting. Retaliation Nil.	
	8/10/16.		Rounds fired 97. We paid special attention to Enemy's Communication trenches. All dug outs of Emplacements completed by the Pioneers.	
	9/10/16.		Rounds fired Nil. Headquarters and Gun positions handed over to 37th Division. Relief Completed by 5pm.	

2353 Wt. W2541/1454 700,000 5/15 D. D. & L. A.D.S.S./Forms/C. 2118.

3/

Instructions regarding War Diaries and Intelligence Summaries are contained in F. S. Regs., Part II. and the Staff Manual respectively. Title pages will be prepared in manuscript.

WAR DIARY
or
INTELLIGENCE SUMMARY.
(Erase heading not required.)

Army Form C. 2118.

Place	Date	Hour	Summary of Events and Information	Remarks and references to Appendices
Hulluch	11/10/16.		Took over Hulluch Sector from the 8th Division, which consisted of four poor emplacements in H.19.a. and H.13.c. and also four other very badly built alternative Emplacements in H.13.d. All these Emplacements were well marked down by Enemy's Mortars and artillery and the Dug outs and Ammunition Recesses were of a very Elementary character, consisting of holes let into the side of the trench with three feet of head cover.	
	12/10/16.		Commenced Registering Guns taken over, but were obliged to cease firing owing to Infantry Relief.	
	13/10/16.		Continued Registering and effectively bombarded Enemy's front line. Rounds fired 92. Enemy Minenwerfer was firing when we commenced, but soon ceased firing.	
	14/10/16.		Rounds fired 40. Obliged to Economise owing to shortage of complete boxes of component parts. Fired very effectively on Enemy's support trench.	

2353 Wt. W2544/1454 700,000 5/15 D. D. & L. A.D.S.S./Forms/C. 2118.

Army Form C. 2118.

Instructions regarding War Diaries and Intelligence Summaries are contained in F. S. Regs., Part II. and the Staff Manual respectively. Title pages will be prepared in manuscript.

WAR DIARY
or
INTELLIGENCE SUMMARY.
(Erase heading not required.)

Place	Date	Hour	Summary of Events and Information	Remarks and references to Appendices
Hulluch	15/10/16		Rounds fired 21. Unable to fire more owing to Engineers aided by Gunners working on Nos. I and II. Emplacements. We commenced Dugouts on these Guns.	
	16/10/16		Engineers Work progressing favourably. Fired 30 Rounds and silenced Enemy's Aerial Darts.	
	17/10/16		Continued work on Emplacements, and fired on Enemy trenches at H.13.c.54.65. H.13.c.14.68 and H.19.a.60.70. Enemy very quiet directly opposite but Retaliated further South with Rifle Grenades.	
	19/10/16		Rounds fired 60. Enemy's Support and front lines bombarded in Conjunction with our Stokes Guns. A fire was caused and excellent Results obtained, much Wood being thrown into the air. Engineers continued work throughout day on Emplacement (Dugouts).	
	20/10/16		Rounds fired 28. No I Gun Mechanism blown out. Gun and Mechanism taken out of action for Repairs. Same Replaced in the Evening. Much Damage done to Enemy's front line, which appears to be strongly made.	

2353 Wt W2544/1454 700,000 5/15 D. D. & L. A.D.S.S./Forms/C. 2118.

5/

Instructions regarding War Diaries and Intelligence Summaries are contained in F. S. Regs., Part II. and the Staff Manual respectively. Title pages will be prepared in manuscript.

WAR DIARY
or
INTELLIGENCE SUMMARY.
(Erase heading not required.)

Army Form C. 2118.

Place	Date	Hour	Summary of Events and Information	Remarks and references to Appendices
Hulluch	20/10/16.		Rounds fired 75. Enemy's front and Support lines bombarded and much wood and Revet work thrown up. Enemy made weak Retaliation, to which our Stokes Guns Replied and effectively silenced.	
	21/10/16.		Rounds fired 32. Owing to faulty Mechanisms had 60 misfires. Replaced same and continued firing at Enemy's Support trench.	
	22/10/16.		Rounds fired 105. Much Material Damage done to Enemy's front line. Two Enemy Minnenwerfers located at H.20.c.10.60. and H.20.c. 60.20. They gave out much smoke and fired heavy short Shells about every 3 mins. We Retaliated to Enemy's fire.	
	23/10/16.		Rounds fired 102. Obliged to Economise owing to temporary shortage of Component Parts. Enemy's Minnenwerfers Active.	
	24/10/16.		Rounds fired 80. No 3. Emplacement occupied During the afternoon. We accurately Registered this Gun and Effectively bombarded Enemy's support lines with all four Guns.	

2353 Wt. W2544/1454 700,000 5/15 D. D. & L. A.D.S.S./Forms/C. 2118.

6.

Instructions regarding War Diaries and Intelligence Summaries are contained in F. S. Regs., Part II. and the Staff Manual respectively. Title pages will be prepared in manuscript.

WAR DIARY
or
INTELLIGENCE SUMMARY.
(Erase heading not required.)

Army Form C. 2118.

Place	Date	Hour	Summary of Events and Information	Remarks and references to Appendices
Hulluch.	25/10/16		Rounds fired 62. We bombarded the enemies communication and support trenches in H.19.A and H.13.C. We were unable to fire more owing to Infantry Relief. (Brigade Relief by 72 Bgde 24 Div.)	
	26/10/16		Rounds fired 75. We occupied for the first time the position of Hay Lane on the right, and successfully registered this gun on the enemies support and front line. No retaliation in the vicinity of the gun. The Minnen-werfer on our left fired on Green Curve.	
	27/10/16		Rounds fired 58. We continued bombarding enemies support line, and ~~[illegible]~~ replied at the rate of 10 to 1 to his H.T.M. fire on our left.	
	29/10/16		Rounds fired 63. A premature took place on No 3 gun, blowing the emplacement up, and very slightly wounding	

2353 Wt W2541/1454 700,000 5/15 D. D. & L. A.D.S.S./Forms/C. 2118.

Instructions regarding War Diaries and Intelligence Summaries are contained in F. S. Regs., Part II. and the Staff Manual respectively. Title pages will be prepared in manuscript.

WAR DIARY
or
INTELLIGENCE SUMMARY.
(Erase heading not required.)

Army Form C. 2118.

Place	Date	Hour	Summary of Events and Information	Remarks and references to Appendices
Hulluch	28/10/16.		one man. The gun was dug out intact. We had no further use for the emplacement.	
	29/10/16.		Rounds fired 12. Unable to fire much owing to Infantry Relief, and were especially requested by Infantry to keep quiet in order to allow work to proceed.	
	30/10/16.		Obliged to leave No 1 emplacement, owing to same falling in at the back. We occupied the old H.T.M. emplacement directly behind the No 1 position and placed gun in action. On the night of 29–30th the enemy obtained a direct hit on the dug out of No 2 gun with an Incendiary shell. Rounds fired 78.	
	31/10/16.		Rounds fired 21. Owing to I.M. Relief unable to fire more, we fired on enemies support lines in H.19.A and H.13.C.	

R. L. [illegible] Lt.
O.C. Y.40 T.M.B.

2353 Wt. W2541/1454 700,000 5/15 D. D. & L. A.D.S.S./Forms/C. 2118.

Instructions regarding War Diaries and Intelligence Summaries are contained in F. S. Regs., Part II. and the Staff Manual respectively. Title pages will be prepared in manuscript.

WAR DIARY
or
~~INTELLIGENCE SUMMARY.~~
(Erase heading not required.)

Z. 40 Trench Mortar Battery

Army Form C. 2118.

Place	Date	Hour	Summary of Events and Information	Remarks and references to Appendices
14 Bis	1/10/16		The open position in the QUARRY in front of the gun is considered unsuitable because both guns cannot fire at once. Therefore we prepared another open position to fire at the same targets but at the back of the old emplacement. The headcover at CHALK PIT ALLEY is very insecure and had to be propped up today to prevent its total collapse. Fired 57 rounds from the two guns	
		2-3.30pm	in the afternoon at 14 Bis chiefly and the front line all round this salient.	
	2/10/16		The morning was spent chiefly in bringing up ammunition to the dump in RESERVE line. The dump is only an old shelter but the bombs are hidden from	
		2-4pm	view and so are pretty safe. In the afternoon we fired at the supports and communication trenches opposite us dropping 63 bombs over their front line.	
	3/10/16		The artillery party was specially large last night and we were able to bring down two truck loads of bombs. Also had plenty of ammunition we again fired all afternoon sending 67 bombs among their trenches.	
	4/10/16		In the morning there was an intra battalion relief and we were unable to fire before 3 p.m. After that we fired 27 rounds at the enemy support line.	

T2134. Wt. W708—776. 500000. 4/15. Sir J. C. & S.

Instructions regarding War Diaries and Intelligence Summaries are contained in F. S. Regs., Part II. and the Staff Manual respectively. Title pages will be prepared in manuscript.

WAR DIARY
or
~~INTELLIGENCE SUMMARY.~~
(Erase heading not required.)

Army Form C. 2118.

Place	Date	Hour	Summary of Events and Information	Remarks and references to Appendices
14 Bis	5/10/16		Relief by second half battery which was completed by 2 p.m.	
		3.15 pm	Premature at the QUARRY gun apparently through no fault of the gunners. Gnr Dearden was killed instantaneously and both gunners Walton and McCarthy were wounded luckily neither very seriously. The emplacement caught fire and is badly wrecked. Also the passage connecting it with the dugout has fallen in. Fired 16 rounds.	
	6/10/16		In the morning we picked up some D III wire which had been abandoned by the artillery and relaid it down CHALK PIT ALLEY from the gun to the junction of the above named trench and the reserve line. Here we tapped into the wire of a battery running back to an observation post at the bottom of CHALK PIT ALLEY. We did this with the permission of the battery commander. In the afternoon we fired 10 rounds. Dearden was buried at PHILOSOPHE.	
	7/10/16		We did no firing in the morning but brought up ammunition. In the afternoon we fired the gun in CHALK PIT ALLEY with observation from the artillery O.P. They ranged us on Puits 14 Bis, the front line and the wire just north of the PUITS. 23 rounds were fired.	

T2134. Wt. W708–776. 500000. 4/15. Sir J. C. & S.

Instructions regarding War Diaries and Intelligence Summaries are contained in F. S. Regs., Part II. and the Staff Manual respectively. Title pages will be prepared in manuscript.

WAR DIARY
or
~~INTELLIGENCE SUMMARY.~~
(Erase heading not required.)

Z. 40 Trench Mortar Battery

~~Army~~ Form C. 2118.

Place	Date	Hour	Summary of Events and Information	Remarks and references to Appendices
14 Bis	8/10/16		We started to mend the QUARRY emplacement but it requires scientific handling. In the afternoon I ordered both guns to fire 15 rounds at ranges which I gave them and observed them from LOOS towers. This is the only real O.P. for the scots. Fired 47.	
	9/10/16		In the morning the infantry were relieving and so we did not fire. We took over the new dump built by the Stokes in the RESERVE line as they no longer seem to use it and ours has completely fallen in. Fired 15.	
	10/10/16		The bed at CHALK PIT ALLEY had to be dug up today and the headcover over the gun was taken down and readjusted. The engineers began to do this last night but left it very soon saying that they were being shelled. A shell was seen to burst within 200 yards of the emplacement.	
	11/10/16		The rations went astray today owing to the relief of the 231 Field Coy R.E. by the 229 Field Coy. They were found in the afternoon at the headquarters of the 121 Stokes trench mortar battery.	
	12/10/16		The numbers on the guns were sent down this morning. The bomb store is getting very short of component parts compared with the number of bombs there. Fired 43.	

T2134. Wt. W708—776. 500000. 4/15. Sir J. C. & S.

Instructions regarding War Diaries and Intelligence Summaries are contained in F. S. Regs., Part II. and the Staff Manual respectively. Title pages will be prepared in manuscript.

WAR DIARY

or

~~INTELLIGENCE SUMMARY.~~

(Erase heading not required.)

Army Form C. 2118.

Place	Date	Hour	Summary of Events and Information	Remarks and references to Appendices
14 Bis	13/10/16		Bombardier O'Hagan was evacuated to No1 C.C.S. today with dysentery. I can't find anybody else in the battery suffering from this. The infantry were relieving in the morning. Later we fired 19 bombs.	
	14/10/16		The rifle mechanism at CHALK PIT ALLEY jammed this morning and we had to continue firing with T tubes. The mechanism at the QUARRY also blew out and had to be replaced. Fired 37	
	15/10/16		The artillery fatigue party left the truck on the line out in the open instead of at CRUCIFIX DUMP. Unfortunately I had not made anyone definitely responsible. Rations came up tonight and there was no fatigue party at CHALK PIT ALLEY. Fired 34.	
	16/10/16		Payne & Johnson A made acting unpaid bombardiers today. We took over a gun in SEAFORTH ALLEY and with 35 bombs. The battery front now stretches from LOOS crassier to the QUARRY at 4 Bis. Fired 12 rounds.	
	17/10/16		The bed at the new gun had to be shifted and put in further forward. This emplacement is in a clay soil and is already sodden with rain. Two new emplacements are being dug but neither are nearly ready. Fired 59	

T2134. Wt. W708—776. 500000. 4/15. Sir J. C. & S.

Instructions regarding War Diaries and Intelligence Summaries are contained in F. S. Regs., Part II. and the Staff Manual respectively. Title pages will be prepared in manuscript.

WAR DIARY
or
INTELLIGENCE SUMMARY.
(Erase heading not required.)

Army Form C. 2118.

Place	Date	Hour	Summary of Events and Information	Remarks and references to Appendices
14 Bis	18/10/16		The Quarry gun sank about 4 inches towards the right hand front corner after firing 15 shots this morning. It was replanted this afternoon and was again in action by 5 p.m. 4 reinforcements came to the battery from the D.A.C. Fired 37.	
	19/10/16		Darts began to fall on the QUARRY today. They seem to come from behind & north of the PUITS and I cannot reach them. They stopped firing when CHALK PIT ALLEY fired at 500 yards and across the PUITS. The bed of the latter gun had to be adjusted in the morning. Fired 55.	
	20/10/16		The rifle mechanism of the QUARRY gun went out of order this morning and the gun was out of action all day. The bed at SEAFORTH ALLEY again had to be relaid. After dark and during the night the enemy searched for the gun in CHALK PIT ALLEY with his heavies. Fired 15.	
	21/10/16		The darts have stopped falling in the QUARRY and now fall between the front and support lines. In the afternoon we fired 58 rounds all along the enemy support line.	
	22/10/16		In the morning I saw the C.O. left battalion and he wants me to register	

T2134. Wt. W708—776. 500000. 4/15. Sir J. C. & S.

Instructions regarding War Diaries and Intelligence Summaries are contained in F. S. Regs., Part II. and the Staff Manual respectively. Title pages will be prepared in manuscript.

WAR DIARY
or
INTELLIGENCE SUMMARY.
(Erase heading not required.)

Army Form C. 2118.

Place	Date	Hour	Summary of Events and Information	Remarks and references to Appendices
14 Bde	22/10/16		on a machine gun north of the PUIT whose fire covers a part of their trenches that he intends to raid. In the afternoon registered on this point and fired [illegible] rounds at it. Fired 40.	
	23/10/16		All afternoon strafe. Fired 69 Retaliation.	
	24/10/16		Registered CHALK PIT ALLEY on wire left of 14 Sec and began cutting it here for a dummy raid. Fired 37 rounds.	
	25/10/16		Beds were sent down to SEAFORTH for the new emplacement there and also to the CHALK PIT. Had to dismiss artillery fatigue party as there were no component parts at any of the bomb stores in [illegible]. Started laying telephone wire along the reserve line from HQ to SEAFORTH ALLEY.	
	26/10/16		Continued wiring until staples gave out. The trenches are so bad that very slow progress was made. The new emplacements were not ready so that the beds couldn't be put in. Fired 75 rounds during the day particularly at support trenches behind SEAFORTH CRATER.	
	27/10/16		In the Brigade relief made firing impossible before 3:30 pm. Then all guns fired [illegible] rounds. CHALK PIT ALLEY dropped one short but fire after went alright	

T2134. Wt. W708—776. 500000. 4/15. Sir J. C. & S.

Instructions regarding War Diaries and Intelligence Summaries are contained in F. S. Regs., Part II. and the Staff Manual respectively. Title pages will be prepared in manuscript.

WAR DIARY
or
INTELLIGENCE SUMMARY.
(Erase heading not required.)

Army Form C. 2118.

Place	Date	Hour	Summary of Events and Information	Remarks and references to Appendices
14 Bis	28/10/16		No carrying parties arrived today either at HQrs or at Chalk Pit Alley. The new (24th Division) Engineers took over today. They don't propose to do any work for Trench Mortars, but Captain Gaden will see General Phillips about this.	
	29/10/16		Relief by second half battery was completed by 1 p.m. By 5 p.m. all rifle mechanisms were out of order. Two we managed to put right but they won't stand much use. The Chally mechanism could not be adjusted in any way. Fired 47 rounds today.	6 men of W.40 battery came up in the evening to help dig in the quarry.
	30/10/16		In the morning we did little firing. Chalk Pit Alley put seven shots into the Pit where work was reported being done during the night. I sent down for three new mechanisms which arrived about 3 p.m. All guns then fired 10 rounds making a total of 36 rounds for the day.	
	31/10/16		This morning I went to PAT TRENCH with Captain Gaden and subsequently took two men down there to bring back a periscope box. This went down to CRUCIFIX DUMP by the fatigue party of Artillerymen and will be sent	
		3-4 pm	down on the transport with two other spare boxes. In the afternoon we had a combined shoot from all guns firing 60 rounds.	

T2134. Wt. W708–776. 500000. 4/15. Sir J. C. & S.

Instructions regarding War Diaries and Intelligence Summaries are contained in F. S. Regs., Part II. and the Staff Manual respectively. Title pages will be prepared in manuscript.

WAR DIARY or INTELLIGENCE SUMMARY.

(Erase heading not required.)

D.T.M.O. 40th Div. Trench Mortar Officer.

November, 1916.

Vol 5

Army Form C. 2118.

Place	Date	Hour	Summary of Events and Information	Remarks and references to Appendices
Loos	1		X Bty fired 47 rds bombarding enemy trenches.	
Hulluch			Y " " 75 " " " "	
14 Bis			Z " " 84 " " " " Ironwork seen to fly into air from Puits 14 bis.	
Loos	2		D.T.M.O. proceeded on 10 days leave – Lt. H. Forrest, R.A.?, taking over his duties.	
			X fired 53 bombarding enemy trenches & bombarding hostile Mortar in Triangle.	
Hulluch			Y " 41 " " " 1 in retaliation to enemy minenwerfer fire.	
14 bis			Z " 72 " " " An explosion was caused near Puits 14 bis. Enemy searched for our Mortar with "pipsqueaks".	
Loos	3		X fired 103 bombarding enemy trenches.	
Hulluch			Y " 47 " " "	
14 Bis			Z " 69 " " "	
Loos	4		X " 101 " " " in Triangle. This drew intermittent fire from enemy Mortars.	
Hulluch			Y " 63 " " "	
14 bis			Z " 15 " " "	
Loos	5		X " 103 on enemy lines in Triangle & also behind Hart's & Harrison's Craters.	
Hulluch			Y " 62 " " " " retaliation to minenwerfer fire.	
14 Bis			Z " 34 bombarding enemy trenches.	

T2134. Wt. W708–776. 500000. 4/15. Sir J. C. & S.

(2)

Instructions regarding War Diaries and Intelligence Summaries are contained in F. S. Regs., Part II. and the Staff Manual respectively. Title pages will be prepared in manuscript.

WAR DIARY
or
INTELLIGENCE SUMMARY.
(Erase heading not required.)

Army Form C. 2118.

Place	Date	Hour	Summary of Events and Information	Remarks and references to Appendices
Loos	6		X 87 fired 87 bombarding enemy trenches.	
Hulluch			Y " 34 " " "	
14 bis			Z " 12 " " "	
Loos	7		Fired the Heavy (9.45") Mortar in Loos for first time - 6 rds. fired - 3 rds very good - 2 rds. short of target but fell in enemy lines. One round fell in our own line at junction of South St. & support line.	
			X Bty fired 63 cooperating with Heavy T.M. above mentioned.	
Hulluch			Y " " 56 bombarding enemy trenches.	
14 bis			Z " " 88 " " " behind Gordon Crater.	
Loos	8		X " " 21 " " "	
Hulluch			Y " " 47 " " "	
14 bis			Z " " 23 " " "	
Loos	9		X " " 40 " " " near Hart's Crater.	
Hulluch			Y " " 15 " " "	
14 bis			Z " " 37 " " "	
Loos	10		X " " 35 " " " in Triangle.	
Hulluch			Y " " 79 " " " and wire cutting.	
14 bis			Z " " 29 " " "	

T2134. Wt. W708—776. 500000. 4/15. Sir J. C. & S.

(3.)

Instructions regarding War Diaries and Intelligence Summaries are contained in F. S. Regs., Part II. and the Staff Manual respectively. Title pages will be prepared in manuscript.

WAR DIARY
or
INTELLIGENCE SUMMARY.
(Erase heading not required.)

Army Form C. 2118.

Place	Date	Hour	Summary of Events and Information	Remarks and references to Appendices
Loos	11		X fired 11 on enemy trenches.	
Hulluch			Y " 61 cutting wire.	
14 Bis			Z " 22 " " .	
Loos	12		X " 57 bombarding enemy trenches.	
Hulluch			Y " 57 " " "	
14 bis			Z " 26 " " "	
Loos	13		X " 39 on enemy lines in Triangle & cutting wire left of Hart's Crater.	
Hulluch			Y " 64 bombarding enemy trenches and cutting wire.	
14 bis			Z " 81 " " " " " "	
Loos	14		X " 50 " " " " " "	
Hulluch			Y " ~~38~~ 82 " " " " " "	
14 bis			Z " ~~82~~ 38 " " " " " "	
Loos	15		X " 84 cutting wire.	
Hulluch			Y " 60 " "	
14 bis			Z " 119 on trenches & cutting wire – Explosion caused in enemy support line.	
Loos	16		X " 19 cutting wire & enlarging gaps already cut.	
Hulluch			Y " 70 " " .	
14 bis			Z " 36 trenches.	

T2134. Wt. W708–776. 500000. 4/15. Sir J. C. & S.

(4.)

Instructions regarding War Diaries and Intelligence Summaries are contained in F. S. Regs., Part II. and the Staff Manual respectively. Title pages will be prepared in manuscript.

WAR DIARY
or
INTELLIGENCE SUMMARY.
(Erase heading not required.)

Army Form C. 2118.

Place	Date	Hour	Summary of Events and Information	Remarks and references to Appendices
Loos	17		X fired 85 cutting wire.	
Hulluch			Y " 53 " " & dispersing working parties.	
14 bis			Z " 49 " " " " " "	
Loos	18		X " 7 on enemy trenches.	
Hulluch			Y " 15 " " "	
14 bis			Z " 44 " " "	
Loos	19		X " 118 " " ". – The Heavy (9.45") Mortar fired 4 rounds.	
Hulluch			Y " 229 " " "	
14 bis			Z " 76 " " "	
Loos	20		X " 27 cutting wire. Wire very badly damaged.	
Hulluch			Y " 54 on enemy trenches.	
14 bis			Z " 46 " " " and wire cutting. ~~[illegible]~~ – Large gap made in enemy's wire.	
Loos	21		X fired 11 on enemy trenches.	
Hulluch.			Y " 53 " " " and cutting wire.	
14 bis			Z " 41 " " " " " – We also strafed a M. G. emplacement.	
Loos	22		X " 137 – Concentration on enemy front line & wire behind Start's Crater – most effective on both.	
Hulluch			Y fired 61 Concentration on enemy support line. Very many direct hits, apparently right in the trench	
14 bis			Z fired 36 rounds cutting wire.	

T2134. Wt. W708–776. 500000. 4/15. Sir J. C. & S.

(5)

Instructions regarding War Diaries and Intelligence Summaries are contained in F. S. Regs., Part II. and the Staff Manual respectively. Title pages will be prepared in manuscript.

WAR DIARY
or
INTELLIGENCE SUMMARY.
(Erase heading not required.)

Army Form C. 2118.

Place	Date	Hour	Summary of Events and Information	Remarks and references to Appendices
Loos	23		X fired 36 bombarding enemy trenches. Heavy Mortar fired 4 rds.- registration.	
Hulluch			Y " 41 " " "	
14 bis			Z " 46 " " "	
Loos	24		X " 38 " " "	
Hulluch			Y " 36 " " "	
14 Bis			Z " 70 " " "	
Loos	25		X " 62 behind Hart's Crater & South of Harrison's Crater.	
Hulluch			Y " 145 on enemy's support line and wire.	
14 Bis			Z " 103 bombarding enemy trenches.	
Loos	26		X " 63 cutting wire. V40 fired 5 rds. 9.45" - further registration.	
Hulluch			Y " 30 " "	
14 Bis			Z " 42 bombarding enemy's trenches.	
Loos	27		X " 103 cutting wire.	
Hulluch			Y " 30 " "	
14 Bis			Z " 54 " "	
Loos	28		X " 30 bombarding enemy's trenches.	
Hulluch			Y " 44 " " "	
14 bis			Z " 14[illegible] " " "	

T2134. Wt. W708—776. 500000. 4/15. Sir J. C. & S.

(6)

Instructions regarding War Diaries and Intelligence Summaries are contained in F. S. Regs., Part II. and the Staff Manual respectively. Title pages will be prepared in manuscript.

WAR DIARY
or
INTELLIGENCE SUMMARY.
(Erase heading not required.)

Army Form C. 2118.

Place	Date	Hour	Summary of Events and Information	Remarks and references to Appendices
Loos Hulluch 14 Bis	29		X Bty. fired 70 rds. on enemy trenches and wire cutting.	
			Y " " 33 " " " "	
			Z " " 66 " " " front line – also cut wire. Both effective.	
Loos Hulluch 14 Bis	30		X " " 65 " cutting wire.	
			Y " " 42 " on enemy trenches.	
			Z " " 56 " " " "	

Total number rounds 2" expended during the month :- 5,025
Average daily exp. of 2" for the month :- 167

[signature] Capt.
D. T.M. Off.
40th Division.

T2134. Wt. W708–776. 500000. 4/15. Sir J. C. & S.

Instructions regarding War Diaries and Intelligence Summaries are contained in F. S. Regs., Part II. and the Staff Manual respectively. Title pages will be prepared in manuscript.

WAR DIARY
or
~~INTELLIGENCE SUMMARY~~.
(Erase heading not required.)

V/40 TMB

Army Form C. 2118.

November

V/40. T. M. battery

Place	Date	Hour	Summary of Events and Information	Remarks and references to Appendices
Loos.	1-7.		Up till the 7th. of this month, the battery was out of action & engaged in finishing an emplacement which had been started in Loos.	
	7.		The emplacement was nearly finished, & was ready for firing. Six rounds were fired at a suspected emplacement of "Jane" one of the enemy's mortars, M.6.D.40.30. Three shells fell very close to the target & two seemed to be direct hits. The rounds fell as follows:- (1) Enemy's wire (M.6.D.30.95) (2) Target (M.6.D.40-45.) (3) The same as (2). (4) Fell only about 100 yards in front of the gun pit, this must have been due to faulty ammunition. (5) Target. (6) Support line (M.6.D.50-90.).	
	14.		No more firing was done until the 19th. Several improvements were made in the gun position & the bed was very much improved. Four rounds were fired at the trench junction M.6.D.40.50. Rounds fell as follows. (1) Unobserved (2) Fine burst in M.6.D.30.30. (3) A deflection of 3° more left was given, but the round fell on the right of the previous one in M.6.D.25.30. (4) M.6.D.20.60. All four rounds failed to hit the target.	

A5834 Wt. W4973/M687 750,000 8/16 D. D. & L. Ltd. Forms/C.2118/13.

Instructions regarding War Diaries and Intelligence Summaries are contained in F. S. Regs., Part II. and the Staff Manual respectively. Title pages will be prepared in manuscript.

Army Form C. 2118.

WAR DIARY
or
INTELLIGENCE SUMMARY.
(Erase heading not required.)

November (continued) — V/40. T.M. Battery

Place	Date	Hour	Summary of Events and Information	Remarks and references to Appendices
Loos.	23		No more rounds were fired until the 21st. when four more were fired at the Trench Junction in M.6.D.45.50. The rounds fell as follows:– (1) Trench in M.6.D.20.50. (2) Trench in M.6.D.45.40. (3) Railway embankment in M.6.D.45.40. (4) Trench in M.6.D.50.60.	
	26.		The next "shoot" was on the 26th, when five rounds were fired. It was originally intended that six should be fired in the hour. But some delay was caused by a miss-fire at the fourth round. The second round was a direct hit on the target. The target was the junction of a communication trench & the support line, in M.6.D.45.70. The rounds fell as follows. (1) Trench in M.6.D.50.88. (2) Direct hit on target M.6.D.45.70. (3) M.6.D.40.55. After the second round it was not possible to get back onto the target, range increased by about 20 yards for each round. (4) Miss-fired, M.6.D.45.58. (5) Exactly the same as (4). M.6.D.45.55. Before this last round was fired, the range was shortened by 40 yards, but it made very little difference. No more firing was done this month. In all the firing this month the charges used were made up to 19 ozs. instead of 14½. [illegible] O.C. V/40. T.M. Baty.	

A5834 Wt. W4973/M687 750,000 8/16 D. D. & L. Ltd. Forms/C.2118/13.

X. 40. Trench Mortar Battery.

November 1916.

WAR DIARY
or
INTELLIGENCE SUMMARY.
(Erase heading not required.)

Army Form C. 2118.

Instructions regarding War Diaries and Intelligence Summaries are contained in F. S. Regs., Part II. and the Staff Manual respectively. Title pages will be prepared in manuscript.

X/40 TMB

Place	Date	Hour	Summary of Events and Information	Remarks and references to Appendices
Loos.	1.11.16.		Telephone wire laid from H.Q. to Chalk Pit. Some difficulty over registering Cordrale Avenue owing to cartridges jamming in the Rifle mechanism. Fired. Cordrale 1. Queen 0. South St: 20 Chalk 3.	Total fired 24.
	2.11.16.		Laid wire to connect Queen St, Cordrale Avenue, South St: O.P. and H.Q.	
			Registered Queen St. on trenches & a 'Minnie' emplacement in Triangle. Rifle mechanism again puts Cordrale out of action. Chalk Pit mechanism broke, but one was made up out of parts of other broken ones. Fired:- Cordrale 0. Queen St. 23. South St: 24. Chalk Pit 5.	Total fired. 52.
	3.11.16.		Laying telephone wires finished. All guns now in telephone connection with H.Q. & South St: O.P. Started a bombardment by all guns except Cordrale. Mechanism at Chalk Pit broke after 15 rounds. A few rounds later South St. Mechanism broke. Fired. Cordrale 13. Queen 23. South 0. Chalk 15.	Total fired. 54.
	4.11.16.		Cordrale only firing in retaliation owing to work proceeding on emplacement. Fired [illegible] other 3 guns on various selected targets. South St: Mechanism broke. Fired. Cordrale 0. Queen 45. South 40. Chalk 17.	Total. 102.
	5.11.16.	6.30.A.M.	Fired 5 from Cordrale & 8 from Queen St: Slight retaliation. Wire along Queen St: & Cordrale Av: was broken in about 20 places. Chalk Pit Mechanism broke. Bed had also sunk, so was taken up and relaid. Laid wire from H.Q. to O.P. on top of Loos Towers. This is	

T2134. Wt. W708—776. 500000. 4/15. Sir J. C. & S.

2

Instructions regarding War Diaries and Intelligence Summaries are contained in F. S. Regs., Part II. and the Staff Manual respectively. Title pages will be prepared in manuscript.

WAR DIARY
or
INTELLIGENCE SUMMARY.
(Erase heading not required.)

Army Form C. 2118.

Place	Date	Hour	Summary of Events and Information	Remarks and references to Appendices
Loos.	(Contd.) 5.11.16.		O.P. for Chalk Pit & Smith St. guns. Fired. Cordiale 22. Queen 30. Smith 20. Chalk 29.	Total. 101.
	6.11.16.		No bombs in Loos store. Very little firing during morning owing to Infantry relief taking place. Queen St. went out of action owing to bed sinking, & back of emplacement falling in. It had not been revetted or boarded up. Phone wires along Queen St. & Cordiale were for once intact. Queen St. left with only 5 bombs owing to Officer i/c. of Maroc fatigue refusing to make two journeys. Minnies firing on R.E. Chalk dump in Regent St. & Loos Crassier were speedily silenced by Smith St. & Chalk Pit guns. Cpl. Heth off all duty with Trench Fever. Very short handed at H.Q. Fired. Cordiale 17. Queen 44. Smith 21. Chalk 21. Cut a gap in wire round Sap just to left of Harts' crater.	Total 103.
	7.11.16.		No carrying party at Loos this a.m. Rain & wind all day. Cordiale mechanism woodwork broken but just managing to continue with it. No. carrying party at Maroc. Artillery party again very short. – only 13 men.	
		2.30.Pm.	To assist 9.45" T.M. Chalk Pit & Smith St. guns fired heavily on Saps behind Harts & Harrison's Craters. After 5 rounds Smith St. went out of action owing to ~~after~~ emplacement collapsing on gun, & bed having sunk & being under water. Cordiale went out of action after 1 round owing to mechanism breaking. The chief reasons for so many	

T2134. Wt. W708–776. 500000. 4/15. Sir J. C. & S.

3

Instructions regarding War Diaries and Intelligence Summaries are contained in F. S. Regs., Part II. and the Staff Manual respectively. Title pages will be prepared in manuscript.

WAR DIARY
or
INTELLIGENCE SUMMARY.
(Erase heading not required.)

Army Form C. 2118.

Place	Date	Hour	Summary of Events and Information	Remarks and references to Appendices
Loos.	(cont) 7.11.16.		Mechanisms breaking is (1) The woodwork is not protected by a band, & breaks, causing the unprotected metal part to bend. (2) Springs of striker pin being weak & not having sufficient force to fire cartridge. Yesterdays rations permanently lost while on their way up on Pioneer transport. Fired. Cordrale 25. Queen 10. South 30. Chalk 40.	Total. 105.
	8.11.16.		Bombarded trenches behind Hart's Crater. Lot of repairing to wire necessary. Both Queen & Cordrale mechanisms broken. R.E. working on latter. Fired Cordrale 1. Queen 4. South. 18. Chalk 22.	Total 45.
	9.11.16.		New South St. emplacement not yet ready. Old one totally useless. Bombarded trenches round Hart's Crater. The need of 2 signallers – one for each half-Batt: – is badly felt. There are 5 telephones to keep in repair, & about 11 miles of wire to mend, patrol, pin up, dig out of blown in trenches daily. At present this has to be done by the Officer & Corporal, in addition to visiting guns, registering them, meeting carrying parties, seeing Coy. Commanders &c. An impossibility as no one in the Battery has the slightest knowledge of telephones. Men in Battery cannot be spared, as they are already shorthanded. Fired. Cordrale 0. Queen 0. South 0. Chalk 21.	Total 21.
	10.11.16.		Spent hours repairing telephone wires. Saw R.E. re South St. emplacement. Component	

4.

Instructions regarding War Diaries and Intelligence Summaries are contained in F. S. Regs., Part II. and the Staff Manual respectively. Title pages will be prepared in manuscript.

WAR DIARY
or
INTELLIGENCE SUMMARY.
(Erase heading not required.)

Army Form C. 2118.

Place	Date	Hour	Summary of Events and Information	Remarks and references to Appendices
Loos.	(cont). 10.11.16.		parts were issued to-day minus cartridges. Continued demolishing trenches round Harts' Crater. Fired. Cordrale 0. Queen 0. Chalk. 40. South 0.	Total 40.
	11.11.16.		Registered Queen St. on some soft spots in Triangle & Chalk Pit on wire at M. 6. d. 2-10. Fired. Cordrale 0. Queen 10. South 0. Chalk 25.	Total 35.
	12.11.16.		Chalk Pit gun cutting wire Bombarded trenches in triangle. Fired. Cordrale 0. Queen 27. South. 0. Chalk 10.	Total 37.
	13.11.16.		Chalk Pit cut wire & bombarded front line at M. 6.c. 9-8. Reported to Infantry & asked them to keep gap open at night. R.E. at last started on South St. Queen St. bed taken up. Fired. Cordrale 10. Queen 11. South St. 0. Chalk. 28.	Total. 49.
	14.11.16.		Impossible to register Queen & Cordrale by phone as wires get broken as soon as they are mended. Chalk Pit still on wire & trenches behind. R.E's will finish South St. to-morrow. Fired. Cordrale 3. Queen 12. South 0. Chalk 25.	Total 40.
	15.11.16.		Chalk widened gap at M.6.c.9.8. Mist prevented Queen St. being registered accurately on wire. Queen St. mechanism broken. Fired. Cordrale 10. Queen 34. South 0. Chalk 40.	Total. 84.
	16.11.16.		Started to register Queen St on wire. after 3 rounds mechanism blew out putting gun	

T2134. Wt. W708—776. 500000. 4/15. Sir J. C. & S.

5

Army Form C. 2118.

Instructions regarding War Diaries and Intelligence Summaries are contained in F. S. Regs., Part II. and the Staff Manual respectively. Title pages will be prepared in manuscript.

WAR DIARY
or
INTELLIGENCE SUMMARY.
(Erase heading not required.)

Place	Date	Hour	Summary of Events and Information	Remarks and references to Appendices
Loos.	(cont) 16.11.16		out of action. Gun threads were also burred. Gun sent away. Bombarded trenches in M.6.c. Fired. Cordrail 0. Queen 3. South 0. Chalk 16.	Total 19.
	17.11.16.		South St: gun in action again in new emplacement. Bombarded trenches in M.6.c. Registered on wire at M.6.c. 2-5. M.4.d. 8½-4¼. M.5.c. 3-8½. All four guns were in action to-day. R.E. started putting in new double bed at Queen St. Fired. Cordrail 32. Queen 7. South 14. Chalk 32.	Total. 85.
	18.11.16.		Infantry relief precluded much firing to-day. After 3rd shot from South St: the bed broke. Replaced it, but it was then dark. R.E. did no work at Queen St. Fired. Cordrail 0. Queen 0. South 2. Chalk 5.	Total 7.
	19.11.16.		Combined Artillery & T.M. strafe took place to-day. Fired from 11.30. A.M. till 12.30 P.M. & from 2. P.M to 3. P.M. at selected targets and wire. South St: could not fire in morning owing to mechanism being useless. 2 P.M. all 4 guns were in action. Fired. Cordrail 39. Queen 17. South 33. Chalk 29.	Total 118.
	20.11.16.		Chalk Pit still out of action - no mechanism. Cut wire from Queen St: & South St. Fired. Cordrail 0. Queen 4. South 23. Chalk 0.	Total 27.
	21.11.16.		2nd shot from Queen St: blew mechanism out, damaging threads of adaptor. Sent gun out	

6.

Instructions regarding War Diaries and Intelligence Summaries are contained in F. S. Regs., Part II. and the Staff Manual respectively. Title pages will be prepared in manuscript.

WAR DIARY
or
INTELLIGENCE SUMMARY.
(Erase heading not required.)

Army Form C. 2118.

Place	Date	Hour	Summary of Events and Information	Remarks and references to Appendices
	(cont)			
Loos.	21.11.16.		Putting in a bed in the open in the Quarry. Fired. Cordrale 0. Queen 3. South. 8. Chalk 0.	Total 11.
	22.11.16.		Bombarded trenches round Hart's Crater. Cut wire & bombarded enemy front line at M. 5. d. 6. 3½. & M. 5. d. 4½ - 3. Had barrel brought from Cordrale to Queen St & started to cut wire. After 3rd shot mechanism broke. R.E's still at work on Cordrale emplacement & start to-morrow on Queen St. Fired. Cordrale 0. Queen 5. South 52. Chalk 40.	Total 97.
	23.11.16.		Cutting wire in a new place to right of Harrison's Crater. Cordrale & Queen still out of action owing to R.E. repairing them. Gun in Chalk Pit has sunk 16 inches making firing impossible. Have put bed in open. Fired 20 rounds from South St. on wire at M. 5. d. 92 - 60. with good results. An obvious gap at this spot. Also one at M. 5. d. 76. - 56. There is also a gap cut some weeks ago & recently enlarged at M. 6. a. 0.2 - 9. round a sap. Fired. Cordrale 0. Queen 0. South 28. Chalk 6.	Total 34.
	24.11.16.		No firing before 3. P.M. owing to infantry relief. Went up every sap between Boyau 31. A. & Loos Crassier in order to get a close view of gaps in enemy wire. Very	

7.

Instructions regarding War Diaries and Intelligence Summaries are contained in F. S. Regs., Part II. and the Staff Manual respectively. Title pages will be prepared in manuscript.

WAR DIARY
or
INTELLIGENCE SUMMARY.
(Erase heading not required.)

Army Form C. 2118.

Place	Date	Hour	Summary of Events and Information	Remarks and references to Appendices
Loos.	24.11.16.		unsatisfactory view owing to snipers &c. Fired Chalk Pit open position & South St. on Enemy wire the former at M.6.c. 55-62. The open bed in Chalk Pit had sunk 14 inches. Relaid it with 4. 9 by 3 beams underneath. Sinking very slightly now. Fired. Cordrale 0. Queen 0. South 12. Chalk 26.	Total 38.
	25.11.16.		For 2 days only 3 candles have been rec^d for 4 guns & H.Q. Impossible state of affairs. Seldom more than 6 or 7 are rec^d. During a.m. went round all guns with Major Parsons & S.O. T.M. R.E. have not been near Cordrale or Queen St all day.	
		2.P.m.	Fired 20 rounds each from Chalk & South guns on wire & front line. Rain allday. Fired. Cordrale 0. Queen 0. South. 31. Chalk 31.	Total 62.
	26.11.16.		Again R.E. have done no work at Cordrale & Queen St. Have got gunners on trying to make them strong enough for firing. During a.m. registered Chalk Pit open bed & South St. new bed on new spots on trenches & wire at M. 6.c. 5-6. and at M.5.d. 74-60. Guns very erratic making it difficult to cut a gap. Disturbed in Towers O.P. while doing it by 4. 4.2" into Towers. Cut phone wire. During P.M. again fired on above points. Fired. Cordrale 0. Queen 0. South 28. Chalk 35.	Total 63.

T2134. Wt. W708-776. 500000. 4/15. Sir J. C. & S.

8.

Instructions regarding War Diaries and Intelligence Summaries are contained in F. S. Regs., Part II. and the Staff Manual respectively. Title pages will be prepared in manuscript.

WAR DIARY
or
INTELLIGENCE SUMMARY.
(Erase heading not required.)

Army Form C. 2118.

Place	Date	Hour	Summary of Events and Information	Remarks and references to Appendices
Loos.	27.11.16		Ridiculous complaint from Infantry Sub: That South St: was dropping near our trenches. When Capt. told him I was on 'phone at O.P. observing & would he speak to me, he said perhaps he was wrong & went away. All shots were personally observed to fall in enemy wire and trenches near Dead-man's Sap. While South St: was	
		10.A.M.	firing something fell on ~~fuze~~ while bomb was in gun about to be fired.	
		1.30 P.M.	Emplacement was wrecked. Gun intact. From 1. to 4 registered Central & Queen St: on wire and trenches at M.4.d.8-7. & M.5.c.2½-7½. Lot of timber with telephones & mechanisms. Good results observed. Also bombarded trench from which smoke emerges when Minnies fire. 6 direct hits on the spot. No retaliation.	
		3.30.	Fired Chalk Pit open bed on wire, arranged with R.E. to put double bed in open there. Fired. Central 31. Queen 35. South 5. Chalk 31.	Total 102.
	28.11.16.		Very foggy day making observation impossible. Phone wires in Quarry badly cut by aerial darts. Fired Chalk gun on wire. Queen St: & Central continued wire cutting round triangle. Fired. Central 5. Queen. 20. South. 0. Chalk. 5	Total. 30

T2134. Wt. W708-776. 500000. 4/15. Sir J. C. & S.

9.

Instructions regarding War Diaries and Intelligence Summaries are contained in F. S. Regs., Part II. and the Staff Manual respectively. Title pages will be prepared in manuscript.

WAR DIARY
or
INTELLIGENCE SUMMARY.
(Erase heading not required.)

Army Form C. 2118.

Place	Date	Hour	Summary of Events and Information	Remarks and references to Appendices
Loos.	29.10.16		All guns except Smith St: continued cutting wire at previously specified points. Also bombardments of trenches behind these points were carried out. A lot of damage seems to have been done. Fired. Cordiale 43 Queens 7 Smith. 0 Chalk 20	Total. 70.
	30.10.16.		Queen St. barrel broke and was replaced by a new one as expeditiously as possible, being in action again before midday. Cordiale & Queen St continued their bombardment of enemy wire and front line each side of the triangle. A few rounds were also dropped on trench junctions further back. Gap in wire opposite Sap 6. in triangle. Mechanism broke, but gun continued firing with T tubes. Chalk Pit continued firing on wire. Fired. Cordiale. 26 Queens. 12. Smith. 0 Chalk. 27.	Total. 65.
			Fired during month. Cordiale A: 256. 13 days in action. most of the day. Queen St. 420. 20 " " " " " " Smith St. 413. 17 " " " " " " Chalk Pit. 627. 25 " " " " " " Total 1716	

Norman Reid 2/Lieut. R.F.A.
X. 40. T.M.B.

T2134. Wt. W708—776. 500000. 4/15. Sir J. C. & S.

Instructions regarding War Diaries and Intelligence Summaries are contained in F. S. Regs., Part II. and the Staff Manual respectively. Title pages will be prepared in manuscript.

November

WAR DIARY
or
INTELLIGENCE SUMMARY.

Y. 40. T.M.B.

(Erase heading not required.)

Army Form C. 2118.

Place	Date	Hour	Summary of Events and Information	Remarks and references to Appendices
Hulluch	1/11/16		Rounds fired 62. We bombarded the enemy's trenches in H.19.A and H.13.C. Good effect observed. No hostile retaliation.	
	2/11/16		Rounds fired 75. We continued bombarding the enemy's front & support lines. No3 Gun Stoky have moved to an old deserted position in Sap Trench which was not handed over by the 8th Division. No2 Gun out of action owing to mechanical trouble.	
	3rd		Rounds fired 41. We fired in retaliation to enemy's minenwerfer on our left which was silenced. The old Heavy position in Vendin Alley was occupied by us, the bed had to be reset because gun was firing into No3 arc of fire.	T.M.
	4.		Rounds fired 47. We fired in retaliation to aerial darts and suspected positions. Good effects observed.	
	5.		Rounds fired 63. We bombarded enemy support line in H.13.C and H.19.A and H.19.D. 77 m.m. gun	

Instructions regarding War Diaries and Intelligence Summaries are contained in F. S. Regs., Part II. and the Staff Manual respectively. Title pages will be prepared in manuscript.

WAR DIARY
or
INTELLIGENCE SUMMARY.
(Erase heading not required.)

Army Form C. 2118.

Place	Date	Hour	Summary of Events and Information	Remarks and references to Appendices
Hulluch	5		fired in retaliation on our gun positions. Hostile Minenwerfer fired on our Fat Foundry position. No damage caused.	
	6.		Rounds fired 63. Hostile 77 m.m. guns fired in retaliation on our position – no damage caused. We fired on enemies support line doing considerable damage. We destroyed an enemy grenade dump in his front line & large explosion took place	
	7.		We shelled enemies support line in H.19.D and cut two gaps in the wire at H.13.C.62.70 and H.19.A.55.81.	
	8.		Rounds fired 56. Heavy Minenwerfer and Nat(?) retaliation to Fat Foundry position. We continued cutting wire and shelling enemy's trenches alternately. Engineers commenced making the dug outs on the new position in Vendin(?) [illegible]	
	9		Rounds fired 47. Enemy shelled our support and Reserve line with 4.2's in the morning and destroyed an old unoccupied position in Vendin Alley.	

2353 Wt W2541/1454 700,000 5/15 D. D. & L. A.D.S.S./Forms/C. 2118.

3

Instructions regarding War Diaries and Intelligence Summaries are contained in F. S. Regs., Part II. and the Staff Manual respectively. Title pages will be prepared in manuscript.

WAR DIARY
or
INTELLIGENCE SUMMARY.
(Erase heading not required.)

Army Form C. 2118.

Place	Date	Hour	Summary of Events and Information	Remarks and references to Appendices
Hulluch	10.		Rounds fired 54. We bombarded the enemy's support line in H.19.A. H.13.C and H.19.D. Much corrugated iron was thrown into the air and two small explosions caused.	
	11.		Rounds fired 79. We cut a gap in enemy's wire at H.19.A.60.80 and bombarded enemy's trenches in H.13.C in retaliation to Minenwerfer which was firing erratically, several bursting high up in the air.	
	12.		Rounds fired 69. Wire cutting in H.13.C and H.19.A continued. We caused a fire in the enemy's front line, much debris being thrown up out of his trenches.	
	13.		Rounds fired 57. Wire cutting continued. We fired on enemy's trenches in H.19.D in retaliation to aerial dart activity.	
	14.		Rounds fired 64. Enemy's front & support lines bombarded with good results in conjunction with our artillery.	

4

Instructions regarding War Diaries and Intelligence Summaries are contained in F. S. Regs., Part II. and the Staff Manual respectively. Title pages will be prepared in manuscript.

WAR DIARY
or
INTELLIGENCE SUMMARY.
(Erase heading not required.)

Army Form C. 2118.

Place	Date	Hour	Summary of Events and Information	Remarks and references to Appendices
Hulluch	15th		Rounds fired 63. We continued cutting wire and shelling enemy's front line in the morning & Infantry relief in the afternoon.	
	16		Rounds fired 70. We cut large gaps in the enemy's wire at H.19.a.5.9 and H.13.c.5.0	
	17.		Rounds fired 54. We cut a gap in enemy's wire at H.19.b.1.3. Two enemy working parties were reported, we obtained direct hits on them, timbers were blown up into the air also a considerable amount of timber. No retaliation.	
	18.		Rounds fired 15. Owing to Infantry relief we were unable to fire more.	
	19.		Rounds fired 229. In conjunction with the artillery on the right we bombarded the enemy's front line and wire, considerable damage was done and several large gaps cut most of which were filled up at night again.	

5.

Instructions regarding War Diaries and Intelligence Summaries are contained in F. S. Regs., Part II. and the Staff Manual respectively. Title pages will be prepared in manuscript.

WAR DIARY
or
INTELLIGENCE SUMMARY.
(Erase heading not required.)

Army Form C. 2118.

Place	Date	Hour	Summary of Events and Information	Remarks and references to Appendices
Hulluch	20		Rounds fired 54. Wire cutting continued. Enemy retaliated with Aerial Darts on our Vinden A position, our Stokes guns effectively silenced same. Two explosions were caused in the enemies wire – cause unknown.	
	21.		Rounds fired 53. Fire caused in enemies front line at H.13.c.55.30. Enemy minenwerfer active on the left, we retaliated and silenced same.	
	22.		Rounds fired 61. Enemy minenwerfer very active on the Right & Left sectors. We bombarded his support and communication trenches, obtaining several direct hits.	
	23.		Rounds fired 41. We continued effectively cutting enemies wire.	
	24.		Rounds fired 61. We shelled enemies support line in retaliation to his Aerial dart activity.	

2353 Wt. W2544/1454 700,000 5/15 D. D. & L. A.D.S.S./Forms/C. 2118.

6.

Instructions regarding War Diaries and Intelligence Summaries are contained in F. S. Regs., Part II, and the Staff Manual respectively. Title pages will be prepared in manuscript.

WAR DIARY
or
INTELLIGENCE SUMMARY.
(Erase heading not required.)

Army Form C. 2118.

Place	Date	Hour	Summary of Events and Information	Remarks and references to Appendices
[illegible]	25		During the bed of No 2 & No 3 gun having sunk we were obliged to dig same out. Wire cutting continued in H.13.C	
	26		Rounds fired 30. We dispersed an enemy working party opposite Aegean 66. Much timber was thrown into the air.	
	27.		Rounds fired 41. No 1 gun was heavily shelled by Minnie Werfer to which we retaliated and silenced.	
	28.		Rounds fired 44. Large gap of about 12 yds broad cut in enemies wire at H.19.A. We commenced work on a new site for 2nd emplacement of Brandery	
	29.		Fired 35 at the enemies front line. We were unable to fire more owing to mist.	
	30.		Rounds fired 42. Infantry report we shelled the enemies support trench in H.17.D. H.19.A. and H.13.C.	

R. T. [illegible]

H.Y.40 [illegible]

Instructions regarding War Diaries and Intelligence Summaries are contained in F. S. Regs., Part II. and the Staff Manual respectively. Title pages will be prepared in manuscript.

WAR DIARY
or
INTELLIGENCE SUMMARY.
(Erase heading not required.)

Army Form C. 2118.

Z40 T.M.B.

Place	Date	Hour	Summary of Events and Information	Remarks and references to Appendices
14 Bis				
Wednesday 1/11/16			The SEAFORTH emplacement which we took over from X battery is almost useless in this wet weather. The bed sinks badly after every few shots so that it has been decided to use this gun for retaliation only until we get into the new deep emplacement, which should be ready in about a week.	
Thursday 2/11/16			During the day we fired 84 chiefly from CHALK PIT ALLEY and QUARRY guns. We secured [illegible] considerable [illegible] of the trenches round 14 Bis particularly north of the POSTS where a machine gun has been recently reported. The SEAFORTH gun only fired 8 bombs and the majority 40 came from C.P. Alley. From the QUARRY we fired 16 at enemy front line causing much chalky smoke.	In future C.P. alley will [illegible]
Friday 3/11/16			Very little enemy activity today. C.P. ALLEY gun firing at extreme range landed several bombs in the enemy trench blowing wood (twice) and corrugated iron into the air. We fired 69 bombs and the only retaliation was a few 77mm shells which fell near WREATH TRENCH and was probably aimed at the C.P. Alley emplacement.	
Saturday 4/11/16			The relief by the other half battery took place between 12 noon & 1pm today.	

T2134. Wt. W708–776. 500000. 4/15. Sir J. C. & S.

Instructions regarding War Diaries and Intelligence Summaries are contained in F. S. Regs., Part II. and the Staff Manual respectively. Title pages will be prepared in manuscript.

WAR DIARY
or
INTELLIGENCE SUMMARY.
(Erase heading not required.)

Army Form C. 2118.

Place	Date	Hour	Summary of Events and Information	Remarks and references to Appendices
14 Bis	4/11/16	(cont)	Very little firing was possible today owing to the infantry reliefs coinciding with our own in the left section and taking place in the afternoon in the right section. Fired 15 during the day.	
Sunday	5/11/16		SEAFORTH ALLEY again had to have the bed shifted and replanted. The afternoon was spent in cutting wire at N 31 a 95 99 observing from an infantry observation post in TOSH ALLEY from here we are in communication with our HQ by means of the infantry telephone wires. This is the only O.P. for the C Battery gun until we can get into communication with the front line by telephone. Fired 34.	
Monday	6/11/16		It has been decided to put a 2" T.M. bed in the disused support line about 200x N. of ENGLISH ALLEY. An infantry fatigue party will work on this from 9 a.m. until dark under our supervision. This morning the party arrived without any tools and it was found impossible to borrow these before 2 p.m. Little work was done here today in consequence. In the afternoon we marked out the site for the bed in the new SEAFORTH alley emplacement and afterwards arranged programme of firing with left battalion	

T2134. Wt. W708—776. 500000. 4/15. Sir J. C. & S.

Instructions regarding War Diaries and Intelligence Summaries are contained in F. S. Regs., Part II. and the Staff Manual respectively. Title pages will be prepared in manuscript.

WAR DIARY
or
INTELLIGENCE SUMMARY.
(Erase heading not required.)

Army Form C. 2118.

Place	Date	Hour	Summary of Events and Information	Remarks and references to Appendices
14 Bty				
Tuesday	7/11/16		The working party for the proposed new gun M[t] did not turn up at all today. In the morning the new SEAFORTH bed was planted and the gun and stores moved into this emplacement. The gun was then registered very roughly as we as yet have no communication with no convenient Observing station. However the position is a great improvement on the old emplacement which has been useless lately. During the afternoon it was found necessary to take up the bed at C.P. alley and to put a large timber baulk behind it. Fired 88 from the three guns the majority being from SEAFORTH. No retaliation by the enemy.	In future M[t] will denote gun in trenches support line N of [illegible]
Wednesday	8/11/16		With the R.E. officer inspected the new HOOGE LANE emplacement. It will be ready in about a fortnight and is the best position we have so far. The emplacement on the right of SEAFORTH which was almost completed is to have further revetting by orders of GEN. CAPPER and so will not be ready for use for another fortnight. The beds at C.P. alley and the QUARRY were unsteady today and only 23 rounds were fired	

T2134. Wt. W708–776. 500000. 4/15. Sir J. C. & S.

Instructions regarding War Diaries and Intelligence Summaries are contained in F. S. Regs., Part II. and the Staff Manual respectively. Title pages will be prepared in manuscript.

WAR DIARY
or
~~INTELLIGENCE SUMMARY.~~
(Erase heading not required.)

Army Form C. 2118.

Place	Date	Hour	Summary of Events and Information	Remarks and references to Appendices
14 Bie				
Thursday	9/11/16		SEAFORTH ALLEY is still out of action. It went out of action last night owing to the bed jumping out of the ground. This is being remedied by replanting the bed with timbers at the back and in front and with sandbags beaten in all round it. The party working on the emplacement at [illegible] have completed the bomb store but have put no roof on at present. At the QUARRY there was a lot of trouble with cartridges 35 being reqd to fire 7 bombs. This was probably the fault of the mechanism and a new one is going there tomorrow. Fired 37.	
Friday	10/11/16		Relief complete by 12.30 p.m. The QUARRY fired 17 on the sidings on a sap where work was reported last night. Little more firing again owing to infantry reliefs occupying most of the day. Fired 29 at registered points.	
Saturday	11/11/16		The bomb store was completed today at [illegible] and the gun pit started. The bed at S.E.P. alley has almost disappeared underneath the back of the emplacement. We took down the back revetting and rebuilt it much more solidly and with a large timber behind the bed. The gun was out of action all day. Fired 22	

T2134. Wt. W708–776. 500000. 4/15. Sir J. C. & S.

Instructions regarding War Diaries and Intelligence Summaries are contained in F. S. Regs., Part II. and the Staff Manual respectively. Title pages will be prepared in manuscript.

WAR DIARY
or
~~INTELLIGENCE SUMMARY.~~
(Erase heading not required.)

Army Form C. 2118.

Place	Date	Hour	Summary of Events and Information	Remarks and references to Appendices
14th Bde				
Sunday 12/11/16			The gun in the QUARRY was out of action all day owing to a broken bed which had to be replaced. C P alley bed faces almost exactly the same direction as before so the registrations require no alterations. Fired 26.	
Monday 13/11/16			Other guns going well all day and fired 88 rounds at enemy front line and wire. The emplacement M is completed and a bed was put in there today. The emplacement in the QUARRY which was destroyed on the seventh ultimo should be completed by the 22nd. Two shots from C P alley blew up pieces of iron into the air and one shot falling in the POTS itself did considerable damage.	
Tuesday 14/11/16			Rain and mist made accurate observing impossible and there was very little activity indeed on our part or on that of the enemy. Fired 38.	
Wednesday 15/11/16			In the morning we did no firing but carried a large number of bombs to the guns. In the afternoon a gun & stand were taken to M and we fired 21 rounds into the enemy wire. The second shot falling in his front line blew into the air corrugated iron and other debris probably falling on an enemy dump. A second	

T2134. Wt. W708–776. 500000. 4/15. Sir J. C. & S.

Instructions regarding War Diaries and Intelligence Summaries are contained in F. S. Regs., Part II. and the Staff Manual respectively. Title pages will be prepared in manuscript.

WAR DIARY
or
~~INTELLIGENCE~~ SUMMARY.
(Erase heading not required.)

Army Form C. 2118.

Place	Date	Hour	Summary of Events and Information	Remarks and references to Appendices
14 Bis				
Wednesday	15/11/16	(cont)	attempt to hit the point fell short. Altogether we fired 68 bombs today.	
Thursday	16/11/16		The minenwerfers behind CARBON CRATER was inclined to be active this morning but SEAFORTH fired 47 rounds on or near the point from which it appeared to be firing and soon silenced it. We carried out a bombardment all along the front during the afternoon and fired 119 rounds during the day. The relief took place today and was completed successfully to 3 p.m. A spare bed was brought from LOOS to go into the repaired emplacement in the QUARRY. A double frame has been put in here to take it giving a width of sixty degrees	
Friday	17/11/16		SEAFORTH alley out of action for the next 24 hours owing to the frame supporting breaking. A bomb for some unknown reason struck the screen and fell a bit short but doing no damage to our trenches. The mechanism of C.P. alley gun blew out and the clamping handle broke causing this gun to be out of action during the latter part of the day. Gun in action in QUARRY, but requires bolts should be [illegible] before it is safe. Fired 49.	

T2134. Wt. W708–776. 500000. 4/15. Sir J. C. & S.

Instructions regarding War Diaries and Intelligence Summaries are contained in F. S. Regs., Part II. and the Staff Manual respectively. Title pages will be prepared in manuscript.

WAR DIARY

or

~~INTELLIGENCE~~ SUMMARY.

(Erase heading not required.)

Army Form C. 2118.

Place	Date	Hour	Summary of Events and Information	Remarks and references to Appendices
14 Bie Saturday	18/11/16		The new gun in the QUARRY cannot fire until bolts are made fast as it nearly threw up the emplacement today. No carrying party turned up for the SEAFORTH gun this morning. Started to cut wire with C.P. alley gun but the mechanism threw out after firing 5 rounds and could not be persuaded to fire. Fired 44.	
Sunday	19/11/16		Gun no carrying party for SEAFORTH. Fired at enemy wire in co-operation with the big gun and the artillery from 11.30 am to 2.30 pm and from 2–3 in the afternoon. Only fired 6 rounds from SEAFORTH gun as there were very few bombs here and a supply must always be kept on the gun. Fired 76.	
Monday	20/11/16		Continued wirecutting with all guns. No carrying party arrived for the SEAFORTH gun in spite of the report send of the last two days and the gun was out of action all day having no bombs. A test S.O.S. was fired for 6.30 p.m. Owing to the time being fixed and all arrangements being made beforehand the adequacy of the test is doubtful. However we fired one round from each gun when the rockets went up. In the evening we completed the laying of four	

Instructions regarding War Diaries and Intelligence Summaries are contained in F. S. Regs., Part II. and the Staff Manual respectively. Title pages will be prepared in manuscript.

WAR DIARY
or
~~INTELLIGENCE~~ SUMMARY.
(Erase heading not required.)

Army Form C. 2118.

Place	Date	Hour	Summary of Events and Information	Remarks and references to Appendices
14 Bis				
Monday	20/4/16		telephone wire from HQ to SEAFORTH alley gun. The speaking is very clear. The wire runs in the open behind the reserve line for the greater part of the distance. Fired 46.	
Tuesday	21/4/16		An attempt to cut wire with the C.P. alley gun was cut short after the tenth round by the blowing out of the mechanism and the failure of the remaining spare mechanisms to strike the cartridges. The QUARRY gun fired at a suspected M.G. emplacement but only obtained one direct hit. Laid a wire from C.P. alley emplacement to the junction of front line & BOYAU 55. Fired 41.	
Wednesday	22/4/16		Relief complete by 2 p.m. C.P. alley out of action after 7 rounds. Only 1 bomb left at the QUARRY gun and no carrying parties owing to infantry relief. SEAFORTH alley replying to hostile T.M's caused an explosion in enemy support line, probably a dump of handgrenades. Fired 36.	
Thursday	23/4/16		SEAFORTH out of action owing to explosion of minnie on top of shaft. The enemy proceeded to bombard our trenches on meeting with no retaliation. Two days repairs must be made before gun can fire again. Fired 46	

WAR DIARY
or
INTELLIGENCE ~~SUMMARY~~.
(Erase heading not required.)

Army Form C. 2118.

Instructions regarding War Diaries and Intelligence Summaries are contained in F. S. Regs., Part II. and the Staff Manual respectively. Title pages will be prepared in manuscript.

Place	Date	Hour	Summary of Events and Information	Remarks and references to Appendices
M Bis				
Friday	24/[illegible]/16		At suggestion of infantry colonel SEAFORTH gun was placed in PIONEER trench. The [illegible] were stood on the firestep. The gun was put in a bay between two mine holes and the nearest dugout was about 100x away. However the pin securing would not fit and the gun could not be got into action. C.P. alley fired 30 & Quarry 40.	
Saturday	25/[illegible]/16		[illegible] pioneer trench under water. Gun replaced in emplacement and 26 rounds fired in reply to 2 minnenwerfer shells. Bombardment all along the enemy wire. Fired 103 rounds.	
Sunday	26/[illegible]/16		In the morning we replaced the beds at C.P. alley and about SEAFORTH. In the afternoon fired all three guns especially QUARRY at enemy wire with some success. Fired 72. In the evening the gun complete from C.P. alley was sent to the Brigade bomb store LOOS by truck. The men slept here the night and with the help of an infantry fatigue party which arrived at 1 a.m. they moved the gun down to the emplacement on the right of SEAFORTH alley. The dugout here will not be ready for a few days, but the men put the bombs in their dugout temporarily and sleep at the emplacement alone	

Instructions regarding War Diaries and Intelligence Summaries are contained in F. S. Regs., Part II. and the Staff Manual respectively. Title pages will be prepared in manuscript.

WAR DIARY

or

INTELLIGENCE SUMMARY.

(Erase heading not required.)

Army Form C. 2118.

Place	Date	Hour	Summary of Events and Information	Remarks and references to Appendices
14 Bn [illegible]				
Sunday	[illegible]		two hundred yards further up the trench and on the left (previously referred [to] as SEAFORTH). The new gun is called SEAFORTH 'A' & the older 'B'.	
Monday	2[illegible]/16		Today the gun in the separated [illegible] emplacement was in action. It has had to wait twelve days for the bolts necessary to keep the [illegible] to the cradle frame. This gun fired 30 rounds and with the Serjeant [illegible] endeavoured to register the HASSEAFORTH guns but owing to mist this was difficult. Fired 54.	
Tuesday	[illegible]		In the morning SEAFORTH 'A' fired 5 rounds the last two of which fell behind our own frontline. The [illegible] here had started to push the stairs leading to the dugout down into the dugout itself & a large crack has been dug in behind the bed. Fired 14 only owing to [illegible] and to infantry relief.	
Wednesday	[illegible]		The SEAFORTH 'A' gun is still firing short and only reaching the middle of No man's land at extreme range. The entrance to the dug out is still giving at the bottom and the top of the frame is being pushed	

T2134. Wt. W708—776. 500000. 4/15. Sir J. C. & S.

Instructions regarding War Diaries and Intelligence Summaries are contained in F. S. Regs., Part II. and the Staff Manual respectively. Title pages will be prepared in manuscript.

WAR DIARY
or
INTELLIGENCE SUMMARY.
(Erase heading not required.)

Army Form C. 2118.

Place	Date	Hour	Summary of Events and Information	Remarks and references to Appendices
14 Bde				
Wednesday	29/6/16		out towards the gun. Fired 60.	
Thursday	30/6/16		The reason for the short shooting of SEAFORTH 4" is still unapparent. The gun barrel is being thoroughly overhauled today and the bed is being reset.	
			We put the gun into WOODLARK emplacement today. This is the best emplacement that we have got but the screen intended for it has not yet arrived and the temporary screen is far too heavy to be moved out of the way from within.	
			The WEARY fired 4 rounds from the old open position and obtained a direct hit on an aerial dart gun.	

Oscar P. Taylor Lieut GL
OC Z/40 Trench Mortar Battery
40th Div.

T2134. Wt. W708—776. 500000. 4/15. Sir J. C. & S.

Instructions regarding War Diaries and Intelligence Summaries are contained in F. S. Regs., Part II. and the Staff Manual respectively. Title pages will be prepared in manuscript.

WAR DIARY
or
INTELLIGENCE SUMMARY.
(Erase heading not required.)

Army Form C. 2118.

Vol X6

Place	Date	Hour	Summary of Events and Information	Remarks and references to Appendices
	Dec.			
Loos	1		X Battery expended 92 rounds bombarding enemy trenches.	
Hulluch			Y 〃 〃 93 〃 〃 〃 〃	
14 Bis			Z 〃 〃 35 〃 〃 〃 〃	
Loos	2		X 〃 〃 65 〃 〃 〃 〃	
Hulluch			Y 〃 〃 103 〃 〃 〃 〃	
14 Bis			Z 〃 〃 41 〃 〃 〃 〃	
Loos	3		X 〃 〃 28 〃 〃 〃 〃	
Hulluch			Y 〃 〃 54 〃 〃 〃 〃	
14 Bis			Z 〃 〃 32 〃 〃 〃 〃	
Loos	4		X 〃 〃 54 〃 〃 〃 〃	
Hulluch			Y 〃 〃 28 〃 〃 〃 〃	
14 Bis			Z 〃 〃 32 〃 〃 〃 〃	
			Trench Mortar Officers of the relieving Divl. Artillery (24th Divl. Artillery) given all information regarding the front being taken over.	
	5		40th Divl. T.M. Batteries left Les Brebis by Motor Lorries, - proceeding	

T2134. Wt. W708—776. 500000. 4/15. Sir J. C. & S.

Instructions regarding War Diaries and Intelligence Summaries are contained in F. S. Regs., Part II. and the Staff Manual respectively. Title pages will be prepared in manuscript.

D.T.M.O., 40TH DIVISION.

2.

Army Form C. 2118.

WAR DIARY
or
INTELLIGENCE SUMMARY.

(Erase heading not required.)

Place	Date	Hour	Summary of Events and Information	Remarks and references to Appendices
	Dec.			
			en route to AIRAINES (Somme), at which place we arrived on Sunday the 10th inst., staying for one night at each of the following places en route:- night of 5th at MARLES-LES-MINES.	
	6		Left MARLES-LES-MINES for ORLENCOURT - billeted there the night.	
	7		" ORLENCOURT for BOUBERS-SUR-CANCHE - - - - -	
	8		" BOUBERS-SUR-CANCHE for BRETEL - - - - -	
	9		" BRETEL for VILLERS BOCAGE - - - - -	
	10		" VILLERS BOCAGE for AIRAINES (Somme) and billeted there.	
	11 to 31		Battery doing Physical Training - Musketry - Improving billets - Lectures - Football - Fatigues for 188 Bde, R.F.A. etc.	
	28		Div. T.M. Off. - (Capt. [illegible]) left AIRAINES for the line - Lt. H. Forrest, R.G.A. taking over the duties of D.T.M.O.	

H Forrest Lt. R.G.A.
for Div. T.M. Offr. [illegible]

T2134. Wt. W708–776. 500000. 4/15. Sir J. C. & S.

Army Form C. 2118.

V/40 TMB

Instructions regarding War Diaries and Intelligence Summaries are contained in F. S. Regs., Part II. and the Staff Manual respectively. Title pages will be prepared in manuscript.

WAR DIARY
or
~~INTELLIGENCE SUMMARY.~~
(Erase heading not required.)

December. V/40. T.M. Baty.

Place	Date	~~Hour~~	Summary of Events and Information	Remarks and references to Appendices
Field.	1–5.		The first five days of December were spent in handing over the guns & positions in Loos & Hulluch, to the 24th. Divl. T.M.s. Two guns were sent to the "Brickstacks", near La Bassée. The gun was handed over in action at Loos. The Hulluch position had not been completed & the gun was not in action.	
	5.		On the fifth of the month the battery, with the other T.M.s batys. left Les Brebis in motor lorries & travelled South. The night of the fifth was spent in billets at Marles-les-Mines.	
	6.		Destination "Orlancourt"	
	7.		" Bouchers-sur-canche.	
	8.		" Bretelle, difficulty in finding billets here.	
	9.		" Villers Bocage.	
	10.		" Airaines.	
			The remainder of the month was spent in Airaines, the T.M. batys. found fatigue parties to assist the 188 Bgde. of artillery. Musketry, marching drill & football were carried out daily.	
	23.		A very successful concert was held on the 23rd, by T.M.s. in conjunction with the 188. Bgde. 2nd Lt. G. F. Tayler of Z. T.M. baty. being the organiser.	
	25th.		On Xmas day a dinner was given to the men of all the T.M. batys.	
			A T.M. course was held for some officers & men of the 188 Bgde, & artillery T.M. officers were attached to the field batys. for a few days instruction.	

[illegible] Capt. R.A.
O/C. V/40.

A5834 Wt. W4973/M687 750,000 8/16 D. D. & L. Ltd. Forms/C.2118/13.

1.

X. 40. Trench Mortar Battery.

WAR DIARY

or

INTELLIGENCE SUMMARY.

(Erase heading not required.)

December 1916. Army Form C. 2118.

X/40 TMB

Instructions regarding War Diaries and Intelligence Summaries are contained in F. S. Regs., Part II. and the Staff Manual respectively. Title pages will be prepared in manuscript.

Place	Date	Hour	Summary of Events and Information	Remarks and references to Appendices
Loos.	1.12.16.		Very thick fog prevented any registration or destruction of special targets. Bombarded trenches in the Triangle, and round Harrison's crater. South St, which had been put out of action by a premature, came into action again in the afternoon. The Rifle Mechanism at Queen St. became useless, so 'T' Tubes had to be used. Quarry guns firing under difficulties as bed pumped out of wooden frame every shot. New plates are being made to remedy this defect. Fired:- Cordiale Queen South Chalk.	Total. 92.
	2.12.16.		Again misty. Bombarded the Triangle and cut wire 300 yards right of Harrison's crater. Good results were obtained. Fired:- Cordiale Queen South Chalk.	Total. 65
	3.12.16.		Owing to Infantry relief firing only in retaliation. Telephone wires give a lot of trouble owing to sides of trenches collapsing & being blown in. Much valuable time spent daily in repairing damage. Enemy continue to throw out coils of wire during the night into the gaps cut in their wire. Infantry have been asked to keep them open with machine guns. Fired:- Cordiale Queen South Chalk.	Total. 28

T2134. Wt. W708—776. 500000. 4/15. Sir J. C. & S.

2. X. 40. T.M.B.

Instructions regarding War Diaries and Intelligence Summaries are contained in F. S. Regs., Part II. and the Staff Manual respectively. Title pages will be prepared in manuscript.

WAR DIARY
or
INTELLIGENCE SUMMARY.
(Erase heading not required.)

Army Form C. 2118.

Place	Date	Hour	Summary of Events and Information	Remarks and references to Appendices
Loos.	4.12.16.		Most of day & night spent in handing over to X.24. T.M.B. Only beds & elevating stand handed over at Chalk Pit & South St. Guns intact at Hendale Avenue & Queen St. Owing to mistake by X.24. Queen St. were not relieved until 9 A.M. on 5th. and were due to leave the district at that hour. Handed over to X.24. T.M.B:- 6 beds serviceable. 2. beds unserviceable. 2 guns. 2 elevating stands, 9 handcarts. 12 miles of telephone wire, an average of 50 bombs per gun, & 240 per bomb store. Also maps, passes, aerial photographs &c.	
	5.12.16.	10 A.M.	Left Les Brebis in 2 lorries for Marles les Mines. Arrived 12.30.	
	6.12.16		" for Orlencourt. 8 A.M.	
	7.12.16		" " Boubers sur Canche.	
	8.12.16		" " Bretel.	
	9.12.16.		" " Villers-Bocage. At nearly all the places great difficulty was experienced in obtaining billets for officers & men, & when obtained were invariably broken down, draughty mud barns & very bad. There was never an Englis mess. The French people would rather men slept in the muddy road, than lend an old empty barn.	

T2134. Wt. W708—776. 500000. 4/15. Sir J. C. & S.

3

X. 40. T.M.B

Instructions regarding War Diaries and Intelligence Summaries are contained in F. S. Regs., Part II. and the Staff Manual respectively. Title pages will be prepared in manuscript.

WAR DIARY
or
INTELLIGENCE SUMMARY.
(Erase heading not required.)

Army Form C. 2118.

Place	Date	Hour	Summary of Events and Information	Remarks and references to Appendices
Airaines	10.12.16.		Left for Airaines. Original billets (given by Town major) so appalling that we had to find others ourselves.	
"	11.12.16.		Unloaded lorries, cleaned guns &c.	
"	12.12.16.		Physical drill, marching drill, musketry &c.	
"	13.12.16.		Fatigues for R.F.A.	
"	14.12.16.		Do. do.	
"	15.12.16.		Do. do.	
"	16.12.16.		Drill, musketry, 2" instruction &c. & Football.	
"	17.12.16		" " " " & baths.	
"	18.12.16.		Fatigues for R.F.A.	
"	19.12.16		" " "	
"	20.12.16		" " "	
"	21.12.16		Marching drill. Improvement to billets, football &c.	
"	22.12.16		" "	
"	23.12.16.		Fatigues most of day	
"	24.12.16.		" & 2" instruction.	
"	25.12.16		Holiday. Men had an appalling Xmas dinner. no vegetables at all. no	

4 X. 40. T. M. B.

Instructions regarding War Diaries and Intelligence Summaries are contained in F. S. Regs., Part II. and the Staff Manual respectively. Title pages will be prepared in manuscript.

WAR DIARY
or
INTELLIGENCE SUMMARY.
(Erase heading not required.)

Army Form C. 2118.

Place	Date	Hour	Summary of Events and Information	Remarks and references to Appendices
Airaines	(Cont) 25.12.16		Comforts & less than half their ration of plum pudding. Practically no wood or coal issued. Men in need of boots & clothes badly. Urgent indents sent in 2 weeks ago. Winter half gone & leather waistcoats not yet received.	
"	26.12.16		Drill, instruction & football.	
"	27.12.16		Close order & rifle drill & fatigues for R.F.A.	
"	28.12.16		Fatigues for R.F.A. Musketry. & Route March. Baths.	
"	29.12.16		" " " 2" instruction	
"	30.12.16		" " " physical drill, &c.	
"	31.12.16		" " " drill &c.	

Norman Reid 2/Lieut. R.F.A.
O.C. X. 40. T.M.B.
31.12.16.

T2134. Wt. W708–776. 500000. 4/15. Sir J. C. & S.

Instructions regarding War Diaries and Intelligence Summaries are contained in F. S. Regs., Part II. and the Staff Manual respectively. Title pages will be prepared in manuscript.

WAR DIARY
~~or~~
INTELLIGENCE SUMMARY.
(Erase heading not required.)

X 40 T.M.B.

Army Form C. 2118.

Place	Date	Hour	Summary of Events and Information	Remarks and references to Appendices
	Decr 1916			
	4th		Most of day & night spent in handing over to X 24 T.M.B. at Chalk Pit & South St which we handed over in early a.m. we only left the beds & elevating stand in. At Queen St & Cordeale Avenue we left the guns intact, taking over X 24's. Owing to a mistake by X 24 Queen St were not relieved until 8 am on the 5th. Altogether there were handed over to X 24 6 serviceable beds & 2 unserviceable 2 guns. 2 elevating stands 9 hcarts. 12 miles of telephone wire. an average of 50 bombs per gun & 240 per bomb store together with maps passes photographs &c	
	5th		Queen St detachment arrived at 9.30 AM when limbers (3) were loaded & ready. Left Les Brebis about 10 for Marles les Mines	
	6th		Left for Orlencourt @ 8 AM	
	7th		Left for Bouberс-sur-Canche	
	8th		Left for Bretel	
	9th		Left for Villers-Bocage	

Instructions regarding War Diaries and Intelligence Summaries are contained in F. S. Regs., Part II. and the Staff Manual respectively. Title pages will be prepared in manuscript.

WAR DIARY
or
INTELLIGENCE SUMMARY.
(Erase heading not required.)

X 40 T.M.B.

Army Form C. 2118.

Place	Date	Hour	Summary of Events and Information	Remarks and references to Appendices
	Decr	1916		
1	10th		Left for Airaines	
	11th		Unloaded lorries. Cleaned guns, bets, tools &c	
	11th to 31st		Battery in rest Fatigues & Parades daily	
	Jany. 1917			
	1st to 29th		Battery in rest Fatigues & Parades daily	
	9th		Took over battery stores from Y. Z & V	
	19th		Lt Reid handed over battery to Lt Stanford	
	29th		Left Airaines for Chipilly	
	30th		Lt Horn took over battery from Lt Stanford	
	30th		Ordinary parades.	
	31st		"	

Capt Horn 2/Lt
for O.C. X40 T.M.B.

Y. 40. T. Mortar Battery.

Army Form C. 2118.

WAR DIARY
or
INTELLIGENCE SUMMARY.
(Erase heading not required.)

December. 1916.

Instructions regarding War Diaries and Intelligence Summaries are contained in F. S. Regs., Part II. and the Staff Manual respectively. Title pages will be prepared in manuscript.

Place	Date	Hour	Summary of Events and Information	Remarks and references to Appendices
Aulloch	Decr 1st		Fired 93 rounds. This morning the Bosche was very active with rifle grenades & darts. Three guns concentrated on his support line & communication trenches & after 15 minutes he was completely silenced. During the afternoon bombed working party at H.19d.2.2. Timber & timbers seen with no visible means of support.	
	2nd		Fired 103. Between 12.30 & 1 A.M. enemy artillery & minnies very active. We replied with two guns for an hour, his fire ceased & he gave very little trouble for the rest of the day. During the forenoon & afternoon wire cutting was indulged in.	
	3rd		Fired 54 rounds. Fired twenty rounds into his support line about midday retaliating to Darts. The remainder was used principally for wire cutting. One half of battery relieved tonight by 34th Division.	
	4th		Rounds fired 40. Practically all fired for wire cutting & instructing new division taking over. Relief now complete.	

2353 Wt. W2544/1454 700,000 5/15 D. D. & L. A.D.S.S./Forms/C. 2118.

Army Form C. 2118.

WAR DIARY
or
INTELLIGENCE SUMMARY.
(Erase heading not required.)

Instructions regarding War Diaries and Intelligence Summaries are contained in F. S. Regs., Part II. and the Staff Manual respectively. Title pages will be prepared in manuscript.

Place	Date	Hour	Summary of Events and Information	Remarks and references to Appendices
	5.		40th D.T.M. Batteries left Les Brebis by motor lorries proceeding to AIRAINES (Somme) for rest. We arrived at AIRAINES on Sunday 10th Decem. stopping for one night at each of the following places en route:- night of 5th at MARLES-LES-MINES	
	6		left MARLES-les-MINES for ORLENCOURT.	
	7		" ORLENCOURT " BOUBERS-sur-CANCHE	
	8.		" BOUBERS-sur-CANCHE " BRETEL	
	9.		" BRETEL " VILERS BOCAGE	
	10		" VILERS BOCAGE . " AIRAINES	
	11 to 31 st		AIRAINES. Battery doing fatigues for 188 Bgde R.F.A., Lectures, Musketry, Route marches, Physical Training, Cleaning guns & stores, Improving billets, Football, Close order drill.	

R. T. [illegible] Lt.

Instructions regarding War Diaries and Intelligence Summaries are contained in F. S. Regs., Part II. and the Staff Manual respectively. Title pages will be prepared in manuscript.

WAR DIARY
or
~~INTELLIGENCE SUMMARY.~~

(Erase heading not required.)

Army Form C. 2118.

Place	Date	Hour	Summary of Events and Information	Remarks and references to Appendices
			Z/40 Trench Mortar Battery 40th Division December 1916.	

A5834 Wt. W4973/M687 750,000 8/16 D. D. & L. Ltd. Forms/C.2118/13.

Instructions regarding War Diaries and Intelligence Summaries are contained in F. S. Regs., Part II. and the Staff Manual respectively. Title pages will be prepared in manuscript.

WAR DIARY
or
INTELLIGENCE SUMMARY.
(Erase heading not required.)

Army Form C. 2118.

Place	Date	Hour	Summary of Events and Information	Remarks and references to Appendices
	Dec 1916			
14 BIS	1st		In the morning, registered Seaforth Alley Gun. Very misty. Could not do much. No carrying party turned up for Seaforth Alley Gun.	
			Evening – Met RFA party at LOOS.	
	2nd		Morning. Called on RE's re screen for HUGO LANE, which they promised for next day. CHALK PIT gun caused lot of trouble owing to bad rifle. mechanism. Compelled to use HUGO LANE mechanism.	
			Afternoon Again registered SEAFORTH ALLEY Gun.	
	3rd		Spent morning having things put straight for handing over. HUGO LANE Gun still out of action. Sent to BREBIS for another mechanism. Had ammunition for all guns made up with parts to at least 30 rounds.	
			Evening. Relieving Officer of 24th Division with 2 detachments + 2 guns arrived. Sent down 2 guns not screw-threaded for Silencer.	
	4th		Showed relieving Officer all gun emplacements + OP's. Also Battalion + Coy H.Q. Received receipts for all guns handed over.	
			Relief to 24th Division complete at 9.30 pm.	

T2134. Wt. W708–776. 500000. 4/15. Sir J. C. & S.

Army Form C. 2118.

Instructions regarding War Diaries and Intelligence Summaries are contained in F. S. Regs., Part II. and the Staff Manual respectively. Title pages will be prepared in manuscript.

WAR DIARY
or
INTELLIGENCE SUMMARY.

(Erase heading not required.)

Place	Date	Hour	Summary of Events and Information	Remarks and references to Appendices
	Dec 1916			
In the field	5th to 10th (inclusive)		Employed in moving from 1st Corps at Les Brebis to AIRAINES, 15th Corps. At AIRAINES, on 10th, Battery went into rest billets. Transport was done by Motor Lorries. Men billeted for each night at each stopping-place.	
	11th to 31st (inclusive)		During these days, the Battery was in rest, the men being employed in Route-Marching, Physical Training, Gun Drill, Cleaning etc of Guns, Billets, Lectures and Bathing. Football Matches were played + a Concert organised on 23 Dec. The Battery also supplied daily fatigues to different Field Batteries of 188 Bde RFA, where excellent work was done in making stables, horse-lines, roads etc. The health + condition of ~~the~~ men is now very good.	

Oscar F. Taylor Lieut GA.
O.C. Z/40 Trench Mortar Battery 40th Div
29 Dec 1916

A5834 Wt. W4973/M687 750,000 8/16 D. D. & L. Ltd. Forms/C.2118/13.

Secret

Instructions regarding War Diaries and Intelligence Summaries are contained in F. S. Regs., Part II. and the Staff Manual respectively. Title pages will be prepared in manuscript.

WAR DIARY
or
INTELLIGENCE SUMMARY.
(*Erase heading not required.*)

Army Form C. 2118.

D.T.M. Offr.
40th Divn.

Vol 7

Place	Date	Hour	Summary of Events and Information	Remarks and references to Appendices
January 1917.				
AIRAINES	1 to 8		T.M. B's on rest. Employed in Physical Training, Fatigues, Recapitulation, Cleaning of guns, stores, etc. Y Bty left AIRAINES on the 6th. for LE FORREST – Employed there on fatigues – assisting R.E's. in making dug-outs – also provided men for Divl. Guard and men for fatigues for R.F.A. Batteries.– V. X. & Z. Batteries left behind in AIRAINES	
	9	10AM	V & Z Batteries left AIRAINES for Camp 21 – X Battery left in AIRAINES guarding T.M. Stores, guns, etc.	
	10 to 28		V & Z Batteries supplying fatigue parties for various R.F.A. Batteries – Men not on R.F.A. fatigue parties employed on improving the Camp, etc.	
	29		All Btys left the several places where they had been employed on fatigues, for CHIPPILLY and billeted there.	
	31		Y Bty left CHIPPILLY in Motor Lorries for a T.M. Course of Instruction at 4th Army Sch. of Mortars at VAUX-EN-AMIENOIS	

[illegible] Capt.
D.T.M.O.

T2134. Wt. W708–776. 500000. 4/15. Sir J. C. & S.

V.40. Heavy T.M.B. January/1917.

Instructions regarding War Diaries and Intelligence Summaries are contained in F. S. Regs., Part II. and the Staff Manual respectively. Title pages will be prepared in manuscript.

WAR DIARY
or
INTELLIGENCE SUMMARY.

(Erase heading not required.)

Secret

Army Form C. 2118.

Place	Date	Hour	Summary of Events and Information	Remarks and references to Appendices
Airaines	Jan 1st to Jan 9th		Battery in billets, Parades daily, Physical Drill, Marching Drill Musketry etc.	
	Jan 9th	9. am	left Airaines by train	
	Jan 10th	8. pm	arrived at Camp 21.	
Camp 21	Jan 11th to Jan 28th		Men employed on improvements to 181 Bde Wagon lines. except two parties shown below.	
	Jan 12th to Jan 27th		1 Officer and 21 Other ranks attached to D/181 Bty RFA for duty.	
	Jan 16th to Jan 27th		20 Other ranks attached to 181 Bde RFA for duty.	
	Jan 28th	9. am	left camp 21 march route.	
	Jan 28th	1.0 pm	arrived Chipilly.	
Chipilly	Jan 28th to Jan 31st		Battery in billets, Parades daily. Marching Drill, Physical drill etc.	

H Forrest Lt. R.G.A.
O.C V40. H.T.M.B.

A5834 Wt. W4973/M687 750,000 8/16 D. D. & L. Ltd. Forms/C.2118/13.

Y.40 T.M.B.

Y-40. T.M.B

WAR DIARY
or
INTELLIGENCE SUMMARY.

(Erase heading not required.)

Army Form C. 2118.

Instructions regarding War Diaries and Intelligence Summaries are contained in F. S. Regs., Part II. and the Staff Manual respectively. Title pages will be prepared in manuscript.

Place	Date	Hour	Summary of Events and Information	Remarks and references to Appendices
Airaines	1/1/17 to 5/1/17		Gun, Squad and Physical Drill; Route Marches, Fatigues, and Football.	
	6/1/17.	9 a.m.	Entrained at Airaines Station for the Plateau Siding via Longpré, Amiens and Mericourt.	
	7/1/17.	1. a.m.	Arrived at the Plateau Sidings.	
		11 a.m.	Left the Plateau in G.S. Wagons and arrived at Maurepas Ravine at 2 p.m. where the Battery were billeted in tents.	
	8/1/17 to 26/1/17		Supplied Regular Guard for Gun. Hd. Qrs. (1 N.C.O. + 3 men) 24 hrs Guard.)	
			Supplied Regular Fatigue of 1 N.C.O. and 9 men for R.A. Hd. Qrs.	
			Supplied 1 N.C.O. and 7 men for fatigues for Field Batteries in Line.	
	27/1/17.		Left Maurepas Ravine at 9. a.m. for Camp 20 - (Maricourt)	
	28/1/17.	9 a.m.	Left Maricourt for Chipilly. Arrived 2 p.m.	
	29/1/17 to 30/1/17		General Fatigues. Kit Inspections. Overhauling Guns.	
	31/1/17.		Left Chipilly in Motor Lorries for Trench Mortar School of Instruction at Vaux-en-Amienois.	

R. T. [illegible] Lt.
O.C. Y.40 T.M.B.

2353 Wt. W2544/1454 700,000 5/15 D. D. & L. A.D.S.S./Forms/C. 2118.

Instructions regarding War Diaries and Intelligence Summaries are contained in F. S. Regs., Part II. and the Staff Manual respectively. Title pages will be prepared in manuscript.

WAR DIARY
or
INTELLIGENCE SUMMARY.
(Erase heading not required.)

Army Form C. 2118.

Place	Date	Hour	Summary of Events and Information	Remarks and references to Appendices
			Z/40 TRENCH MORTAR BATTERY 40th Div JANUARY 1917 Oscar P Taylor Lieut Genl List OC	

A5834 Wt. W4973/M687 750,000 8/16 D. D. & L. Ltd. Forms/C.2118/13

Z 40 · T.M.B.

Instructions regarding War Diaries and Intelligence Summaries are contained in F. S. Regs., Part II. and the Staff Manual respectively. Title pages will be prepared in manuscript.

WAR DIARY

~~or~~

~~INTELLIGENCE SUMMARY.~~

(Erase heading not required.)

Army Form C. 2118.

Place	Date	Hour	Summary of Events and Information	Remarks and references to Appendices
	1917 January			
AIRAINES	1 to		Battery in rest. Employed in Physical Training, Route-Marching, Fatigues, recapitulation + cleaning of guns + Ammunition. Football was played on alternate afternoons. Health + condition of men good.	
	8th		Lieut Taylor awarded Military Cross.	
	9th	10 am	Left AIRAINES by train + after being sent back to ROMESCAMPS Sidings proceeded through AMIENS to	
	10th		PLATEAU SIDINGS, where the Battery detrained + marched to Camp 21	
Camp 20	11th		Cleaning camp + providing Latrines, Cookhouses, Trench boards + firing arrangements.	
	12th		1 NCO + 8 men sent up the line to build gun pits for 181 Bde RFA. Another 10 men sent to Captain Hawkins of ~~DAC~~ DA Wagon Lines to assist in building roads. Remainder employed on fatigues in the Camp	

T2134. Wt. W708–776. 500000. 4/15. Sir J. C. & S.

Instructions regarding War Diaries and Intelligence Summaries are contained in F. S. Regs., Part II. and the Staff Manual respectively. Title pages will be prepared in manuscript.

WAR DIARY

or

INTELLIGENCE SUMMARY.

(Erase heading not required.)

Army Form C. 2118.

Place	Date	Hour	Summary of Events and Information	Remarks and references to Appendices
1917 January Camp 20.	13th		Balance of men carried on with fatigues at D.A. wagon lines from 13th to 27th inclusive.	
	28th	9.0.AM	Left Camp 20 and proceeded to Chipilly.	
Chipilly	29th		Cleaning Kit and inspection of same.	
	30th 31st		Training.	

[signature] Capt for O/C Z/40 T.M.B.

A5834 Wt. W4973/M687 750,000 8/16 D. D. & L. Ltd. Forms/C.2118/13.

Z.40 Trench Mortar Battery.

Instructions regarding War Diaries and Intelligence Summaries are contained in F. S. Regs., Part II. and the Staff Manual respectively. Title pages will be prepared in manuscript.

WAR DIARY
or
INTELLIGENCE SUMMARY.

(Erase heading not required.)

Army Form C. 2118.

Place	Date	Hour	Summary of Events and Information	Remarks and references to Appendices
Chipilly	Feb 1st	– 9th	Battery in rest. Parades for physical training, marching and gun drill — particularly use of dial sight.	
Maurepas	Feb 9th	– 28th	Battery proceeded to Maurepas by motor lorry. Here it was attached to 1st Home Counties R.E. for work on dugouts and gun positions between Le Forest & Rancourt	

R J Hammond
2nd Lt RFA
for O.C. Z.40 T.M. Bty.

A5834 Wt. W4973/M687 750,000 8/16 D. D. & L. Ltd. Forms/C.2118/13.

Instructions regarding War Diaries and Intelligence Summaries are contained in F. S. Regs., Part II. and the Staff Manual respectively. Title pages will be prepared in manuscript.

WAR DIARY
or
INTELLIGENCE SUMMARY.
(Erase heading not required.)

D.T.M.O. 40TH DIVISION. Feby 1917.

Army Form C. 2

Vol 8

Place	Date Feby:	Hour	Summary of Events and Information	Remarks and references to Appendices
CHIPILLY	1		V, X, Y Z Batteries inspected by Gen Nicholson, (CRA) - Y Bty. being at 4th Army Sch. of Mortars, VAUX-EN-AMIENOIS.	
"	2 to 8		V, X, Y Z Batteries - fatigues - cleaning guns - physical training - running, etc.	
	9	9am	5 Offrs + 90 OR (50 from V, + 20 each from X + Z) left CHIPILLY at 9am for fatigues in the line.	
CHIPILLY	10 & 11		Details of Batteries left in CHIPILLY doing fatigues, etc.	
	12		On termination of their T.M. course at 4th Army Sch. of Mortars, VAUX-EN-AMIENOIS, 1 Offr. + 15 OR. of Y40. T.M.B. proceeded to forward area to join the 5 Offrs + 90 OR. sent up on the 9th inst. for fatigues. The remaining men returned to CHIPILLY with their mortars, + then, along with the details of Batteries already in CHIPILLY, were given physical training, running, etc.	
CHIPILLY	12		Capt Gaden, Conn. Rangers, D.T.M.O. left for England - he having to report at War Office for special duty. 2/Lt. T.S. Ward, R.F.A. took over duties of D.T.M.O., pending the return from leave of Lieut O.P. Taylor.	
CHIPILLY	13		Lieut. O.P. Taylor returned from leave and took over command of 40th Div. T.M. Batteries.	

T2134. Wt. W708–776. 500000. 4/15. Sir J. C. & S.

2.

Instructions regarding War Diaries and Intelligence Summaries are contained in F. S. Regs., Part II. and the Staff Manual respectively. Title pages will be prepared in manuscript.

WAR DIARY
or
INTELLIGENCE SUMMARY.
(*Erase heading not required.*)

D.T.M.O.
40th DIVISION.
No.
Date

Army Form C. 2118.

Place	Date	Hour	Summary of Events and Information	Remarks and references to Appendices
	Feby.–			
	14 to 23		Ordinary routine duties – ie. personnel of T.M.B's in the line on fatigues, and details in CHIPILLY doing physical training, running, etc.	
	24 & 25		Instead of having the details of 4 batteries in CHIPILLY, instructions were received to assemble one complete Battery at that place – this necessitated the details of 'Y' Battery in the line coming to CHIPILLY. (Y being the Battery ordered to assemble in CHIPILLY) and the details of V, X, & Z Batteries (less Offrs) to proceed to the line. The move commenced 24th & completed 25th – both parties (ie. party coming from forward area to CHIPILLY, and party from CHIPILLY to forward area) being accommodated by the D.A.C. at BRAY on night of 24th.	
	26 to 28		Ordinary routine duties – ie. personnel of T.M.B's in the line on fatigues, and ~~details~~ Y Bty in CHIPILLY on physical training, running, etc.	
CHIPILLY	27th		Y Bty at CHIPILLY inspected by C.R.A. – Gen Nicholson.	

Oscar P. Taylor Lt. G. L., MC
A/D.T.M.O., 40th Divn.

T2134. Wt. W708–776. 500000. 4/15. Sir J. C. & S.

February 1917.

Instructions regarding War Diaries and Intelligence Summaries are contained in F. S. Regs., Part II. and the Staff Manual respectively. Title pages will be prepared in manuscript.

WAR DIARY
or
INTELLIGENCE SUMMARY.
(Erase heading not required.)

X. 40. Trench Mortar Battery

Army Form C. 2118.

Place	Date	Hour	Summary of Events and Information	Remarks and references to Appendices
Chipilly	1/2/17.	to 9/2/17.	At rest doing Gun drill, fatigues, route marches &c.	
	9/2/17.		Moved up to Camp at Maurepas. Stayed in huts doing fatigues for Artillery from 7 A.M. to 6 p.m. building roads, gun-pits &c.	
	28/2/17.		Still doing as above.	

Norman Reid Lieut. R.F.A.
O.C. X. 40. T.M.B.
28.2.17

T2134. Wt. W708—776. 500000. 4/15. Sir J. C. & S.

V.40. Heavy Trench Mortar Battery.

Instructions regarding War Diaries and Intelligence Summaries are contained in F. S. Regs., Part II. and the Staff Manual respectively. Title pages will be prepared in manuscript.

WAR DIARY
or
INTELLIGENCE SUMMARY.
(Erase heading not required.)

February 1917.

Army Form C. 2118.

Place	Date	Hour	Summary of Events and Information	Remarks and references to Appendices
Chipilly	Feb 1st to Feb 9th		Battery in rest. Parades for physical training, musketry, drill and route marches.	
Maurepas	Feb 9th		Battery left Chipilly by motor buses for camp at Maurepas.	
	Feb 10th to Feb 28th		attached to 1st Home Counties R.E. for work on dugouts and gun positions between Le Forest and Rancourt.	

Hubert Forrest,
Capt. R.G.A.
O.C. V.40 Heavy Trench Mortar Battery

A5834 Wt. W4973/M687 750,000 8/16 D. D. & L. Ltd. Forms/C.2118/13.

Instructions regarding War Diaries and Intelligence Summaries are contained in F. S. Regs., Part II. and the Staff Manual respectively. Title pages will be prepared in manuscript.

WAR DIARY
or
~~INTELLIGENCE SUMMARY.~~
(Erase heading not required.)

February 1917.

Army Form C. 2118.

Y40 Trench Mortar Battery.

Place	Date	Hour	Summary of Events and Information	Remarks and references to Appendices
Vaux en Amienois	1st – 10th		Battery on refresher course at 4th Army School of Mortars Drill & firing.	
Maurepas Ravine.	11th – 24th		Fatigue work on dugouts & R.A. emplacements near Le Forest.	
Chipilly	25th – 28th		Checking stores & drill.	

J. M. Rymer Jones
2 Lt R.F.A
for O.C. Y40TMB

2353 Wt. W2544/1454 700,000 5/15 D. D. & L. A.D.S.S./Forms/C. 2118.

Instructions regarding War Diaries and Intelligence Summaries are contained in F. S. Regs., Part II. and the Staff Manual respectively. Title pages will be prepared in manuscript.

WAR DIARY
or
INTELLIGENCE SUMMARY.
(*Erase heading not required.*)

D.T.M.O., 40th DIVISION.
No.
Date MARCH. 1917.

Army Form C. 2118.

Vol 9

Place	Date	Hour	Summary of Events and Information	Remarks and references to Appendices
	1		V, X, & Z Batteries on fatigues at MAUREPAS. Y Bty. at CHIPILLY in charge of guns, stores, etc, and doing physical training. Lt. R.J.H. Ellis, G.L. o/c Y40 T.M.B. transferred to England - sick.	
	2 } 3		V, X, & Z on fatigues - MAUREPAS. Y Bty at CHIPILLY in charge of guns, stores, etc., and doing physical training.	
	4		V, X, & Z still at MAUREPAS on fatigues. Y Bty left CHIPILLY for BRAY - accommodated there the night.	
	5		V, X, & Z at MAUREPAS - fatigues. Y Bty. left BRAY for MAUREPAS, where they joined V, X, & Z Batteries.	
	6 & 7		All Batteries - V, X, Y, & Z, on fatigues at MAUREPAS	
	8		V Bty. X (½ Bty.), Y (½ Bty), went into the line in the BOUCHAVESNES - CLERY Sector. Z Bty, together with the remaining ½ Batteries of X & Y, moved from MAUREPAS to P.C. EARTHWORKS. (½ Batteries relieve each other every 4 days)	
	9		5 rds. fired by Y Bty.	
	10		8 " " " " "	
	11		2 " " " X, and 5 by Y.	

T2134. Wt. W708-776. 500000. 4/15. Sir J. C. & S.

2.

Army Form C. 2118.

Instructions regarding War Diaries and Intelligence Summaries are contained in F. S. Regs., Part II. and the Staff Manual respectively. Title pages will be prepared in manuscript.

WAR DIARY
or
INTELLIGENCE SUMMARY.
(Erase heading not required.)

Place	Date	Hour	Summary of Events and Information	Remarks and references to Appendices
	12		3 rds. fired by X, & 5 by Y. Divl. Commander gave instructions that we were only fire our Mortars at the request of the Battn. Commander.	
	13		Y Bty. withdrawn from action to commence building Medium T.M. emplacements.	
	14		3 rds 9.45" fired by V Bty.	
	15		Z Bty. went to 4th Army Sch. of Mortars at VAUX-EN-AMIENOIS on a 10 days 2" T.M. course. V Bty. fired 34 rds. 9.45". X Bty. fired 48 rds.	
	16		18 rds. fired by X Bty.	
	17		11 " " " "	
	18		Owing to enemy having retired from the front, personnel and guns withdrawn from the line to R.C. EARTHWORKS.	
	19		Capt. H. Forrest, R.G.A., O/c V40 T.M.B., - wounded.	
	6 – 31		Personnel of T.M. B's on fatigues - collecting ammunition from vacated 18 pdr. & 4.5 gun positions and guarding same.	
	29		X Bty. to 4th Army Sch of Mortars on 10 dys course. Lt. M. Stanford transfd. to 42nd Divl. T.M. B's.	
			Oscar P. Taylor Capt. G. L. Divl. T.M. Off. 40th Divn.	

T2134. Wt. W708—776. 500000. 4/15. Sir J. C. & S.

X. 40. Trench Mortar Battery.

Instructions regarding War Diaries and Intelligence Summaries are contained in F. S. Regs., Part II. and the Staff Manual respectively. Title pages will be prepared in manuscript.

WAR DIARY
or
INTELLIGENCE SUMMARY.
(Erase heading not required.)

March.

Army Form C. 2118.

Place	Date	Hour	Summary of Events and Information	Remarks and references to Appendices
Trampas. (Camp 165)	1/3/17. to 7/3/17.		Doing fatigues for R.F.A. from 7 a.m. to 6 P.M. Building Gun Pits, making roads and so on.	
	8/3/17.	11 A.M.	Took over Clery Sector from Z 33. T.M.B. No guns in action. No ammunition. 4 beds were handed over in dug outs in a disused support trench off Wurzel Avenue.* Trench only 3 ft 6 in deep & in full view of enemy lines & artillery O.P's on Mt. St. Quentin about a mile back. Any work or firing during the day time quite out of the question. No targets, ranges or map spottings were apparently available to hand over. Decided to put in a gun near Headquarters dug out* (Berlin Wood) where all ranks live. Found 50 old bombs & two boxes of tails on manne dump. No component parts.	* I 7.a. 7-9½. (Mustard Support) * I. 1.a. 3-3½.
		7.30 P.M.	Enemy moderately quiet. Guns, N.C.O's & men &c. arrived by transport at 7-30. P.M.	
	9/3/17.		Took guns & stores up to Wurzel Avenue. Saw C.O. Right Batt. Obtained 150 Sand bags 6 9 by 3 beams &c. & commenced H.Q. Emplacement. Built latrines for Officers & O.R. & cleaned up place which was in a filthy state. Reconnoitred trenches for possible positions, without success. Most places too muddy, & also no cover for men or bombs. Dug-out heavily bombarded with T.M's & artillery every morning from 6 to 8.	
	10th		Completed H.Q. emplacement. Ready to fire, but no ammunition. Hostile artillery & T.M's	

T2134. Wt. W708—776. 500000. 4/15. Sir J. C. & S.

2

X. 40. Trench Mortar Bty.

Instructions regarding War Diaries and Intelligence Summaries are contained in F. S. Regs., Part II. and the Staff Manual respectively. Title pages will be prepared in manuscript.

WAR DIARY
or
INTELLIGENCE SUMMARY.
(Erase heading not required.)

March

Army Form C. 2118.

Place	Date	Hour	Summary of Events and Information	Remarks and references to Appendices
Clary	(cont) 10/3/17.		very active all day, especially aerial darts. Visited by D. T. M. O. Batt: C.O. does not wish any 2" T.M's near any Communication trench.	
"	11/3/17.		Built an extemporary Emplacement in trench off Wurzel Avenue.* Gun ready to fire. Work done under great difficulty to avoid being seen. Found a few old charges & fired 2 rounds from H.Q. gun, using the Temple Silencer. Observation very difficult, as owing to saps, enemy front line could not be accurately discerned. Hostile artillery very active along Beaulin Valley & ridge above.	*I.7.d.7.9½.
		1.8 P.M.	100 bombs & Com: parts arrived by transport. (50% Silencer tails). Rounds fired 2	
	12/3/17.		Bombs stored in empty shaft T.M. near dump. Fired 3 rounds in salvoes with Y. 40 who had a gun 40 yards away. No retaliation. Rounds fired 3.	
	13/3/17.		Consulted with Capt. J. Taylor of the Stokes with a view to grouping 2" & Stokes mortars. Brought ammunition up to H.Q. gun. Am: recess improved from old shelter. Took over 1 gun complete & 7 beds from Y. 40 who moved to Bouchavesnes sector. Enemy fairly active.	
	14/3/17.		Work continued. Wurzel Gun had to be dug-out had to be unearthed as the back of the trench had fallen in on it.	

T2134. Wt. W708—776. 500000. 4/15. Sir J. C. & S.

3

X. 40. Trench Mortar Battery

Instructions regarding War Diaries and Intelligence Summaries are contained in F. S. Regs., Part II. and the Staff Manual respectively. Title pages will be prepared in manuscript.

WAR DIARY
or
INTELLIGENCE SUMMARY.
(Erase heading not required.)

March.

Army Form C. 2118.

Place	Date	Hour	Summary of Events and Information	Remarks and references to Appendices
Clery	15/3/17		Commenced another extemporary emplacement off Wurzel Avenue (Mustard Support) under guidance of one sapper. Work continued on H.Q. bomb recess &c. Position off Macaroni trench (15 yds behind front line) under 6 inches of water. Took up 5 bombs to Wurzel Avenue.	
"	16/3/17	9 A.M.	Heavy mist. According to instructions started a bombardment of enemy trenches in conjunction with 9.45" T.M. One gun at Wurzel & one at H.Q. both using silencers. The mist enabled a small supply of bombs to be kept up at the Wurzel Avenue gun, but made accurate registration almost an impossibility. The whole battery was brought up to carry bombs, no other parties being available (firing at very short notice). Each gun fired 24 rounds when all the Rifle mechanisms were used up, owing chiefly to S.A. cartridges bursting backwards. There was no retaliation at all. Fired 48.	
"	17/3/17 to 22/3/17		Enemy having retired. Guns, beds &c. were collected & transferred to Hem Wood & all bombs &c collected & stored at Marne Dump.	
"	23/3/17 to 28/3/17		Fatigues, drill, cleaning guns &c.	
	29/3/17		Left for 4th Army School of Mortars. Lieut. Em. Cummins on a Course.	

Norman Reid Lieut R.F.A.
O.C. X.40.T.M.B

T2134. Wt. W708—776. 500000. 4/15. Sir J. C. & S.

1/ V 40 Heavy Trench Mortar Battery.

V 40 T M B

Instructions regarding War Diaries and Intelligence Summaries are contained in F. S. Regs., Part II. and the Staff Manual respectively. Title pages will be prepared in manuscript.

WAR DIARY
or
INTELLIGENCE SUMMARY.

(Erase heading not required.)

Army Form C. 2118.

Place	Date	Hour	Summary of Events and Information	Remarks and references to Appendices
1917 Field.	Mch 1–7		Battery engaged as working party on Field Gun positions in front of [illegible].	
Bouchavesnes – [illegible]	8.		Two heavy Mortars taken over from 33rd Division. One gun in the quarry between [illegible] Lane and the river, the other in Mary Avenue about C [illegible]. The River gun was in action and ready to fire. It was considered that a good deal more work was needed on Mary gun before the position would be ready.	Maps – Bouchavesnes and Peronne.
			The Battery moved from Camp [illegible] to "[illegible]" near [illegible] Wood.	
	9		Work started on River Gun. Mary detachment moved bombs from Middle Dump to a dugout near the gun.	
	10		Work continued on River Gun. Mary detachment moving bombs.	
	11		R E help obtained to improve River position generally. Arrangements made to complete Mary position under supervision of R E ([illegible]). At this time there was no dugout for the men or for the bombs, neither was it expected that the slope on which the gun was placed would stand the shock when the mortar was fired. A suggested position for a heavy T M was visited in the quarry at C [illegible]. An attempt was made to discover an O.P. in the neighbourhood of support line crossing Bethune Peronne Rd.	
	12.		Relief. Work continued on River and Mary positions. Arrangements made to move bombs stored at Middle Dump to the Bomb Store at P C Madame.	
	13.		Work continued. Party detailed to clear bombs from Middle Dump. Intpost O P [illegible].	
	14		Work on River and Mary guns.	

A5834 Wt. W4973/M687 750,000 8/16 D. D. & L. Ltd. Forms/C.2118/13.

[illegible] 2/Lt RFA

V 40 T M B.

31.3.17

II

V/40 Heavy Trench Mortar Battery. V 40 T M B

Army Form C. 2118.

WAR DIARY
or
INTELLIGENCE SUMMARY.
(Erase heading not required.)

Instructions regarding War Diaries and Intelligence Summaries are contained in F. S. Regs., Part II. and the Staff Manual respectively. Title pages will be prepared in manuscript.

Place	Date	Hour	Summary of Events and Information	Remarks and references to Appendices
Field.	1917 Feb 15		Artillery O.P. in Bazencourt Wood visited.	
Bouchavesnes – Fley			Fired three rounds from River Gun.	
			Work on Mary Position.	
	16		Misty. Boche thought to be about to withdraw.	
			Steam [illegible]. Fired thirty four rounds from River and Mary Guns.	
	17		River Gun had moved. Work continued on "Mary" position. It was reported that Boche had retired.	
	18		Inspected damage done by H T M to Boche Trenches. These had been damaged considerably a dugout was found to have been blown in. A 9.45 "dud" was close by. The fuse of another "dud" had been removed. Visited Mont St Quentin and noticed how valuable this place had been to the Boche for observation.	
	19		Capt. Tomes wounded.	
	20		"Mary" Gun and bombs brought to Mangle Dump.	
	21		2 N.C.O's and 24 men carrying 2" bombs for X and Y Batteries. 1 N.C.O. and 8 men to assist DAC at A.R.P. Mangle Dump.	
	22		Working party at A.R.P. increased to 1 N.C.O. and 16 men. Party to clean gun at Mangle Dump. Party for [illegible].	
	23		Parties as for 22nd.	
	24		1 N.C.O. and 16 men at A.R.P. Party to load "Mary" Gun into lorry at Mangle Dump at 2 pm. Lorry arrived at 8 p.m. and was handed over by A R P	

A5834 Wt. W4973/M687 750,000 8/16 D. D. & L. Ltd. Forms/C.2118/13.

[illegible] Lt. R.F.A.
V 40 T.M.B. 31-3-17

V.40 Heavy Trench Mortar Battery.

Instructions regarding War Diaries and Intelligence Summaries are contained in F. S. Regs., Part II. and the Staff Manual respectively. Title pages will be prepared in manuscript.

Army Form C. 2118.

WAR DIARY
or
INTELLIGENCE SUMMARY.

(Erase heading not required.)

Place	Date	Hour	Summary of Events and Information	Remarks and references to Appendices
Field	1917		1 NCO and 11 men to A.R.P. – Party to bring Rowe gun to billets near Glen Wood.	
Bouchavesnes Ang.	March 25		Field gun ammunition of C and D Battery 181 taken over. Guards provided.	
	26		Working Party at A.R.P. – Guards on 18 pr ammunition. Remainder cleaning guns and stores.	
	27 28		Working Party at A.R.P. – Guards on 18 pr ammunition. Remainder cleaning guns and stores.	
	29		Guards on 18 pr ammunition and also working party.	
	30		Oiling Bombs at Mangle Dump. Cleaning Guns. Guards on 18 pr ammunition.	
	31		Bringing 4" and 2" Bombs from right side [illegible] to Mangle Dumps.	

W.R.B. Lavington [illegible]

31-3-17

A5834 Wt. W4973/M687 750,000 8/16 D. D. & L. Ltd. Forms/C.2118/13.

Instructions regarding War Diaries and Intelligence Summaries are contained in F. S. Regs., Part II. and the Staff Manual respectively. Title pages will be prepared in manuscript.

WAR DIARY
or
~~INTELLIGENCE SUMMARY.~~
(Erase heading not required.)

Y40. Trench Mortar Battery

Army Form C. 2118.

March 1917.

Place	Date	Hour	Summary of Events and Information	Remarks and references to Appendices
Chipilly	1st – 4th		Drill & cleaning guns & stores.	
Maurepas.	4th – 8th		Gathering of all T.M. Batteries preparatory to taking over the two sectors north of the River Somme from the 33rd Divn.	
Clery sector	8th		Took over line; three open positions with no cover. Half a mile of double wire & 3 beds taken over. Guns brought up in evening to Clery dump & stored by the dump with stores. 33 bombs complete taken over at the guns. Night firing only possible owing to direct observation from Mont St Quentin.	
"	9th		Guns brought up to Berlin Valley Hdq. dugout & two mounted in the line, the other remaining at Hdq for proposed emplacement near by to be no 1 gun. No 2 gun covered Zombor Trench & no 3 with 42° M.B. covered the wire of Herzfeld Trench in direct enfilade. Both ~~these~~ guns were situated 20 yds behind our front line & about 200 yds from Macaroni Trench. Observation for both guns is extremely difficult owing to the crest in "No Mans Land" concealing the enemy wire.	

2353 Wt. W2544/1454 700,000 5/15 D. D. & L. A.D.S.S./Forms/C. 2118.

2

Instructions regarding War Diaries and Intelligence Summaries are contained in F. S. Regs., Part II. and the Staff Manual respectively. Title pages will be prepared in manuscript.

WAR DIARY
or
INTELLIGENCE SUMMARY.
(Erase heading not required.)

Army Form C. 2118.

Place	Date	Hour	Summary of Events and Information	Remarks and references to Appendices
In the Field Clery Sector	9th cont:		Five rounds fired from No 2 at C 26 c 9.0 at 8.30. p m. Rifle grenade & aerial dart retaliation. Weather misty & day quiet	
	10th		Eight rounds fired at 9.15 p m in conjunction with our artillery from Nos 2 & 3 guns. Very little retaliation but one bed (No 3) sank 4 inches & the rifle mechanism of no 3 blowing out spoilt the adapter. No one gun put into action near Hdq: dugout with 120° M.B covering part of Inferno Trench	
	11th		Enemy artillery very active during day; both sides of Berlin valley being shelled intermittently. Five rounds fired from No 3 gun at 7.5 p.m. Trouble with no 2's mechanism. Machine gun played on parapet in vicinity of guns during the firing	
	12th		4 Rounds fired from Hdq Gun (No 1) with silencer in conjunction with X Bty. Relief of right half bty by left during the afternoon.	

2353 Wt. W2544/1454 700,000 5/15 D. D. & L. A.D.S.S./Forms/C. 2118.

3/

Instructions regarding War Diaries and Intelligence Summaries are contained in F. S. Regs., Part II. and the Staff Manual respectively. Title pages will be prepared in manuscript.

WAR DIARY
or
INTELLIGENCE SUMMARY.
(Erase heading not required.)

Army Form C. 2118.

Place	Date	Hour	Summary of Events and Information	Remarks and references to Appendices
Clery sector	13th		Owing to no 2" Mortars being in Bethune Road sector No 3 & 1 guns brought out of action during afternoon & brought down to rest billets by hand cart at night with all stores	
Bethune Rd sector.	14th		Men & kits taken to dugouts near Middle Dump for work on two proposed new emplacements. Owing to thigh deep water in trenches work had to be postponed.	
	15th -16th		Work still impossible owing to bad state of trenches	
	17th		Work on clearing out trenches by sites for new emplacements commenced. Line opposite evacuated by enemy during the afternoon.	
	18th		Owing to enemy retreat work on trenches ceased & men withdrawn to Rest Headquarters in Hem Wood.	

2353 Wt. W2544/1454 700,000 5/15 D. D. & L. A.D.S.S./Forms/C. 2118.

4/

Instructions regarding War Diaries and Intelligence Summaries are contained in F. S. Regs., Part II. and the Staff Manual respectively. Title pages will be prepared in manuscript.

WAR DIARY
or
INTELLIGENCE SUMMARY.
(Erase heading not required.)

Army Form C. 2118.

Place	Date	Hour	Summary of Events and Information	Remarks and references to Appendices
Rest billets near Hem Wood	19th		cleaning guns + stores.	
	20 -21		Bombs carted from Middle Dump by decauville to Mangold Dump with tail boxes & component parts, the latter rendered useless owing to contact with damp (All these dumped by 33rd Divl T.M.S. Bombs also transferred from Morning dump to Mangold Dump by hand cart.	
	22 to 31		Fatigues, - drill, - cleaning guns, etc.	

R W Bennett 2Lt.
for. O.C. Y/40 T.M.B.

2353 Wt. W2544/1454 700,000 5/15 D. D. & L. A.D.S.S./Forms/C. 2118.

Z/40 Trench Mortar Battery

Instructions regarding War Diaries and Intelligence Summaries are contained in F. S. Regs., Part II. and the Staff Manual respectively. Title pages will be prepared in manuscript.

Army Form C. 2118.

WAR DIARY
or
INTELLIGENCE SUMMARY.

(Erase heading not required.)

Place	Date	Hour	Summary of Events and Information	Remarks and references to Appendices
Maurepas.	1st–7th		Battery at camp 165 near Maurepas. They spent most of their time digging advanced gunpits near Dancourt, and in the construction of dugouts. When not required here they put up huts in the camp.	
Ham Wood	8th–10th		The Battery shifted its [illegible] to [illegible] and lived in dugouts in front of Ham Wood. They carried rations and material for the batteries in the line.	
Vaux.	11th–21st		The Battery was at the IVth Army School of Mortars at Vaux-en-Amienois.	
Ham Wood.	[illegible]		The Battery returned to earthworks in the 26th Trench and was employed in guarding the ammunition at battery positions evacuated by the field artillery of the division.	
			[illegible] Hammond [illegible] O.C. Z/40 T.M. Bty.	

A5834 Wt. W4973/M687 750,000 8/16 D. D. & L. Ltd. Forms/C.2118/13.

Instructions regarding War Diaries and Intelligence Summaries are contained in F. S. Regs., Part II. and the Staff Manual respectively. Title pages will be prepared in manuscript.

WAR DIARY
or
INTELLIGENCE SUMMARY.
(*Erase heading not required.*)

D.T.M.O., 40TH DIVISION. April, 1917.

Army Form C. 2118.

Vol 10

Place	Date	Hour	Summary of Events and Information	Remarks and references to Appendices
	1 to 9		V, Y, and Z Batteries collecting and guarding 18-pdr. and 4.5" ammunition from vacated gun positions in the BOUCHAVESNES— CLERY Sector. X Battery on a 2" French Mortar 'Refresher' Course at 4th Army Sch. of Mortars, VAUX-EN-AMIENOIS.	
	9		X Bty. returned to billets (dugouts) at HEM WOOD.	
	10 to 18		All Batteries - V, X, Y, and Z - still collecting and guarding 18-pdr. and 4.5" ammunition, and working on the 'Ammunition Refilling Point' at FINS.	
	19		All Batteries left HEM WOOD for MOISLAINS - accommodated there the night.	
	20 to 30		Batteries employed building horse standings for 181 Bde., R.F.A. at EQUANCOURT, and unloading ammunition at the 'Ammunition Refilling Point' at FINS.	
	29		Reconnoitred outpost line in front of LA VACQUERIE with a view to putting in a Heavy Mortar, but found that LA VACQUERIE was out of range from even the most advanced trench.	

Oscar J. Taylor Capt., G.L.,
Divl. T.M. Offr.,
40th Division.

T2134. Wt. W708—776. 500000. 4/15. Sir J. C. & S.

V. 40. Trench Mortar Battery. April. 1917.

Army Form C. 2118.

WAR DIARY
or
INTELLIGENCE SUMMARY.

(Erase heading not required.)

Instructions regarding War Diaries and Intelligence Summaries are contained in F. S. Regs., Part II. and the Staff Manual respectively. Title pages will be prepared in manuscript.

Place	Date	Hour	Summary of Events and Information	Remarks and references to Appendices
Hem Wood.	1/4/17. to 18/4/17.		Whole Battery occupied daily in transporting Field Artillery ammunition from Clery & Bouchavesnes sectors to dump at P.C. Wurzel, and in guarding the ammunition at the Battery positions before removal.	
Moislans.	19/4/17.		Moved on foot to Moislans. Put up for night near D.A.C.	
Fins	20/4/17		" " " Fins. Erected tarpaulin shelters for men, & generally settled down.	
	21/4/17. to 30/4/17		All working on building of horse standings at 181 Bgde R.F.A. Wagon line at Equancourt. Sometimes unloading ammunition at A.R.P. Fins at night.	
	29/4/17.		Reconnoitred our front opposite La Vacquerie with D.T.M.O with a view to getting a gun in action by Wednesday 2/5/17. to fire into La Vacquerie. Only possible spot was just behind our front line on Gouzeaucourt. La Vacquerie Rd. Extreme range just reached outskirts of village. No work possible in daylight. only just screened from Enemy observation. Decided it was out of question.	

Norman Reid. Lieut. R.F.A.
O.C. V.40. T.M.B
30.4.17.

T2134. Wt. W708—776. 500000. 4/15. Sir J. C. & S.

X.40. T.M.B.

Instructions regarding War Diaries and Intelligence Summaries are contained in F. S. Regs., Part II. and the Staff Manual respectively. Title pages will be prepared in manuscript.

WAR DIARY
or
INTELLIGENCE SUMMARY.
(Erase heading not required.)

April 1917.

Army Form C. 2118.

Place	Date	Hour	Summary of Events and Information	Remarks and references to Appendices
Vaux-en-Amiénois	1/4/17 to 9/4/17		The Whole Battery doing a "Refreshing" Course at the 4th Army School of Mortars, Vaux-en-Amiénois.	
Hem Wood.	9/4/17.		Returned to Hem Wood in Lorries.	
	10/4/17. to 18/4/17		Whole battery on fatigue every day carrying 18 Pdr & 4.5 How. ammunition from old Battery positions in Velery & Bouchavesnes Sectors to dump at P.C. Wurzel.	
Moislains.	19/4/17.		Left Hem Wood on foot for Nos. 1 & 2. Sections D.A.C at Moislains. Remained there the night.	
Fins	20/4/17.		Left Moislains for Fins. No billets. Temporary ones erected with the aid of tarpaulins &c.	
"	21/4/17. to 30/4/17.		Work daily from 8. a.m. to 5. p.m. building horse-standings for B/181. Bgde. R.F.A near Equancourt.	
"			Men sometimes needed to work at A.R.P unloading ammunition from Lorries - often at night.	
			3. men sent on Paris leave for 4 days during the month.	

Norman Reid. Lieut. R.F.A.
late. O.C. X.40. T.M.B.
30.4.17.

T2134. Wt. W708—776. 500000. 4/15. Sir J. C. & S.

Instructions regarding War Diaries and Intelligence Summaries are contained in F. S. Regs., Part II. and the Staff Manual respectively. Title pages will be prepared in manuscript.

Army Form C. 2118.

WAR DIARY
or
~~INTELLIGENCE SUMMARY.~~
(Erase heading not required.)

Y40 Trench Mortar Battery.

April, 1917.

Place	Date	Hour	Summary of Events and Information	Remarks and references to Appendices
~~In the Field~~ Near HEM WOOD	1.4.17	–	At the beginning of the month the Battery was supplying a guard ~~of~~ over the ammunition left by three batteries of Artillery in the positions occupied before the German retreat. The remainder of the available men of the Battery was employed in removing ammunition from vacated gun positions to the Divisional A.R.P., Cléry.	
"	11.4.17	2 p.m.	Two guns belonging to the Battery were handed over to a party from the 40th D.A.C., who were proceeding to the 4th Army School of Mortars.	
MOISLAINS	19.4.17	–	The Battery moved forward, together with the remainder of the Divl. Trench Mortars. It was accomodated for the night by the D.A.C.	
FINS.	20.4.17	–	The guns and stores were left behind at Moislains, with 1 N.C.O. and 1 Gunner as a guard. The personnel moved on to Fins, and on arrival bivouacked in a field near the Divl. A.R.P.	
"	21.4.17	8 am	Six men were detailed to continue the construction of the Camp. The remainder went daily to EQUANCOURT WOOD to construct horse standings for "C" Battery and Headquarters, 181st Bde., R.F.A.	
"	24.4.17	–	The Battery was taken off the above work for two days, and put on Loading	

2353 Wt. W2544/1454 700,000 5/15 D. D. & L. A.D.S.S./Forms/C. 2118.

Instructions regarding War Diaries and Intelligence Summaries are contained in F. S. Regs., Part II. and the Staff Manual respectively. Title pages will be prepared in manuscript.

WAR DIARY
or
~~INTELLIGENCE SUMMARY.~~
(Erase heading not required.)

Y40 Trench Mortar Battery ~~Army~~ Form C. 2118.

April, 1917 (contd.)

Place	Date	Hour	Summary of Events and Information	Remarks and references to Appendices
FINS			Fatigues at the Divl. A.R.P., Fins.	
"	27.4.17	8 am.	Work was resumed on the Horse Standings in EQUANCOURT WOOD, and continued till the end of the month.	

Mark Stanford Lieut.
O.C. Y40 T.M.B.
30.4.1917.

2353 Wt. W2544/1454 700,000 5/15 D. D. & L. A.D.S.S./Forms/C. 2118.

2/40 T.M. Battery

Instructions regarding War Diaries and Intelligence Summaries are contained in F. S. Regs., Part II. and the Staff Manual respectively. Title pages will be prepared in manuscript.

WAR DIARY
or
~~INTELLIGENCE SUMMARY.~~
(Erase heading not required.)

APL. 1917.

Army Form C. 2118.

Place	Date	Hour	Summary of Events and Information	Remarks and references to Appendices
Earthworks	1/4/17		Battery guarding ammunition abandoned by advancing field batteries and removing same to the A.R.P. [illegible]	
Derwood	16/4/17			
	26/4/17		Ten men and Cpl Huggeridge went to FINS to complete the new A.R.P. being built there. The remainder worked as before	
	27/4/17		Remainder of battery came up to FINS	
	20–30/4/17		All battery at work on ARP finishing shelters and stacking and issuing ammunition.	

Hammond
Lt RFA
O.C. 2/40 T.M. Bty

2353 Wt. W2544/1454 700,000 5/15 D. D. & L. A.D.S.S./Forms/C. 2118.

Instructions regarding War Diaries and Intelligence Summaries are contained in F. S. Regs., Part II. and the Staff Manual respectively. Title pages will be prepared in manuscript.

WAR DIARY
or
INTELLIGENCE SUMMARY.
(Erase heading not required.)

D. T. M. O., 40TH DIVISION. Army Form C. 2118.

No. MAY 1917.

Place	Date	Hour	Summary of Events and Information	Remarks and references to Appendices
	1 to 13		All Batteries, (V40 - X40 - Y40 - Z40) on fatigues for the 181st Field Artillery Brigades of the Division - building horse standings in EQUANCOURT WOOD, and unloading and stacking 18-pdr. and 4.5" How. ammunition at FINS.	
	14		V Battery went into action at GONNELIEU (one gun in action) relieving W8 T. M. Bty., and continued in action during the whole of the month. X. Y & Z, on fatigues as above.	
	15 to 25		X. & Y still on fatigues. Z Bty. on gun drill - Three Officers, - Sec. Lts. Ford, Johnson, and Benningfield, of C/178, C/181, and 40th D.A.C. respectively - being attached for a course of instruction in 2" Trench Mortars. On 25th, Lt. J. K. Pickard, MC, 13th Yorks, reported for duty & took over command of X40 T. M. B.	
	26 to 31		Y & Z. on fatigues at HEUDICOURT, and near the FINS - GOUZEAUCOURT road - building headquarters for the 178 Bde. R.F.A. at the former place, and building horse standings for the 181 Bde., R.F.A. at the latter place. X Bty. on gun drill. 3 Offrs., - Sec. Lts. Stevens, Elliott, & Blundell, - of 13/178, 13/181, & 40th D.A.C, respec., being attd. for instruction.	
	23-31		Capt. W. REID, R.F.A., in command of 40th Divl. T. M. B's. - Capt. O. P. Taylor, M.C., g.s., being on leave.	

Duncan Reid Capt., R.F.A.
for Div. T. M. Offr.

T2134. Wt. W708-776. 500000. 4/15. Sir J. C. & S.

1/

Instructions regarding War Diaries and Intelligence Summaries are contained in F. S. Regs., Part II. and the Staff Manual respectively. Title pages will be prepared in manuscript.

May

WAR DIARY
or
INTELLIGENCE SUMMARY.
(Erase heading not required.)

V. 40. Trench Mortar Battery.

Army Form C. 2118.

Vol XI

Place	Date	Hour	Summary of Events and Information	Remarks and references to Appendices
Fins.	1/5/17 to 13/5/17		Occupied in making brick horse-standings for A/181 & D/181 in Equancourt Wood. A/181 always lent two wagons to carry chalk, bricks, timber &c. D/181 only lent one wagon, & for last few days provided no wagons, 20 men were taken away & placed on lines of another battery. Wood & bricks procured from wrecked houses in Equancourt.	
			Men in reliefs worked day & night at unloading & unboxing 18 pdr & 4.5" ammunition at Amm Refilling Point Fins.	
Gonnelieu	14/5/17		Went into action at Gonnelieu relieving W.8. Trench Mortar Battery. One gun in action in a sunken road at R 33.b. 45-96. Headquarters in a house R 26.d. 70-25. O.P. in a 3 storied house at cross roads R.27 c. 40-20. Gun firing at strong point in enemy front line and wire at R.28.a 20.00. At 5 p.m. O.P. was three parts demolished by 5.9s owing to infantry & other people wandering in at all hours of the day in full view of German trenches, balloons &c. Detachment arrived at 9.30 p.m. & immediately took 3 rounds to the gun. No cover of any sort at the gun. No infantry & no wire in front. During the day 3 rounds at the gun were ruined by shrapnel.	
	16/5/17		Spent getting settled, building latrines, making cover for men near gun. Work at gun very difficult owing to aerial observation. Hostile aeroplanes coming down to within 200 ft	

T2134. Wt. W708–776. 500000. 4/15. Sir J. C. & S.

2/

Instructions regarding War Diaries and Intelligence Summaries are contained in F. S. Regs., Part II. and the Staff Manual respectively. Title pages will be prepared in manuscript.

May

WAR DIARY
or
INTELLIGENCE SUMMARY.
(Erase heading not required.)

V. 40. T.M.B

Army Form C. 2118.

Place	Date	Hour	Summary of Events and Information	Remarks and references to Appendices
Gonnelieu	15/5/17	(cont)	of the road, thus making any work or men in road obvious. Reconnoitred for alternative O.P. Several houses in front & to right of present one give quite as good view.	
		2 pm	After firing 1 round found that remaining 8 charges were soaking wet & quite useless. Found 4 men of Lincolnshire Regt. 8th Div. & 2 Germans, all killed 24th April, lying about unburied behind H.Q. No identification. Buried the men & erected crosses.	
			Fired 1. Bombs in hand 6. Component parts nil (all wet).	
	16/5/17		Work on gun continued. Searched whole village for O.P's. re timber, ladders.	
			Small German T.M. (10½ lb. bomb) Range 1460x fires on road near gun	
		9.45 Am.	Saw 2 Germans come from enemy wire & run towards our line, stopping & crouching every 50x or 20. Were met by our infantry in no man's land. 60x to right of gun. Were young men of 94th Saxon Regt.	
			Major Ward came in & arranged about laying wires between O.P. this line 18 pdr. (B/181) for co-operation. Wires were laid. H.Q. vicinity shelled during night. One shell hit the house.	
		11 pm	10 bombs arrived by D.A.C. transport also some camouflage & another telephone. Bomb Store refuses to send extra component parts in place of those ruined by damp.	

3/

Instructions regarding War Diaries and Intelligence Summaries are contained in F. S. Regs., Part II. and the Staff Manual respectively. Title pages will be prepared in manuscript.

May

WAR DIARY
or
INTELLIGENCE SUMMARY.
(Erase heading not required.)

V. 40. Trench Mortar Bty

Army Form C. 2118.

Place	Date	Hour	Summary of Events and Information	Remarks and references to Appendices
Gonnelieu	16/5/17 (Cont)		Raining all day & night. Fired. nil. In hand 16. Com. parts 10.	
	17/5/17		Morning spent on work on shelters, and bomb recesses near gun. Charges &c. kept at H.Q. owing to wet state of everything at gun, & taken down to gun when firing. Anyone going to gun can be seen walking down for 300x. Range to enemy front line for gun 600x. Raining again. Found new position for gun in yard of a house at R 27 c. 50-25. Spot invisible to enemy, with care people can come & go unobserved, behind house in front is an excellent deep, 2-entranced German dug-out for crew. In building at side 2x from gun, can dig an excellent bomb store. Will start work at once.	
		2.30pm	Fired 4 rounds on R. 28. a. 20-00. 3 rounds appeared to fall in trench, 1 one in the wire. Timber thrown in the air.	
		10 pm.	10 bombs arrived by transport. Arranged with Kings Own (Loyal Lancs) re messages & laying wires to their H.Q. from ours. Could only take 3 bombs to gun as hand-cart broke, and gun area was being ~~heavily~~ shelled with gas.* Respirators had to be worn. Have 120 German small minnenwerfer gas shells. Have asked for captured gun to fire them. Fired. 4. In hand 22. Com. parts 16.	* Small minnenwerfer.

T2134. Wt. W708-776. 500000. 4/15. Sir J. C. & S.

4

Instructions regarding War Diaries and Intelligence Summaries are contained in F. S. Regs., Part II. and the Staff Manual respectively. Title pages will be prepared in manuscript.

May

WAR DIARY *or* INTELLIGENCE SUMMARY.

(Erase heading not required.)

V. 40. Trench Mortar Battery.

Army Form C. 2118.

Place	Date	Hour	Summary of Events and Information	Remarks and references to Appendices
			2/Lieut. H.J. Escott R.F.A. att^d from D/178. Bgde. R.F.A.	
Gommecourt	18/5/17.		Weather fine & cloudy. Marked out new gun position at R. 27. c. 60. 25. Zero line 86° mag. Range 800^x. Locality shelled for an hour. This spot which which is 100^x in front of O.P. is always shelled fairly heavily several times a day	
	morn.	11 a.m.	Fired 4 rounds. 2nd front line at R. 26. C. 20. 95. & 2nd wire. A gap has been blown in wire here, in fact all round that spot the wire has been wrecked & is a mass of 9.45" craters.	
	p.m.	p.m.	Laid wires to Battalion H.Q. (King's own Loyal Lancs) from ours. Gommecourt shelled by 5.9's. Major Ward B/181 killed near O.P. during afternoon.	
	5 p.m.	5 p.m.	Lieut. F.P. Enright arrived to relieve me. Fired 1 round to show him target. Relief delayed 15 mins, arrived 9 p.m. Fired 5. 2nd Land 17. C.p. 11	
	19/5/17	6 a.m.	Handed over to Lieut. F.P. Enright. Started work on more bomb recesses in back near gun. Remainder of detachment working on new gun emplacement. Work suspended twice owing to locality being heavily shelled with 77 m.m. 5.9's & 4.2 Shrapnel. Whole village of Gommecourt shelled throughout the day. C.O. Argyl & Sutherland Highlanders asked for gun to be used for retaliation only (sic) as his men got the retaliation when it was fired. Kings own did not seem to notice or mind any retaliation.	

T2134. Wt. W708—776. 500000. 4/15. Sir J. C. & S.

5

Instructions regarding War Diaries and Intelligence Summaries are contained in F. S. Regs., Part II. and the Staff Manual respectively. Title pages will be prepared in manuscript.

May

WAR DIARY or INTELLIGENCE SUMMARY.

(Erase heading not required.)

V 40 Trench Mortar Battery

Army Form C. 2118.

Place	Date	Hour	Summary of Events and Information	Remarks and references to Appendices
Gomiecourt	19/5/17	-	Cpl. Freeman sent to hospital ill. Fired 0 On hand 17. C.p. 11.	
	20/5/17		Work on new Emplacement	
	5/20/	5.30 pm	Fired 5 rounds on usual target. Slight retaliation on Gomiecourt. Raining. Fired 5. On hand 12 C.p. 6.	
	21/5/17	7 am	Hostile shelling disturbed work on new emplacement. Hostile planes over guns	
		3 p.m.	Fired 5 rounds at R 28.c 20-95 to R 28 c 30-85 with good effect. 6 bombs taken to [illegible] 10 bombs & extra Cm parts arrived by transport. Fired 5 On hand 17.	
	22/5/17		Raining. Gomiecourt shelled 77 m.m. & 5.9s	
		3.30 pm	Fired 6 rounds on R.28.c. 35-85 and Trench Mortar at R.28.A. Retaliation by 5.9s at O.P. Aeroplane (German) hovered over guns for some time after firing. 2 5.9s fell near guns. 77 m.m. on Gomiecourt. Fired 6. On hand 11	
	23/5/17	6 am	Handed over to Lt Escreet R.F.A. Quiet day. Considerable aerial activity. 10 bombs arrived. Fired nil On hand 21.	
	24/5/17	10.30 am	Fired 4 rounds at usual target (the only one which can be observed)	

T2134. Wt. W708—776. 500000. 4/15. Sir J. C. & S.

6

Instructions regarding War Diaries and Intelligence Summaries are contained in F. S. Regs., Part II. and the Staff Manual respectively. Title pages will be prepared in manuscript.

May

WAR DIARY
or
INTELLIGENCE SUMMARY. V 40. T.M.B
(Erase heading not required.)

Army Form C. 2118.

Place	Date	Hour	Summary of Events and Information	Remarks and references to Appendices
Gonnelieu	24/5/17	10 pm	Commenced to move gun to new emplacement at R 27 c. 6-25. Completed 2-15 A.M. 9 bombs at gun Fired 4. in hand 17.	
	25/5/17	8 AM	Registered gun & fired 5 rounds on same target at request of A. & S.H. Cut wire at R 28.c.2.8 Fired 9. in hand 8	
	26/5/17	10 AM	Fired 4 rounds 10 bombs rec'd Fired 4. in hand 14.	
	27/5/17	8 am	Handed over to Lieut Enright. (Capt Reid is act'g D.T.M.O. while latter is on leave) Replanted bed which had sunk 3° at the head. Fired 5 rounds. Bombs rec'd Fired 5. in hand 19.	
	28/5/17		Gonnelieu shelled 8 to 9 a.m. with 4.2's. Act'g D.T.M.O. arrived & went round gun &c. Commenced work on another emplacement near old position in Sunken road at R.33.b.45.95. Vicinity of gun & O.P. as usual heavily shelled because Infantry & other people will persist in wandering down road under observation & then walking into gate of gun position out of curiosity.	
		8 pm	Fired 1 round - light bad. Fired 1 in hand 18	

T/134. Wt. W708—776. 500000. 4/15. Sir J. C. & S.

Army Form C. 2118.

Instructions regarding War Diaries and Intelligence Summaries are contained in F. S. Regs., Part II. and the Staff Manual respectively. Title pages will be prepared in manuscript.

WAR DIARY or INTELLIGENCE SUMMARY. May. V. 40. T.M.B

(Erase heading not required.)

Place	Date	Hour	Summary of Events and Information	Remarks and references to Appendices
Gommecourt	29/5/17	10.30 AM.	Fired 5 rounds at T.M. at R.28.a. 40-05. Found another O.P. at vicarage at R.27.c. 3-0. Relayed wire there & did some work on it.	
	do	6 p.m.	Fired 4 rounds at T.M. at R.28.a. 40.05. 5.9's near gun.	
			Fired 9. 2nd hand. 9.	
	30/5/17		Gommecourt shelled between 6 & 8 A.m with 4.2's, especially near gun. Work continued on second gun position. Showed Stokes T.M. officer round sunken road &c. Right Batt: (Kings Own Loyal Lancs) asked that we should not fire for 24 hrs as retaliation came on one of his Coy. H.Q. and they wished to move it undisturbed.	
			Fired nil. 2nd hand. 19	
	31/5/17.		Work on second emplacement & bomb recess at present one.	
			During month fired 58.	14th to 31st
			" " there went on 10 days English leave. 2 Sgts & 6 men.	
			Bdr. Hind left for cadet school in England 26/5/17	

Norman Reid Capt. R.F.A.
O.C. V. 40. H.T.M.B

T2134. Wt. W708—776. 500000. 4/15. Sir J. C. & S.

Instructions regarding War Diaries and Intelligence Summaries are contained in F. S. Regs., Part II. and the Staff Manual respectively. Title pages will be prepared in manuscript.

May

WAR DIARY
or
INTELLIGENCE SUMMARY.
(Erase heading not required.)

X.40 Trench Mortar Battery

Army Form C. 2118.

Place	Date	Hour	Summary of Events and Information	Remarks and references to Appendices
Fins	1917 May 1–24		Building Brick Horse Standings for B181 in Equancourt Wood	
	25		Lieut T.K. Pickard reported for duty and took over Command of X.40 T.M. Battery	
"	25–31		Occupied on duty in connection with Officers Course of Instruction	

T.K. Pickard Lieut.
O.C. X.40. T.M. Battery

A6945 Wt. W11422/M1160 350,000 12/16 D. D. & L. Forms/C./2118/14.

Army Form C. 2118.

Instructions regarding War Diaries and Intelligence Summaries are contained in F. S. Regs., Part II. and the Staff Manual respectively. Title pages will be prepared in manuscript.

WAR DIARY
or
INTELLIGENCE SUMMARY.
(Erase heading not required.)

Y40 Trench Mortar Battery.

May, 1917.

Place	Date	Hour	Summary of Events and Information	Remarks and references to Appendices
FINS	1.5.17	8am.	The Battery was employed on fatigues for "C" Battery, ~~17?~~ 181 Bde., R.F.A., and for Headquarters, "B" and "D" Batteries, 178 Bde., R.F.A., consisting of building standings at the horse lines. These fatigues lasted during the whole month, as it was found impossible to bring the Battery into action, owing to the great breadth of "No Man's Land".	

Mark Stanford Lieut.
O.C. Y40 T.M.B.

2353 Wt. W2541/1454 700,000 5/15 D. D. & L. A.D.S.S./Forms/C. 2118.

Instructions regarding War Diaries and Intelligence Summaries are contained in F. S. Regs., Part II. and the Staff Manual respectively. Title pages will be prepared in manuscript.

WAR DIARY
or
~~INTELLIGENCE SUMMARY~~.

(*Erase heading not required.*)

Z 40T. M. Bty.

Army Form C. 2118.

Place	Date	Hour	Summary of Events and Information	Remarks and references to Appendices
FINS				
	1st–22nd May		Battery on fatigue at A. R. P. FINS. Fatigues consisted of unloading lorries at all hours of the day and occasionally at night — stacking the ammunition in seperate dumps — & loading limbers & waggons when the batteries came to draw ammunition. The men were employed regularly as the number of D.A.C. men working on the dump was insufficient in case of a large demand for shells.	
	22nd–27th May		Battery building headquarters for 178th Artillery Bde. near HEUDICOURT.	
	28th May		Went with D.T.M.O. to see heavy T.M. position at GONNELIEU. There is no place possible for a medium T.M. as the enemy is at all points out of range.	
	28th–31st May		Battery building waggon lines for 14th Artillery Bde near FINS–GOUZEAUCOURT Road. This work was finished on the morning of the thirty first.	
	15th to 25th May		2/Lts Ford Johnson, & Benningfield of C/178, C/181, & 40th D.A.C. respectively att^d for a 2" T.M. Course of instruction.	

R. G. Hammond
Lt. R.F.A.
O.C. Z.40 T.M. Bty.

2353 Wt. W2514/1454 700,000 5/15 D. D. & L. A.D.S.S./Forms/C. 2118.

Instructions regarding War Diaries and Intelligence Summaries are contained in F. S. Regs., Part II. and the Staff Manual respectively. Title pages will be prepared in manuscript.

WAR DIARY
or
INTELLIGENCE SUMMARY.
(Erase heading not required.)

Army Form C. 2118.

D.T.M.O.,
40th DIVISION.
No. JUNE
Date 1917.

Vol 12

Place	Date	Hour	Summary of Events and Information	Remarks and references to Appendices
	1 to 8		V 40 T.M. Bty. in action at GONNELIEU. X 40 T.M. Bty. undergoing local training, - building bivouacs, - disciplinary parades - at FINS. Y 40 T.M. Bty. on fatigues for the Field Batteries of the Divn; & cleaning their own guns, etc. prior to going on 2" T.M. Refresher Course at Fourth Army Sch. of Mortars, VAUX-EN-AMIENOIS. Z 40 T.M. Bty. on fatigues for the Field Batteries of the Divn. Capt. N. Reid, R.F.A., acting D.T.M.O. (1st to 7th) - Capt. O. P. Taylor, M.C. being on leave.	
	8 to 20		V Bty. in action at GONNELIEU. X Bty. attd. to 178 & 181 Bdes. R.F.A. for building forward gun positions. Whilst so employed, one N.C.O. & two men were wounded by enemy shell fire. Work on these forward gun positions commended by Brig.-Gen. G. H. W. Nicholson, 40th Div. Arty. Y Bty. on a 2" T.M. Refresher Course at Fourth Army Sch. of Mortars, VAUX-EN-AMIENOIS. Z Bty. on fatigues for Field Batteries of the Divn.	
	20 to 22		V Bty. in action at GONNELIEU. X Bty. still on the above-mentioned forward gun positions. Y Bty. undergoing local training - bathing - physical training - disciplinary parades, at FINS. Z Bty. cleaning up generally prior to going from FINS on 2" T.M. Refresher Course at Fourth Army Sch. of Mortars, VAUX-EN-AMIENOIS.	
	22 to 26		V Bty. in action at GONNELIEU. X Bty. on fatigues as above - forward gun positions for 18-pdrs. & 4.5" Hows. Y Bty. - local training at FINS, - bathing, disciplinary parades, etc. Z Bty. - on Course at 4th Army Sch. of Mortars, VAUX-EN-AMIENOIS.	
	26 to 30		V Bty. in action at GONNELIEU. X Bty. withdrawn from work on above-mentioned forward gun positions, & employed on building bivouacs, latrines, etc., & undergoing local training at FINS. Y Bty. undergoing local training, - bathing - disciplinary parades, etc., at FINS. Z Bty. still on 2" T.M. Course at Fourth Army Sch. of Mortars, VAUX-EN-AMIENOIS.	
	24		Lt. L. C. GARDNER, R.G.A., reported to D.T.M.O. at FINS, and posted to Z 40 T.M.B. from 240 Siege Bty., - as Second-in-Command.	

Oscar P Taylor
Capt. R.F.A.
Cmdg. 40th Div. T.M.B's.

A5834 Wt. W4973/M687 750,000 8/16 D. D. & L. Ltd. Forms/C.2118/13.

1/

June.

Instructions regarding War Diaries and Intelligence Summaries are contained in F. S. Regs., Part II. and the Staff Manual respectively. Title pages will be prepared in manuscript.

WAR DIARY or INTELLIGENCE SUMMARY.

(Erase heading not required.)

V.40 Trench Mortar Battery.

Army Form C. 2118.

Place	Date	Hour	Summary of Events and Information	Remarks and references to Appendices
			2/Lt. Bracet in Line.	
Gommecourt	1/6/17.	8-0 a.m.	Visit by a/D T.M.O. U.P. (vicarage) knocked out by 4.2's. Fired 6 rounds at 10.30 a.m.	
		6.0 p.m.	Fired 2 rounds. 10.30 p.m. 10 rounds & Camouflage arrived by G.S. wagon. Latter for use on new gun pit at R.33 b. 45.95.	
			Fired 8.	
	2/6/17.	11 a.m.	Fired 6 rounds on front line at R.28.c.5.8. Fairly heavy retaliation by small T.M.'s & 4.2's. Aerial activity hindered work on new Emplacement.	
			Fired 6	
	3/6/17.	10.30 a.m.	Fired 8 rounds on front line strong point in R.28.a & c. Usual fairly heavy retaliation. Gommecourt shelled all day. Relaid bed in p.m.	
			Fired 8.	
	4/6/17.		2/Lieut. F.P. Enright in Line.	
		[illegible] a.m.	Fired 4 rounds on R 28 a & c. Concussion of gun sent off a box of Mills grenades no	
		3.0 p.m.	" 4 " - - - - Same target (3 duds) damage except to clothing &c.	
			Gommecourt shelled. Work on new Emplacement continues every night. 50 105 m.m. at 10.p.m.	
	5/6/17.		Fired 8.	

T2134. Wt. W708–776. 500000. 4/15. Sir J. C. & S.

2/

June

Instructions regarding War Diaries and Intelligence Summaries are contained in F. S. Regs., Part II. and the Staff Manual respectively. Title pages will be prepared in manuscript.

WAR DIARY or INTELLIGENCE SUMMARY.

(Erase heading not required.)

V. 40. Trench Mortar Battery

Army Form C. 2118.

Place	Date	Hour	Summary of Events and Information	Remarks and references to Appendices
Gommecourt	5/6/17	10.30 a.m.	Fired 5 rounds on Concentration 5. – 2 duds. Retaliation round gun & O.P. with 10.5. m.m. Fired 5.	
"	6/6/17.	11 a.m.	Heavy shelling of gun & O.P. by Enemy. One fell in bomb store at gun. Fired 1 round on R. 28. a. Shock of gun sent up clouds of brick-dust which had been loosened by 4.2. falling in Bomb store. This cloud hung above the gun for about 5 minutes. Before firing the vicinity including walls, roofs had been well watered. Another O.P. found near H.Q. at R. 26 d. 8-2. Easily the best O.P. in Gommecourt. Fired 1. 3 small T.M's fell in Yard near gun. no damage.	
"	7/6/17	8 a.m.	Visit by a/DT.M.O.	
		10.30 a.m.	Fired 5 rounds on Bleak Walk Enemy retaliated on Church. Village shelled with 77 m.m. 5 to 6 p.m.	
		6.30 p.m.	Fired 3 rounds on Bleak Walk. Fired 8.	
	8/6/17.		2/Lieut. H.J. Scruet R.F.A. in line	
		2 a.m.	False gas alarm.	
		10 a.m.	Fired 5 rounds on Bleak Walk – 1 dud. 5 p.m. Fired 5 on same target. Fair retaliation. Fired 10.	

T2134. Wt. W708–776. 500000. 4/15. Sir J. C. & S.

3. June.

Instructions regarding War Diaries and Intelligence Summaries are contained in F. S. Regs., Part II. and the Staff Manual respectively. Title pages will be prepared in manuscript.

WAR DIARY or INTELLIGENCE SUMMARY.

(Erase heading not required.)

V. 40. Trench Mortar Battery.

Army Form C. 2118.

Place	Date	Hour	Summary of Events and Information	Remarks and references to Appendices
Gonnelieu.	9/6/17.	7 a.m.	Fired 11 rounds on R 28. a. - one round fell 50x short of Enemy wire.	
		6 p.m.	- - 6 - - - - Bleak Walk. Retaliation near gun. 2. Small T.M's fell in House where detachment work destroying rifles, telephone, chronometer &c.	
			Fired 10.	
	10/6/17	10.30 a.m.	5 rounds fired on R. 28. a. 1 dud. Retaliation.	
		7.30 p.m.	Fired 5 rounds on Bleak Walk. Heavy retaliation after each round. Now-a-days detachment has to take cover after every round, and wait until retaliation is over as small T.M's drop right in yard near gun, & 4.2's drop all round. 2. shells in bomb store.	
			Fired 10.	
	11/6/17.	1.30 p.m.	5. 150 mm close to billet	
			Fired nil.	
	12/6/17.		2/Lieut. F.P. Enright in line.	
		10.30 a.m.	Visit by D.T.M.O. Fired 6 rounds on Bleak Walk - 1 dud. Very heavy retaliation.	
		4. p.m.	Fired 2 rounds on Bleak Walk. Light T.M. retaliation. 2 fell 5 yards from gun. 1 in men's billet. 200 shells fell in Gonnelieu in afternoon.	
			Fired 8.	

T2134. Wt. W708–776. 500000. 4/15. Sir J. C. & S.

H/ June

Instructions regarding War Diaries and Intelligence Summaries are contained in F. S. Regs., Part II. and the Staff Manual respectively. Title pages will be prepared in manuscript.

WAR DIARY
or
INTELLIGENCE SUMMARY.
(Erase heading not required.)

V. 40. Trench Mortar Battery. Army Form C. 2118.

Place	Date	Hour	Summary of Events and Information	Remarks and references to Appendices
Gonnelieu.	13/6/17.		Infantry reported that several shells had fallen short on 12/6/17. Went out into no-man's land with Coy. Commander of 12th Suffolks, but could not locate shell holes. Remained there & fired 2 rounds which fell short of Bosche wire. Bed was shifting.	
			Fired 2.	
	14/6/17.		Adjusted bed. 2 p.m. Fired 9 rounds on Bleak Walk. Heavy T.M. retaliation of about 20 rounds after each of ours. 2 fell in yard near gun	
			Fired 9.	
	15/6/17.		Owing to heavy mist could not fire at 10. a.m.	
		p.m.	Fired 4 rounds on Bleak Walk, no retaliation.	
			Fired 4.	
	16/6/17.		Capt. W. Reid. R.F.A. in line.	
			Warned Coy in line of 12th Suffolks re firing. Mended 'phone wires to gun in 4 places. Fuzes all very hard to set. (31 B) Fired 2 rounds – 1 dud. Very heavy retaliation consisting of 50 small T.M's round gun & 112 105 m.m. on Gonnelieu. Wires cut in 6 places. Our own artillery retaliated about 3/4 of an hour too late. Located hostile 105 m.m. firing on Gouzeaucourt from a bearing of 98° magnetic	

T2134. Wt. W708–776. 500000. 4/15. Sir J. C. & S.

5

June

Instructions regarding War Diaries and Intelligence Summaries are contained in F. S. Regs., Part II. and the Staff Manual respectively. Title pages will be prepared in manuscript.

WAR DIARY
or
INTELLIGENCE SUMMARY.
(Erase heading not required.)

V. 40. Trench Mortar Battery.

Army Form C. 2118.

Place	Date	Hour	Summary of Events and Information	Remarks and references to Appendices
	Cont.			
Gonnelieu	16/6/17		from R 26.d.8-2. Showed Heavy Artillery officer the spot. He appeared very apathetic.	
		4 pm.	Fired 7 rounds on Bleak Walk & R.28 a. 3 direct hits on latter target. Fair retaliation. Enemy firing very accurately. Commenced work on new bed in outhouse 5x from present bed. Fired 9.	
"	17/6/17		Bed sinking a trifle at the head.	
		Noon.	Fired 10 rounds on Bleak Walk & R. 28.c.3-8. 3 rounds blew sheets of corrugated iron & timber in the air. Cache at R 28.c 3-8. Seen there mining timber lying in it taken away that night. 1 and. T.M. retaliation after each of first 3 rounds only. Our 18 pdrs & 4.5s were firing at same time. About 20. 105 m.m. in Gonnelieu. Fired 10.	
	18/6/17		Work under R.E. continues on emplacement at R.33.b.45.95.	
		11 a.m.	Fired 5 rounds on Bleak Walk. 1 fell 100x short of Enemy wire. No retaliation. Private of 12th Suffolks fell down well at H.Q. which is 100 ft ~~of water~~ deep & 10 ft of water. Have to get drinking water from Fins. Unprecedented calm all day. Fired 5.	

T2134. Wt. W708–776. 500000. 4/15. Sir J. C. & S.

OVW.

6. June

Instructions regarding War Diaries and Intelligence Summaries are contained in F. S. Regs., Part II. and the Staff Manual respectively. Title pages will be prepared in manuscript.

WAR DIARY
or
INTELLIGENCE SUMMARY.
(Erase heading not required.)

V. 40. Trench Mortar Battery

Army Form C. 2118

Place	Date	Hour	Summary of Events and Information	Remarks and references to Appendices
Gommecourt	19/6/17		Thunderstorm & heavy rain.	
		3 pm.	Fired 4 rounds on R. 28. a - 1 a dud. After 3rd round a man got out of trench at R. 28. c. 3. 8. disappeared behind, reappeared in R. 28 a. 05. 05 & jumped into trench. T.M. retaliation.	
		11 pm.	Detachments relieved.	
			Fired 4	
	20/6/17		Rain again. Visit by D. T. M. O.	
		11 am.	Fired 6 rounds on Bleak Walk & R. 28 a - 2 duds. Slight T.M. retaliation.	
			Visit by C. O. of 13th Yorks re turning Bomb Store (reserve) into a Dressing station. Agreed.	
			Fired 6	
	21/6/17		Usual failure note from infantry that bombs were falling short when all were observed to fall well behind enemy front line on Bleak Walk.	
		3 pm.	Fired 9 rounds on Bleak Walk. Heavy T.M. retaliation 3 fell in yard 5x from gun no damage. Our artillery retaliated. Observed 2 small minnies firing from R. 28. a. 3. 1. (approx) Both close together. 2 of our bombs fell short of enemy wire. Last 2 nights at 9 p.m. have seen 24 Germans collect at R. 28. a. 70. 98. From there they advanced in twos to the front line 600x away. Many knocking about behind front line eating currants to every night from 8-30 to dark.	
			Fired 9	

A5834 Wt. W4973/M687 750,000 8/16 D. D. & L. Ltd. Forms/C.2118/13.

8

June

Instructions regarding War Diaries and Intelligence Summaries are contained in F. S. Regs., Part II. and the Staff Manual respectively. Title pages will be prepared in manuscript.

WAR DIARY
or
INTELLIGENCE SUMMARY.
(Erase heading not required.)

V. 40. Trench Mortar Battery

Army Form C. 2118.

Place	Date	Hour	Summary of Events and Information	Remarks and references to Appendices
Tronchiew	26/6/17.		Cleared up yard after hostile shelling. Work on emplacement all day & bomb stores & mending wires. Fired nil	
	27/6/17	6-0am.	Fired 1 round which only went 100 yds past our front line. Took bed up & relaid it.	
		3.pm.	Fired 6 rounds on Black Walk. Heavy 150 & 105 m.m. retaliation doing considerable damage to bomb store, yard & emplacement & buildings. One crater – at least size of an 8 inch being 7 ft deep & 4 yards across – touching the bed, shaking down roof & sandbags over emplacement & causing a lot of damage. 5·9 in bomb store & half men's billet knocked down. 2. 105. m.m. in yard. Fired 7. [illegible]	
	28/6/17		2/Lieut. H. J. Escreet. R.F.A. in line. Gun out of action as a result of 8 inch shell crater touching front of bed. Fired nil.	
	29/6/17		D. T. M. O. & B. C. arrive. Cupola found & put in bomb store. Fired 2 on Black Walk. Bed impossible owing to large crater in front. Out of action. Fired 2.	
	30/6/17		Visit by Col. Parsons. Major of R.E. &c. Work continued on both Bomb stores & both emplacements. Fired. nil	
			Fired during June. 168.	

Norman Reid. Capt. R.F.A.
O.C. V. 40. T.M.B.

A5834 Wt. W4973/M687 750,000 8/16 D. D. & L. Ltd. Forms/C.2118/13.

Instructions regarding War Diaries and Intelligence Summaries are contained in F. S. Regs., Part II. and the Staff Manual respectively. Title pages will be prepared in manuscript.

X 40 T. M. Battery **WAR DIARY** ~~INTELLIGENCE SUMMARY.~~ for June. 1917.

(*Erase heading not required.*)

Army Form C. 2118.

Place	Date	~~Hour~~	Summary of Events and Information	Remarks and references to Appendices
FINS	June 1st to 8th		Battery undergoing local training – Gun drill, firing "duds" on local range. – Bathing, bivouacing huts and disciplinary parades	
"	9th to 26th		Battery attached to the 181 Bgd. R.F.A. and 178 Bag. R.F.A. employed on fatigue, – building forward gun positions. During this work – 3 men were wounded by enemy shell fire. Work commended by C.R.A.	
	26th.		Men recalled from above mentioned Brigades.	
	27th to 30th		Constructing Huts, – Latrines, – Gun sheds. Cook houses etc in new camp at FINS.	

T. Strand Lt. R.F.A.
for O.C. X40 T.M.B.
1/7/17.

A6945 Wt. W11422/M1160 350,000 12/16 D. D. & L. Forms/C./2118/14.

Instructions regarding War Diaries and Intelligence Summaries are contained in F. S. Regs., Part II. and the Staff Manual respectively. Title pages will be prepared in manuscript.

WAR DIARY
or
INTELLIGENCE SUMMARY.
(Erase heading not required.)

Y40 T.M. Bty,
40th Divn.

Army Form C. 2118.

JUNE - 1917.

Place	Date	Hour	Summary of Events and Information	Remarks and references to Appendices
FINS	1 to 8		Bty. on fatigues for Field Artillery Batteries of the Division, ~~also~~ cleaning their own guns, gun stores, etc., and getting ready generally, prior to going on a 2" T.M. Refresher Course at Fourth Army Sch. of Mortars, VAUX-EN-AMIENOIS.	
VAUX-EN-AMIENOIS	8 to 20		Bty. on 2" T.M. Refresher Course at Fourth Army Sch. of Mortars.	
FINS	20 to 30		Bty. undergoing local training - bathing - building bivouacs - disciplinary parades.	

Oscar P Taylor
Capt., E.h.,
for O/c Y40 T.M.B.

T2134. Wt. W708-776. 500000. 4/15. Sir J. C. & S.

Instructions regarding War Diaries and Intelligence Summaries are contained in F. S. Regs., Part II. and the Staff Manual respectively. Title pages will be prepared in manuscript.

WAR DIARY
or
INTELLIGENCE SUMMARY.
(Erase heading not required.)

Z40 T. M. Bty,
40th Divn.

Army Form C. 2118.

JUNE - 1917.

Place	Date	Hour	Summary of Events and Information	Remarks and references to Appendices
FINS	1 to 19		Bty on fatigues for the Field Arty. Batteries of the Division.	
FINS	19 to 22		Withdrawn from the above-mentioned fatigues. Cleaning guns, stores, and getting ready generally, prior to going on a 2" T.M. Refresher Course at Fourth Army Sch. of Mortars, VAUX-EN-AMIENOIS.	
VAUX-EN-AMIENOIS	22 to 30		Bty on 2" T.M. Refresher Course at Fourth Army Sch. of Mortars.	
	24		Lt. L.C. Gardner, R.G.A., transferred from 240 Siege Bty. to Z40 T.M.B., - posted to the latter Bty as second in command.	

Oscar P Taylor
Capt. G.L.
for O/c Z40 T.M.B.

A5834 Wt. W4973/M687 750,000 8/16 D. D. & L. Ltd. Forms/C.2118/13.

Instructions regarding War Diaries and Intelligence Summaries are contained in F. S. Regs., Part II. and the Staff Manual respectively. Title pages will be prepared in manuscript.

WAR DIARY
or
INTELLIGENCE SUMMARY.
(Erase heading not required.)

Army Form C.

Vol 13

Place	Date	Hour	Summary of Events and Information	Remarks and references to Appendices
	1 to 31		V40 Heavy Trench Mortar Battery in action the whole of the month at GONNELIEU - On the 23rd this Battery had one of its two guns destroyed by enemy shell fire.	
			With the exception of the first four days of the month, when Z40 Trench Mortar Battery were undergoing a 2" Trench Mortar 'Refresher' Course at Fourth Army School of Mortars, VAUX-EN-AMIENOIS, they, along with X Battery, and Y Battery, have been employed during the whole of the month as follows:-	
			Working for V40 Heavy T.M.B., at GONNELIEU, " " 181st Bde, R.F.A., at GOUZEAUCOURT, Training in defensive measures against gas attacks, FINS, Gun Drill, at FINS, Physical training, at FINS, Improving bivouacs, etc., in Trench Mortar Camp, at FINS.	
			Oscar L. Taylor Capt. Etc. Cmdg. 40th Divl. T.M.B's.	

A5834 Wt. W4973/M687 750,000 8/16 D. D. & L. Ltd. Forms/C.2118/13.

1/

V 40 Trench Mortar Battery — **WAR DIARY** *or* **INTELLIGENCE SUMMARY.** (*Erase heading not required.*) — July — Army Form C. 2118.

Instructions regarding War Diaries and Intelligence Summaries are contained in F. S. Regs., Part II. and the Staff Manual respectively. Title pages will be prepared in manuscript.

Place	Date	Hour	Summary of Events and Information	Remarks and references to Appendices
Gommecourt	1/7/17.		Work on Bomb store &c. During the night O.P. destroyed. 77 m.m & 5.9s. on village during day.	Fired nil.
	2/7/17.		Gun strutted over 8 inch shell crater by means of stakes driven in and 18 ft. long baulks.	
		11 a.m.	D.T.M.O and groom & Gardener arrived. 77 m.m. round H.Q. after a visit to Coy H.Q. an inspection of sunken roads in front of front line & behind where new front line has been sited with to putting in medium mortars. 2 suitable spots found.	
			Hun plane after Hendicourt balloon, shot down by machine gun from the ground.	Fired nil.
		9 p.m.	Fixed up O.P	
	3/7/17		No 1 Emplacement in Sunken road at R. 33. 6. 4½ - 9½. nearly complete. Warm day very quiet. 4.2. shrapnel near Church & gun at 8. p.m.	Fired nil.
	4.7.17.		Damp & cloudy day wires to gun cut in several places.	
		10 to 11.	Fired 12 rounds 10 on Bleak walk & Front Line One air burst. A few small T.M.s in retaliation towards end. 10 mins later 14 10.5 m.m. behind gun (no 2). Laid telephone wires to no. 1. gun Absurd note from 18th Welsh saying all our bombs had fallen short of our wire i.e. 700x short of where they actually fell. Major wires 2/17 [illegible]	Fired 12.
	5.7.17		Windy day Bed sunk 3° to rear & 1° to the left. Chronometer 4' out. Salvaged telephone wire in centre of village to complete line to No 1 gun. A close & thorough scrutiny of our wire and vicinage failed to disclose any of the 12 craters which we were accused of causing yesterday	
		2 to 3.	Fired 10 rounds on Bleak walk First round was hopelessly short & fell just in advance of our wire. B.C. stopped firing firing and went down to the spot. Spoke to an officer of 18th Welsh & asked him to clear our front line for 100x for safety. This he did, and firing	

A5834 Wt. W4973/M687 750,000 8/16 D. D. & L. Ltd. Forms/C.2118/13.

2

V. 40. T.M.B.

Instructions regarding War Diaries and Intelligence Summaries are contained in F. S. Regs., Part II. and the Staff Manual respectively. Title pages will be prepared in manuscript.

WAR DIARY
or
INTELLIGENCE SUMMARY.
(Erase heading not required.)

July

Army Form C. 2118.

Place	Date	Hour	Summary of Events and Information	Remarks and references to Appendices
Gouzeaucourt	5.7.17. (cont)		was resumed. Shots 2 to 9 were all very good, but the last again fell in same spot as the first. A visit to the spot elicited the fact that no damage had been done. 2. Cartridges misfired. All result of old salvage unsealed component parts which we receive some even have mud on them. Slight retaliation. with Lieut Enright reconnoitred for new O.P.	Fired 10.
"	6.7.17.		Bed taken up and relaid. Again no R.E. & no limbers for no 1 gun.	Fired nil
	7.7.17.		Major Andrews (act'g C.O. 17th Welsh) refused to clear his front line & threatened Lieut Enright with dire penalties if any bombs fell near our line. Fired 7 rounds on Bleak Walk & T.M. Heavy H.E. retaliation. Heavy bombardment of portion of front line 12.30 to 2. Collected 16 boxes of small minenwerfer bombs. Cannot get a gun from Division to fire them.	Fired 7.
	8.7.17.	11 a.m.	Enemy bombarded heavily with 4.2s, 5.9s and medium T.Ms. We retaliated with 8 rounds on Bleak Walk & front line at R. 28.a. 10-10. Heavy shelling in neighbourhood of Gouzeaucourt all day	Fired 8.
	9.7.17.		D.T.M.O. & B.C. arrived & visited 22 Ravine with a view to putting a gun in there. Only spots not under hostile observation - viz. 2 Quarries - are used as Coy H.Qs. Dumps &c. Gouzeaucourt & trenches heavily bombarded with 4.2s, 5.9s & medium T.Ms. 10.30 to 12. Bomb store at no. 2 gun hit by a shell which was a 'blind'.	Fired nil.
	10.7.17.		Absurd report by 18th Welsh that on July 4th & 5th we had fired 22 rounds into our own front line under the impression that we were firing at Bleak Walk. Partly through crass ignorance & partly through deliberate false statements that the report was sent in. C.R.A. (Brig. Gen. Nicholson) with the assistance of aerial photos taken on July 6th easily routed the opposition. It is obvious that most of the infantry are extraordinarily ignorant and criminally unobservant, so that they will go to any length to prevent our firing because infantry officers observing from our front lines (new & old) from which every portion	

A5834 Wt. W4973/M687 750,000 8/16 D. D. & L. Ltd. Forms/C.2118/13.

3

V 40 T.M.B.

Instructions regarding War Diaries and Intelligence Summaries are contained in F. S. Regs., Part II. and the Staff Manual respectively. Title pages will be prepared in manuscript.

WAR DIARY
or
INTELLIGENCE SUMMARY. July

(Erase heading not required.)

Army Form C. 2118.

Place	Date	Hour	Summary of Events and Information	Remarks and references to Appendices
Gonnelieu	10.7.17 (contd.)		of hostile line is totally invisible, send in fatuous reports about our bombs falling in or near our wire, when in fact they have fallen 700 yards away!! This happens nearly every day, and is extremely annoying & unfair. A cursory glance at any aerial photo of Bleak Walk & vicinity & of our line would convince them of their error. Instead of getting the support of our infantry, we meet with opposition.	Fired nil.
			The Battery was congratulated by the Divisional Commander on its excellent shooting on & destruction of Bleak Walk & Bleak Trench, and were told not to fire for a few days as the target had been destroyed. All leave cancelled.	
	11.7.17		New gun arrived & put in No 1. Emplacement tho' not yet quite complete. Quiet day	Fired nil.
	12.7.17		Major Pile (Brigade Major R.A) came up and inspected both guns. Said No 1. dug-out was not deep enough, and that we were not to fire until they had been made deeper & safer. Toured front line with C.O. 17th Welsh. Men's billets at Fins floored. Dining saloon, ablution bench, new cook houses &c. floored with bricks &c.	Fired nil.
	13.7.17		Work on No 1. gun & Bomb store.	Fired nil.
	14.7.17		C.R.A. (Gen Nicholson) D.T.M.O. & Capt Kennedy of 4th Army School of Mortars visited both guns & all artillery O.P's. Abnormally quiet morning. 12 5.9's at 4 p.m. One in Bomb store wounding Sgt. Abbott in nose. Slight damage. 4 23 near H.Q. Visited C.O. 18th Welsh. Major Kennedy. Some Coy. C.O. had accused us of firing previous night during a relief. As a matter of fact we hadn't fired for a week.	Fired nil.
	15.7.17		Met D.T.M.O. at 119th Bgde. H.Q. saw Gen Crozier.	Fired nil.
	16.7.17		Showed R.E. shaft of [illegible] dug-out at No 2. gun with a view to making it into an emplacement.	Fired nil.

A5834 Wt. W4973/M687 750,000 8/16 D. D. & L. Ltd. Forms/C.2118/13.

V 40. T.M.B.

Instructions regarding War Diaries and Intelligence Summaries are contained in F. S. Regs., Part II. and the Staff Manual respectively. Title pages will be prepared in manuscript.

WAR DIARY
or
INTELLIGENCE SUMMARY.
(Erase heading not required.)

July

Army Form C. 2118.

Place	Date	Hour	Summary of Events and Information	Remarks and references to Appendices
Gonnelieu.	17.7.17.	.	Ordinary normal day of work on both guns. Gonnelieu shelled intermittently with 4.2s.	Fired nil
	18.7.17.		" "	Fired nil
	19.7.17.		Gonnelieu shelled with 4.2s & 77 m.m. Worked strengthening roof of dug-out & bomb recess at No 1. gun.	Fired nil
	20.7.17.		Hostile m T.M. fired near No 1. gun. Shells on Gonnelieu.	Fired nil
	21.7.17.		Same as previous days.	Fired nil
	22.7.17.		Visit by D.T.M.O.	Fired nil.
	23.7.17.	5 p.m.	Permission to fire granted. Fired 8 rounds with No 2 gun on Bleak Walk. Almost immediate 5.9 retaliation. 3 were direct hits on gun. Gun smashed, emplacement wrecked. House in front & all outhouses ruined thus bringing position under observation. Barrel & carriage smashed sleepers not badly damaged.	Fired 8.
	24.7.17		Cleared away debris & salvaged remains of gun	Fired nil
	25.7.17		77 m.m. near H.Q. No. 2 gun & carriage sent back to lines. Good portions cleaned and retained.	Fired nil
	26.7.17		Fired 7 rounds on Bleak Trench/walk with No 1. gun Registration. Retaliation 77 m.m on O.P. 2 hits. Place given away by R.E. Camouflaging it. C.O. 17th Welsh said he was very pleased with shoot. He didn't see them fall, but saw them going well over. Laid wires to new O.P.	Fired 7.
	27.7.17		Away being delayed by E.A. & wires being cut. Fired 3 rounds on Junct. of Bleak Walk & Bleak Support when bid jumped clean out. Emplacement revetment being very bad is already collapsing. Gun wound in as ordered by C.R.A.	Fired 3

A5834 Wt. W4973/M687 750,000 8/16 D. D. & L. Ltd. Forms/C.2118/13.

5

V. 40. T.M.B

Instructions regarding War Diaries and Intelligence Summaries are contained in F. S. Regs., Part II. and the Staff Manual respectively. Title pages will be prepared in manuscript.

WAR DIARY
or
INTELLIGENCE SUMMARY.

(Erase heading not required.)

July

Army Form C. 2118.

Place	Date	Hour	Summary of Events and Information	Remarks and references to Appendices
Foncquevillers	28.7.17		Visit by D.T.M.O. & Lieut Hammond, Z.40 T.M.B looking for new 2" positions. Made new O.P. in front of old one & near 178 Bgde O.P.	
		11 to 12	Fired 14 rounds on Bleak Walk & Support Junct. Bleak Trench & T.M. Very slight retaliation. Village shelled 7-30. to 8-30. a.m.	Fired 14.
	29.7.17		Rain & storm. H.26 near O.P. & H.Q. Arranged to fire 8 to 4. p.m. but cancelled it owing to rain. Enemy signaller captured in no-mans land in p.m. Saw. C.O. 17th Welsh who again mentioned 'shorts' which we had never dropped. His O.P. is on front line from which precisely nothing can be seen of hostile line. An extra loud burst and he calls the round a short. Telephone wires to no 2 gun picked up.	Fired nil.
	30.7.17		Fired 4 rounds on Bleak Walk. Gun again jumped out of bed.	Fired 4.
	31.7.17		Fired 8 rounds on usual targets. Heavy retaliation all round gun with H.26. & 5.9s. No damage done. B.C. & Lieut Knight reconnoitred our front line for any possible O.P. C.O. 17th Welsh could see from. There was none at all. All that could be seen was green grass.	Fired 8.
			Fired during month 81.	

Howard Reid
Capt. R.F.A.
O.C. V. 40. T.M.B
1.8.17.

A5834 Wt. W4973/M687 750,000 8/16 D. D. & L. Ltd. Forms/C.2118/13.

X. 40. T.M. Battery

Instructions regarding War Diaries and Intelligence Summaries are contained in F. S. Regs., Part II. and the Staff Manual respectively. Title pages will be prepared in manuscript.

WAR DIARY
or
INTELLIGENCE SUMMARY.
(Erase heading not required.)

Army Form C. 2118.

Place	Date	Hour	Summary of Events and Information	Remarks and references to Appendices
FINS	July 1-14		6 men on fatigue with V.40 T.M.B. at GONNELIEU	
	1-31		6 men on fatigue with B.181. RFA at GOUZEAUCOURT	
	1-31		2 men on Telephony Course	
	23-31		2 men on fatigue with V.40 TMB at GONNELIEU	
	1-31		Remainder - Drill - Marching - Gun - with and without Box Respirators - and Box Respirator drill. Local fatigues - Battery Cook house, Ablution place, and Gun Park.	
			T.R. Pickard. Lieut.	
			OC. X 40 TMB	

A6945 Wt. W11422/M1160 350,000 12/16 D.D.& L. Forms/C./2118/14.

Instructions regarding War Diaries and Intelligence Summaries are contained in F. S. Regs., Part II. and the Staff Manual respectively. Title pages will be prepared in manuscript.

Army Form C. 2118.

WAR DIARY

~~or~~

~~INTELLIGENCE SUMMARY~~. Y40 Trench Mortar Battery.

(*Erase heading not required.*)

July, 1916.

Place	Date	Hour	Summary of Events and Information	Remarks and references to Appendices
FINS	1·7·17	–	In the early part of the month the Battery was still in rest, being employed during the day on improvements to the bivouac accommodation. Special attention was directed during this period to instruction in defence against gas, and to drill with the Box Respirator. A few men were detached for duty with V40 Battery, which was in action at GONNELIEU; and two others were detached for a course of instruction in signalling.	
"	10·7·17	–	Most of the remainder of the Battery was attached to ~~the~~ "B" and "C" Batteries, 181st Bde., R.F.A., for fatigues at the gun positions. These fatigues lasted for the remainder of the month; the men being employed near GOUZEAUCOURT.	
VILLERS PLOUICH.	26·7·17	–	With a view to bringing the Battery into action, the Battery Commander reconnoitred the ground near the front line east of this village on this and subsequent days; possible ~~[illegible]~~ positions were found for the guns of the Battery, as well as for one of the new Medium Trench Mortars (6" Stokes) which it was hoped shortly to obtain. Up to the end of the month, no definite decision as to bringing the Battery into action had been reached.	

Mark Stanford Lieut.
O.C. Y40 T.M.B.

31·7·1917

2353 Wt. W2544/1454 700,000 5/15 D. D. & L. A.D.S.S./Forms/C. 2118.

Instructions regarding War Diaries and Intelligence Summaries are contained in F. S. Regs., Part II. and the Staff Manual respectively. Title pages will be prepared in manuscript.

WAR DIARY
or
~~INTELLIGENCE SUMMARY~~.
(Erase heading not required.)

Army Form C. 2118.

Z.40 Trench Mortar Battery.

Place	Date	Hour	Summary of Events and Information	Remarks and references to Appendices
FINS	(22/6/17) 1/7/17–4/7/17		The battery was on a medium trench mortar course at VAUX-EN-AMIENOIS. It reached the headquarters at FINS on 4/7/17. The next week was spent building accomodation for the men and guns, together with a cookhouse, ablution bench etc. During the rest of the month the men were employed . . . (i) with 'B' Battery 181ST Brigade } on work near GOUZEAUCOURT. (ii) with 'C' Battery 181ST Brigade } (iii) with 2/40 Heavy Trench Mortar Battery on work in BONNELIEU. No action as a complete was possible during the month but, while in rest, the men were trained in defensive measures against gas and received practice in gun drill and physical exercises. J Hammond Lt R.F.A. O.C. Z.40 T.M. Bty.	

A5834 Wt. W4973/M687 750,000 8/16 D. D. & L. Ltd. Forms/C.2118/13.

Instructions regarding War Diaries and Intelligence Summaries are contained in F. S. Regs., Part II. and the Staff Manual respectively. Title pages will be prepared in manuscript.

WAR DIARY
or
INTELLIGENCE SUMMARY.
(Erase heading not required.)

Army Form C. 2118.

D.T.M.O. 40th DIVISION. No. August 1917.

Vol 14

Place	Date	~~Hour~~	Summary of Events and Information	Remarks and references to Appendices
			During this month the Trench Mortar Batteries of the 40th Division have been situated as follows:–	
	1 – 31		V40 (Heavy) T.M.B. – in action at GONNELIEU.	
	1 – 22		X40 (Medium) T.M.B. – fatigues for "B" Bty, 181 Bde, R.F.A., in GOUZEAUCOURT,	
			" " V40 (Heavy) T.M.B., " GONNELIEU,	
	22 – 31		physical training, box respirator drill, local fatigues, etc, FINS. Building emplacements for (2" T.M.) defensive positions, VILLERS PLOUICH.	
	1 – 22		Y40 (Medium T.M.B. – fatigues for Field Batteries of the Division, GOUZEAUCOURT. constructing temporary emplacements for its guns, which were to co-operate in a bombardment of enemy lines E. of GONNELIEU, – the bombardment was eventually cancelled & the guns & personnel withdrawn to FINS.	
	23 – 28		Box respirator drill – physical training – local fatigues, FINS.	
	29 – 31		Building emplacements for (2" T.M.) defensive positions right of VILLERS PLOUICH – RIBECOURT Road.	
	1 – 16		Z40 (Medium) T.M.B. – fatigues for Field Batteries of the Division, GOUZEAUCOURT,	
	17 – 26		Building 2 open emplacements, GONNELIEU SECTOR.	
	27 – 31		Building emplacements for (2" T.M.) defensive positions, GONNELIEU.	

Oscar P. Taylor
Capt., C.W.,
Comdg. 40th Divl. T.M.B's.

A5834 Wt. W4973/M687 750,000 8/16 D. D. & L. Ltd. Forms/C.2118/13.

Page 1.

V. 40. Trench Mortar Battery.

WAR DIARY
or
INTELLIGENCE SUMMARY.

(Erase heading not required.)

August 1917.

Army Form C. 2118.

Instructions regarding War Diaries and Intelligence Summaries are contained in F. S. Regs., Part II. and the Staff Manual respectively. Title pages will be prepared in manuscript.

Place	Date	Hour	Summary of Events and Information	Remarks and references to Appendices
Gouzeaucourt.	1/8/17.	3.30 pm.	Fired 4 rounds on Bleak Walk. (3 were duds). Amatol Bombs were duds - ammonal bomb burst.	Fired 6.
		7 pm.	Registered. R. 28. c. 83-70 with 2 rounds for a raid. Heavy 4.2. retaliation.	
	2/8/17.	1 a.m.	Fired 8 rounds on R. 28. c. 83-70. to assist in a raid. Heavy retaliation with 4.2. and c.m. & 7.7. c.m	Fired. 8.
	3/8/17.	10. a.m.	Fired 6 rounds on Bleak Walk. (2 duds). C.O. 12th Suffolks asked us to drop a few into Bosch wire.	Fired. 6.
	4/8/17.	3.30 p.m.	" 4 " -- Bleak Trench (1 dud). Gun jumped out of bed, so could not continue.	Fired. 4.
	5/8/17.	noon.	" 6 -- Bleak Support. (1 dud). R.E's. have put in new shelter over gun.	Fired. 6.
	6/8/17.	10. a.m	" 6 -- hostile medium T.M. 20 4.2's in retaliation 50x over gun.	Fired. 6.
	7/8/17.	6. p.m	" 6 --- Bleak Support. & Front Line. 12. 4.2's in retaliation in vicinity of gun.	Fired. 6.
	8/8/17.	2.45 --	--- 6. --- Bleak Support & --- in R.28.c. (2. airbursts). 60. 110. mm. in retaliation	Fired. 6.
	9/8/17.	--	Could not fire owing to very stormy weather.	Fired. nil
	10/8/17.		Fired 9 rounds on Bleak Support & Front line without drawing any retaliation.	Fired. 9.
	11/8/17.	5.15 pm	" 7 -- R. 28. b. 2-2. (3 duds). 4.2's near H.Q. in p.m.	Fired 7.
	12/8/17.	9.30. am.	-- 6 -- R. 28. c. 7.7. without eliciting any response from the Enemy.	Fired. 6.
	13/8/17.		Laid wire to wireless station at Villers Guislain, but found no wireless people there.	
		3.30 pm.	Fired 6 rounds on R. 28. b. 3-0. (1 dud)	Fired. 6.
	14/8/17.		Laid wire to D/178 Long gun & thence to wireless station at D/178. Assisted by aerial observation by an aeroplane of 59. Squadron. R.F.C. Fired 8 rounds on R. 28. a. 85-45. (1 round every 10 mins.) Shoot interrupted by Hostile aeroplanes. One O.K. was registered & one very close fell in another part of trench. 20. 4.2's. & 18 light T.M's in retaliation.	Fired. 8.
	15/8/17.		Met C.R.A at East End of 15 Ravine (~~La Vacquerie~~) & decided to put a long range T.M. there temporarily to fire on La Vacquerie. Permanent position to be made alongside Cambrai Rd. at R. 26. b. 8-6. Fired 8 rounds at 5.15. p.m. on Barrack & Bleak Supports. No retaliation.	Fired. 8.

A5834 Wt. W4973/M687 750,000 8/16 D. D. & L. Ltd. Forms/C.2118/13.

Page 2

V. 40. Trench Mortar Battery.

WAR DIARY
or
INTELLIGENCE SUMMARY.

August.

Army Form C. 2118.

Instructions regarding War Diaries and Intelligence Summaries are contained in F. S. Regs., Part II. and the Staff Manual respectively. Title pages will be prepared in manuscript.

(Erase heading not required.)

Place	Date	Hour	Summary of Events and Information	Remarks and references to Appendices
Ennechies.	10/8/17.	1.p.m.	Fired 5 rounds on Barrack Support. (2. airbursts) 12. 110.m.m. in retaliation.	Fired. 5.
	17/8/17.		Considerable hostile aerial activity during morning. & numerous hostile balloons up.	
		2.30p.m.	Fired 10 rounds on Barrack Support. & lots of wire & stakes were seen in the air.	Fired. 10.
	18/8/17.		Our telephone wire cut in several places. Work on new emplacement near 15 Ravine continues daily.	Fired. nil.
			Rain prevented firing.	Fired. nil.
	19/8/17.		Work on new emplacement.	
	20/8/17.		" " " " 5.9's. at H.Q. men had to remove to dug-outs. Laid wire to new gun emplacement.	Fired. nil.
	21/8/17.		Mounted new gun. Fired. 8 rounds with no 1. at R.28. 6. 3-0. (1 dud & 1 airburst)	Fired. 8.
	22/8/17.		Completed telephone wire to no 2. gun.	
	23/8/17.		Laid wire to D/181. from no 2. Gun & thence to wireless station at 181 Bgde.	
		3.p.m.	with assistance of 59. Squad. R.F.C. Fired 6 rounds on R.15.d. 55-75. at 4th round & 6th round, the gun jumped out of the bed causing bombs to fall in no man's land. One Y.S. obtained. Totally destroying enemy light railway.	Fired. 6.
	24/8/17.		Spent all day making new bed for no 2. gun.	Fired. nil
	25/8/17.		Fired 8 rounds with no. 2. gun on Bleak & Barrack supports. drawing 4.2. retaliation.	Fired 8.
	26/8/17.	3.p.m.	-- 11 " -- no 1. -- on Corner Redoubt & La Vacquerie causing a fire in latter.	Fired. 11.
	27/8/17.		No shooting possible on account of inclemency of weather. Work on no 2. gun continued.	Fired. nil.
	28/8/17.		Again bad weather. Strong wind & rain. Saw R.E. Officer of 229 Coy & arranged to start work on new Cambrai Rd Emplacement. O.P. blown down. Moved to B/178 old one in front of village.	
		5.0?	Fired 20 rounds with no 1. gun on Barrack & Bleak Supports & hostile T.M. Heavy 4.2. retaliation. 10 fell near one. One in emplacement wrecking same tho' not damaging gun. No casualties.	Fired. 20.

A5834 Wt. W4973/M687 750,000 8/16 D. D. & L. Ltd. Forms/C.2118/13.

Page 3 · V. 40. Trench Mortar Battery · August

WAR DIARY
or
INTELLIGENCE SUMMARY.

(Erase heading not required.)

Army Form C. 2118.

Instructions regarding War Diaries and Intelligence Summaries are contained in F. S. Regs., Part II. and the Staff Manual respectively. Title pages will be prepared in manuscript.

Place	Date	Hour	Summary of Events and Information	Remarks and references to Appendices
Gonnelieu.	29/8/17.	3 p.m.	Fired 6 rounds (all available ammunition) with no 2. gun on R. 15 d. 90-65. First went 400x over map range. 2nd fell 800x shorter than first & in no-man's land. Remainder were all in vicinity of target. All very good bursts. 1st fell some hundreds of yards over La Vacquerie. 1 N.C.O. & 8 men from D.A.C. arrived to work on new emplacement. No 1. bed broken by last round.	Fired. 6.
	30/8/17.		Mending no 2. gun bed & no 1. gun emplacement. 4.2's near H.Q. Fixed up telephone exchange.	Fired. nil.
	31/8/17.		Cambrai Rd. Emplacement laid out at 68° mag. No 1. gun emplacement mended.	
			Weather continues bad. Enemy artillery very quiet for last 10 days except in retaliation for our firing.	
			Fired during the month. 166 rounds.	
			Norman Reid. Capt. R.F.A. O.C. V. 40. T.M.B	

A5834 Wt. W4973/M687 750,000 8/16 D. D. & L. Ltd. Forms/C.2118/13.

X. 40 Trench Mortar Battery

Instructions regarding War Diaries and Intelligence Summaries are contained in F. S. Regs., Part II. and the Staff Manual respectively. Title pages will be prepared in manuscript.

WAR DIARY
or
INTELLIGENCE SUMMARY.
(Erase heading not required.)

Army Form C. 2118.

Place	Date	Hour	Summary of Events and Information	Remarks and references to Appendices
			Fatigue parties have been provided as follows:-	
GOUZEAUCOURT	August 1-14		B. 181. R.F.A. 6 men	
GONNELIEU	1-13		V. 40. T.M.B. 2 men	
do	8-14		do 9 men	
do.	17-24		Z. 40 TMB 3 men	
GOUZEAUCOURT	18-22		B. 181. RFA 9 men	
FINS	1-22		Remainder - Respirator Drill - Gun Drill with and without Respirators - Local fatigues.	
WELSH RIDGE	22-31		Building Emplacements for Defensive Position of the Battery	
			R Pickard Lieut. O.C. X 40 TMB.	

A6945 Wt. W11422/M1160 350,000 12/16 D. D. & L. Forms/C./2118/14.

Army Form C. 2118.

Instructions regarding War Diaries and Intelligence Summaries are contained in F. S. Regs., Part II. and the Staff Manual respectively. Title pages will be prepared in manuscript.

WAR DIARY for August 1917.
or
~~INTELLIGENCE SUMMARY.~~
(Erase heading not required.)

Y40 Trench Mortar Battery

Place	Date	Hour	Summary of Events and Information	Remarks and references to Appendices
FINS	1.8.17.	-	The Battery was billeted at FINS, small fatigue parties being furnished to R.F.A. Batteries from its personnel.	
GONNELIEU	17.8.17	-	The Battery having been withdrawn from fatigue work, was sent into the line to construct temporary emplacements for its guns, which were to take part in a bombardment of the enemy lines east of GONNELIEU. The work was done by night, in conjunction with Z40 Battery, which was also taking part.	
"	22.8.17	8 p.m.	The bombardment, which was to have taken place at 10 p.m., was cancelled, as it was suspected that information of it had reached the enemy.	
"	23.8.17	-	Guns were withdrawn to FINS, together with all personnel.	
VILLERS PLOUICH	29.8.17	-	Half the Battery was sent into the line to construct permanent defensive emplacements for the guns. These defensive positions were on the right of the VILLERS PLOUICH — RIBECOURT road.	

Mark Stanford Lieut.
OC. Y40 T.M.B.

Z 40 Trench Mortar Battery

WAR DIARY
or
INTELLIGENCE SUMMARY.
(Erase heading not required.)

Army Form C. 2118.

Instructions regarding War Diaries and Intelligence Summaries are contained in F. S. Regs., Part II. and the Staff Manual respectively. Title pages will be prepared in manuscript.

Place	Date	Hour	Summary of Events and Information	Remarks and references to Appendices
FINS	1/8/17 - 16/8/17		The battery headquarters was at FINS but the men were away working for the artillery brigades building advanced ammunition shelters.	
GONNELIEU	17/8/17		Two open emplacements were made in the BLEAK HOUSE Road to cover the enemy front line near the "Pimple". The work was done entirely by night and was finished in the early morning of the 21st. No firing was done from these emplacements although they were kept ready for action.	
	27/8/17		Work was begun on defensive positions in front of the village and two deep emplacements were started to cover the LAVACQUERIE & the BLEAK HOUSE ROADS. The range admitted a barrage being placed on these roads approximately two hundred and fifty yards beyond our own trenches.	

R J Hammond Lt RGA
O.C. Z 40 T.M. Bty.

A5834 Wt. W4973/M687 750,000 8/16 D. D. & L. Ltd. Forms/C.2118/13.

Instructions regarding War Diaries and Intelligence Summaries are contained in F. S. Regs., Part II. and the Staff Manual respectively. Title pages will be prepared in manuscript.

WAR DIARY
or
INTELLIGENCE SUMMARY.
(Erase heading not required.)

No. 5
Date September, 1917.

Vol 15

Army Form C. 2118.

Place	Date	Hour	Summary of Events and Information	Remarks and references to Appendices
	1 to 30		During the whole of the month V Bty. were in action at GONNELIEU, the Bty. working in 4 day reliefs. Rest billets at FINS. The reliefs not in the line were employed on making new Winter rest billets in a Sunken road about half way between FINS & GOUZEAUCOURT.	
	1 to 26		X Bty. were employed on making reserve S.O.S. positions for their guns at VILLERS PLOUICH.	
	27 to 30		The Battery at Third Army Sch. of Mortars, LIGNY-ST-FLOCHEL, undergoing course of instruction in 6" Newton T.M's.	
	1 to 22		Y Bty. were employed on making defensive emplacements for their guns in front of VILLERS PLOUICH, and also working on a forward position for two of their guns which were to fire on night of 22nd in support of a raid to be made on the enemy trenches by the 14th H.L.I.	
	22	7.30p	Fired 34 rounds in support of the raid just mentioned. Of the seven men employed in firing during this operation we suffered four casualties - 1 killed, - No. 108 Cpl. W. R. Allen, R.F.A., - and three wounded. Great gallantry was displayed by the men firing from this forward position (about twenty yds. in rear of our front line) and the Battery Sergeant has been recommended for decoration.	

A5834 Wt. W4973/M687 750,000 8/16 D. D. & L. Ltd. Forms/C.2118/13.

Instructions regarding War Diaries and Intelligence Summaries are contained in F. S. Regs., Part II. and the Staff Manual respectively. Title pages will be prepared in manuscript.

WAR DIARY
or
INTELLIGENCE SUMMARY.
(Erase heading not required.)

Army Form C. 2118.

Place	Date	Hour	Summary of Events and Information	Remarks and references to Appendices
	23		Work on the defensive emplacements in front of VILLERS PLOUICH completed, as were also an ammunition recess and good dugout.	
	24 to 30		Half the Bty. remained in the line & working on an advanced Bty. H'qrs. & Bomb Store in the village. The other half of the Bty. withdrawn to live at rest billets at FINS, & was employed during the daytime on constructing new Winter rest billets in a sunken road about half way between FINS and GOUZEAUCOURT.	
GONNELIEU	1 to 25		Z Bty. were employed in making defensive positions for their guns, & in constructing a forward position from which to fire in support of a raid to be made on the 25th by the 12th SUFFOLKS.	
"	25	7.30p.	91 rds. were fired in support of this raid. Our casualties during this operation were:- one Gunner very slightly wounded.	
"	26 to 30		Work on the defensive positions continued.	

Oscar P. Taylor Capt, R.A.
Cmdg. 40th Divl. T.M. B's.

A5834 Wt. W4973/M687 750,000 8/16 D. D. & L. Ltd. Forms/C.2118/13.

1/

V. 40. Trench Mortar Battery

WAR DIARY
or
INTELLIGENCE SUMMARY.
(*Erase heading not required.*)

September.

Army Form C. 2118.

Instructions regarding War Diaries and Intelligence Summaries are contained in F. S. Regs., Part II. and the Staff Manual respectively. Title pages will be prepared in manuscript.

Place	Date	Hour	Summary of Events and Information	Remarks and references to Appendices
Gonnelieu.	1/9/17. to 4/9/17.		Work on No. 1. Gun continued (emplacement was wrecked by a hostile 10.5 m.m.). Work also continued on No. 2. new emplacement. No. 2. not allowed to fire from alternative emplacement because of frightening away a sentry whom it is intended to catch on some indefinite raid.	Fired nil.
	5/9/17.	5.p.m.	Fired 6 rounds at junction of roads in La bacquerie with new Mark III. one 'blind'. This gun when fired from old bed is extremely inaccurate.	Fired. 6.
	6/9/17.		Div: Commander & C.R.A. visited No. 2 gun & O.Ps.	
		3.p.m.	Fired 5 rounds on Conco Trench. Good bursts (Mark III).	Fired. 11.
		4.p.m.	Mark I fired 6 rounds on Barrack Support. (2 duds). Sand-bags thrown in air. Usual 10.5. c.m. retaliation.	
	7/9/17.	2.p.m.	Mark I. fired 5 rounds on junction of Bleak & Barrack Supports.	Fired. 9.
		4.30.pm	" III. " 4 " " Conco Trench. Further firing stopped by hostile balloons going up.	
	8/9/17.	5.30.pm.	Mark III fired 2 rounds on road junction in La bacquerie. Gun shooting very erratically & bed jumping. All telephone wires badly broken by hostile shells.	Fired. 7.
		7.30pm	Mark I fired 5 rounds on Bleak support. 2 'blinds'.	
	9/9/17.		C.R.A. recently issued orders that not more than 6 rounds should be fired per gun per day.	Fired 10
		11.a.m.	Mark I fired 6 rounds (1 blind) on Bleak Support.	
		3.p.m.	" III " 4 " " road junction in La bacquerie.	
	10/9/17.		Work continuing on new emplacement in Cambrai Rd. R.E's. extraordinarily lethargic about it.	Fired 6.
		6.p.m.	Mark I. fired 6 rounds on Barrack Trench - one 'blind', one air-burst.	
			" III. Stopped firing until further orders because of a raid.	
	11/9/17.	Noon	Mark I. fired 2 rounds on hostile T.M. emplacements & dug-outs in Bleak Support. Camouflage there caught fire & telephone wires were cut. Usual 10.5. c.m. retaliation.	Fired 6.
		6.p.m.	Fired 4 at same target (1 blind).	

A5834 Wt. W4973/M687 750,000 8/16 D. D. & L. Ltd. Forms/C.2118/13.

Instructions regarding War Diaries and Intelligence Summaries are contained in F. S. Regs., Part II. and the Staff Manual respectively. Title pages will be prepared in manuscript.

V. 40. T.M.B.

WAR DIARY
or
INTELLIGENCE SUMMARY.

(Erase heading not required.)

September.

Army Form C. 2118.

Place	Date	Hour	Summary of Events and Information	Remarks and references to Appendices
Gonnelieu.	12/9/17.	2.30 p.m.	Mark I. fired 7 rounds on T.M's & dug-outs in Bleak Support. 2 blinds, 1 air burst. Heavy 10.5 c.m. retaliation. Time fuzes, both 31.B. & 31.I.c. are very bad causing a lot of blinds and air bursts. Since the 9.45" T.M's have really got going, hostile T.M. activity has practically ceased in Gonnelieu salient.	Fired 7.
	13/9/17.	10. a.m.	Fired 4 rounds on T.M's & dug-outs as covering fire for 2.40 medium T.M's registration. 2 blinds & 1 air burst. One round caused timber & sand-bags to fly in the air	
		9.45 p.m.	Fired 1 round in artillery & T.M. concentration lasting 2 minutes.	Fired. 8
	14/9/17.	10.30 a.m.	Fired 6 rounds on above target. 20 hostile 10.5 c.m. in retaliation	Fired 6.
	15/9/17.	12.45 p.m.	" 6 " " " " sand-bags & timber blown in air. Hostile retaliation.	Fired. 6
	16/9/17.		Unable to fire owing to rifle mechanism breaking at the start & becoming jammed in gun.	Fired. nil.
	17/9/17.	9.45 a.m.	Mark I fired 6 rounds on Bleak Support. } usual retaliation.	Fired 6
	18/9/17.	11. a.m.	– – – 5 – – – –	Fired 5.
	19/9/17.	2. p.m.	– – – – – 6 – – – – – – T.M's & dug-outs in Bleak Support.	Fired. 6.
	20/9/17.	5. p.m.	– – – – – – 6 – – – – – – " " " " 1 blind, " "	Fired. 6.
	21/9/17.		No 1. bed required 1/2 an hour's attention.	
		2.45 pm	Fired 6 rounds on junction of Bleak Support and new Communication Trench. Retaliation	Fired 6.
	22/9/17		New Mark III. bed, weighing 5200 lbs. arrives at No. 2. gun in instalments. Commence putting it in. Hostile balloons being up exceptionally high & plentiful prevent firing from No 1. during morning.	
		4.30 pm.	Fired 6 rounds on new trench & dug-outs. 1 air burst.	Fired. 6.
			3 days work was done on an emplacement in Surrey Ravine, Villers Plouich, but owing to a stores position & dug-out being underneath, work was discontinued.	

A5834 Wt. W4973/M687 750,000 8/16 D. D. & L. Ltd. Forms/C.2118/13.

3

V. 40. T.M.B.

Instructions regarding War Diaries and Intelligence Summaries are contained in F. S. Regs., Part II. and the Staff Manual respectively. Title pages will be prepared in manuscript.

WAR DIARY
or
INTELLIGENCE SUMMARY.
(Erase heading not required.)

September

Army Form C. 2118.

Place	Date	Hour	Summary of Events and Information	Remarks and references to Appendices
Gonnelieu	23/9/17.	9.45 a.m.	Fired 7 rounds on Bleak Support. – 3 'blinds'. Heavy 4.2. retaliation in salvos. New beds complete.	Fired 7.
	24/9/17.	3.45 "	" 7 " " " New trench & dug-outs – 2 duds.	Fired 7.
	25/9/17.	2.15 p.m.	Registered no. 2 gun on Sonnet Farm. 2 blinds out of 5. & 2 direct hits	
		7.30 p.m.	Raid commenced. Mark I. fired on as machine gun. After firing 15 rounds in 30 minutes the butterfly clamping nut broke, & gun went out of action. Considerable hostile shelling round gun pit throughout.	Fired 34.
			Mark III. Fired 14 rounds on Sonnet Farm during period 7-30 to 8-30.	
	26/9/17.		Mark I. out of action. Revetted new emplacement at Mark III gun.	Fired. nil
	27/9/17.	11.45 a.m.	Mark III fired 6 rounds on Sonnet Farm with good effect.	
		3 p.m.	" " I " 4 " " Barrack Support. Retaliation as usual.	Fired 10.
	28/9/17.		Could not fire no 2. owing to hostile balloons.	
		7 p.m.	Mark I fired 6 rounds on new trench, one 'blind'. 15. 10.5 c.m. in retaliation.	Fired. 6.
	29/9/17.	9.10 a.m.	" " " 6 " " dug-outs &c. 1. air burst.	
		12.30 p.m.	" III. " " 6 " " " front line in R.22.a. Took up no 1. beds.	Fired 12.
	30/9/17.		Work on no 1. beds. Started aeroplane shoot on cross roads in La Vacquerie at 2.30 p.m. owing to hostile shelling cutting all telephone wires at 181. Bgde. Batteries, connection failed before 1st round, & shoot was discontinued.	Fired. nil

Fired during the month. 193.

Norman Reid. Capt. R.Fus.
O.C. V. 40. T.M.B.

A5834 Wt. W4973/M687 750,000 8/16 D. D. & L. Ltd. Forms/C.2118/13.

X. 40. Trench Mortar Battery

Instructions regarding War Diaries and Intelligence Summaries are contained in F. S. Regs., Part II. and the Staff Manual respectively. Title pages will be prepared in manuscript.

WAR DIARY
or
INTELLIGENCE SUMMARY.
(Erase heading not required.)

Army Form C. 2118.

Place	Date 1917 Sept.	Hour	Summary of Events and Information	Remarks and references to Appendices
WELSH RIDGE VILLERS PLOUICH	1-26		Work continued on emplacements, ammunition recesses, and advanced headquarters, in making reserve S.O.S positions for guns.	
FINS	27		To Third Army School of Mortars.	
LIGNY ST. FLOCHEL	28-30		Undergoing Course of Instruction in 6 inch Newton TM at Third Army School of Mortars	

T. K. Pickard Lieut.
OC X 40 TMB

A6945 Wt. W11422/M1160 350,000 12/16 D. D. & L. Forms/C./2118/14.

Instructions regarding War Diaries and Intelligence Summaries are contained in F. S. Regs., Part II. and the Staff Manual respectively. Title pages will be prepared in manuscript.

WAR DIARY
or
~~INTELLIGENCE SUMMARY~~.
(Erase heading not required.)

Army Form C. 2118.

Y40 Trench Mortar Battery,

September, 1917.

Place	Date	Hour	Summary of Events and Information	Remarks and references to Appendices
FINS	1st	–	The Headquarters of the Battery, and its rest billets, were still at FINS.	
VILLERS PLOUICH	1st	–	All available men were in the line, engaged in the work of constructing defensive emplacements in front of the village near the RIBÉCOURT road. A strong position was to be constructed for the Battery, which would then be available to fire into "No Man's Land" or on to our own front line on receipt of an S.O.S. call from the Infantry Company Commander or the Artillery Group Commander.	
do.	12th	–	Work was commenced on a forward position (about 20 yards in rear of our front line) for a section of Mortars. These were to be placed forward for an offensive action in support of a raid on the enemy lines to be made by the 14th H.L.I.	
FINS	16th	–	From the 16th to the 23rd, Lieut. T. el Ward, R.F.A., was in command of the Battery, owing to the absence of the O.C. on leave to PARIS.	
VILLERS PLOUICH	22nd	7.0 p.m.	Fire was opened from the advanced section of guns above-mentioned, in support of the raid. The Battery was firing some distance to the flank of the raiding party, which was entering the enemy lines on the right of the VILLERS PLOUICH – MARCOING railway line; the object being to draw the enemy retaliation on to the hill on the left, thus rendering easier the task of the raiding party. This operation was entirely successful, for almost the entire enemy barrage was attracted to the left, while the raiders were able to cross No Man's Land without difficulty. Great gallantry was shown by the men of the Battery at the forward position in	

P.T.O.

2353 Wt. W2544/1454 700,000 5/15 D. D. & L. A.D.S.S./Forms/C. 2118.

Instructions regarding War Diaries and Intelligence Summaries are contained in F. S. Regs., Part II. and the Staff Manual respectively. Title pages will be prepared in manuscript.

WAR DIARY (continued).

~~INTELLIGENCE SUMMARY.~~

(Erase heading not required.)

Army Form C. 2118.

Y40 T.M.B.

Sept. 1917.

Place	Date	Hour	Summary of Events and Information	Remarks and references to Appendices
			keeping the guns in action and maintaining the fire under a heavy bombardment by the enemy. Of the seven men employed, four became casualties. For his gallantry in this action the Battery Sergeant was recommended for decoration.	
VILLERS PLOUICH	24th	—	Defensive positions on the right of the RIBECOURT road for one section of guns, together with ammunition store and dugout, were completed. Half the Battery remained in the line, however, working on the construction of an advanced Battery Headquarters and Bomb Store in the village.	
FINS	24th	—	The other half of the Battery was withdrawn to rest billets; it was employed in the construction of new winter quarters for the Battery to the right of the main road, about midway between FINS and GOUZEAUCOURT, in a sunken road leading to HEUDICOURT. This work continued till the end of the month.	

H Parke Stanford Lieut.
O.C. Y40 T.M.B.

2353 Wt. W2544/1454 700,000 5/15 D. D. & L. A.D.S.S./Forms/C. 2118.

2/40 Trench Mortar Battery

Instructions regarding War Diaries and Intelligence Summaries are contained in F. S. Regs., Part II. and the Staff Manual respectively. Title pages will be prepared in manuscript.

WAR DIARY
or
~~INTELLIGENCE SUMMARY.~~
(Erase heading not required.)

Army Form C. 2118.

Place	Date	Hour	Summary of Events and Information	Remarks and references to Appendices
GONNELIEU	1/9/17–12/9/17		The battery was employed constructing defensive emplacements to enable Z T M to place a barrage about the middle of no man's land in the event of an enemy raid & attack in force. These emplacements were constructed at an average depth of 6' below the surface with a view to occupying them as permanent offensive positions when the battery should be armed with the six inch Newton guns. Dugouts were provided both for the gun crews and for the storage of bombs with 12–20' of head cover.	
	9/9/17		Lieutenant [illegible] R.F.A. joined Z battery to replace Lt. Gardiner who became a casualty on the 5th of the month.	]
	13/9/17	10 am	Two ranging rounds were fired from the forward position in a sunken road in front of the village. The 4.5 howitzers that were intended to cover these rounds fired unfortunately a minute before the zero hour arranged but valuable support was obtained from the heavy T.M. who fired [illegible] rounds on the same target.	Fired 2
	14/9/17	3 pm	Fifteen rounds were fired from 3 p.m. until two minutes past the hour in cooperation with the artillery. The target was the enemy front line near the Pimple, as requested on the 13th.	Fired 15

A5834 Wt. W4973/M687 750,000 8/16 D. D. & L. Ltd. Forms/C.2118/13.

Instructions regarding War Diaries and Intelligence Summaries are contained in F. S. Regs., Part II. and the Staff Manual respectively. Title pages will be prepared in manuscript.

WAR DIARY
or
~~INTELLIGENCE~~ SUMMARY.

(Erase heading not required.)

Army Form C. 2118.

Place	Date	Hour	Summary of Events and Information	Remarks and references to Appendices
GONNELIEU	15/9/17	-24/9/17	All this time work was continued on the different positions with good results.	
	25/9/17	7.6pm	The forward guns were again placed in position and the enemies registration was checked with two rounds.	Fwd 2
		7.30pm	Thirty one rounds were fired in bursts from 7.30pm - 8.20pm. This bombardment was designed to draw the fire of the enemy batteries operating in the area while our infantry entered the opposite trenches. Fire [illegible] The enemy barrage was fairly [illegible] prisoners were obtained in this raid. The [illegible] road were not heavy and accurate but all positions [illegible] hit. One gunner was slightly wounded.	Fwd 91
	26/9/17	-30/9/17	Work on emplacements continued and the left hand pits and dugouts almost completed.	

[illegible signature]
O.C. [illegible]

A5834 Wt. W4973/M687 750,000 8/16 D. D. & L. Ltd. Forms/C.2118/13.

Instructions regarding War Diaries and Intelligence Summaries are contained in F. S. Regs., Part II. and the Staff Manual respectively. Title pages will be prepared in manuscript.

WAR DIARY *or* INTELLIGENCE SUMMARY.

(Erase heading not required.)

October

Army Form C. 2118.

D.T.M.O. 40TH DIVISION. No. ... Date 1 Nov 1917

Vol 11

Place	Date	Hour	Summary of Events and Information	Remarks and references to Appendices
GONNELIEU FINS etc.	Oct 1st 13th		X/40 at 3rd Army School of Mortars. Y/40 in reserve positions on HIGHLAND RIDGE & Z/40 working on defensive Emplacements at GONNELIEU. HQ at FINS. V/40 in action at GONNELIEU	
	13th – 24th		X/40 constructing 6" Newton Empts on WELSH RIDGE & a detachment fired 20 rounds of Newton on hostile mortar from GONNELIEU. Y/40 in reserve positions On night of 22nd two forward guns fired 85 rounds on hostile works. Z/40 constructing 6" Newton Emplacements V/40 in action with one gun at GONNELIEU. On 4th one Heavy TM (Mark III) destroyed by premature No casualties	
	25th	10am	All TM Batteries & HQ relieved by corresponding Batteries of 20th Division. Batteries proceeded to huts in PERONNE DTMO went to NOORDPEENE near CASSEL to arrange billets but move cancelled & DTMO returned on 29th to PERONNE	

A5834 Wt. W4973/M687 750,000 8/16 D. D. & L. Ltd. Forms/C.2118/13.

Instructions regarding War Diaries and Intelligence Summaries are contained in F. S. Regs., Part II. and the Staff Manual respectively. Title pages will be prepared in manuscript.

WAR DIARY October
or
INTELLIGENCE SUMMARY (contd)
(*Erase heading not required.*)

D.T.M.O.
40TH DIVISION
No. ....
Date ....

Army Form C. 2118.

Place	Date	Hour	Summary of Events and Information	Remarks and references to Appendices
PERONNE	Oct 26th-31st		All Batteries in rest at PERONNE engaged in Sports & Football, Gun Drill & Marching Drill etc.	
	N.B.		This unit suffered no casualties during the month. Batteries received reinforcements of 17 men from Divisional Artillery on 28th inst making them up to Establishment. Unit had orders to entrain on 29th inst for north, but these were suddenly cancelled.	

Alan P. Taylor Capt
DTMO 40th Division

Page 1

V. 40. Trench Mortar Battery — October

Army Form C. 2118.

WAR DIARY
or
INTELLIGENCE SUMMARY.
(Erase heading not required.)

Instructions regarding War Diaries and Intelligence Summaries are contained in F. S. Regs., Part II. and the Staff Manual respectively. Title pages will be prepared in manuscript.

73

Place	Date	Hour	Summary of Events and Information	Remarks and references to Appendices
Gonnelieu.	1/10/17	9.30 am	No 1 Gun (R.33.b. 45-95) fired 6 rounds on Bleak Support & new Communication Trench. Gonnelieu shelled all morning	
		2.30 pm.	Mark II. in 15 Ravine fired 10 rounds on R.15.d.55-75. One aeroplane of 59 Squadron R.F.C. was observing & sending corrections. 2 'blinds'. Gun not shooting well.	Fired 16.
	2/10/17	10.0 am	No 1. fired 6 rounds on Barrack Support - 2 'blinds'. Bed gave way. Heavy 5.9 & 4.2. retaliation on gun. Old position	
		2.30	No 2. (MK III) fired 6 rounds on Sonnet Farm. First round tail came off bomb & latter fell behind our support line (1000x short). Coy Comdrs agreed to our continuing. Rest fell in Sonnet Farm.	Fired. 13.
	3/10/17		Unable to fire No 2. No bombs. No 1 shelled with 4.2s.	
		6.30 pm	No 1 fired 6 rounds on Bleak Support 1 air burst. 229 Coy R.E. quite useless. Do practically no work on new MK 3. Emplacement.	Fired 6.
	4/10/17	12.15 am	No 2. fired 3 rounds on Sonnet Farm & 3 on O.P. in Les Vacquerie. Last round though a delay fuze burst at bottom of bore completely destroying gun & emplacement. One man slightly wounded. Just previous to firing 2 bombs had been set aside as having small holes clean through them. All bombs show very clumsy workmanship. Could not fire No 1. owing stormy weather till 6 pm fired 6 thro.	Fired 12. Fired 6
	5/10/17.		O.P. again hit by 4.2. 12.30 fired 6 from No 1. Sub bed gave way.	
	6/10/17.	11-30 am.	No 1 fired 6 rounds at 9.30 pm fired 1 round in conjunction with Artillery & M.T.Ms.	Fired 7
	7/10/17.		5.9s fired at No 1 Gun. at 11-15 fired 6 rounds on Bleak Support (one air burst)	Fired 6
	8/10/17		O.P. again hit by 4.2. Could not fire owing to clinometer suddenly breaking	Fired nil.
	9/10/17	11 am.	No 1 fired 7 rounds on Barrack Support. Timber &c. in air	Fired 7.
	10/10/17		20th Div. Infantry in line. Called on C.O. & Coy Comdrs. D.C.L.I. Fired 7 rounds on 3 targets.	Fired 7.

A5834 Wt. W4973/M687 750,000 8/16 D. D. & L. Ltd. Forms/C.2118/13.

Page 2

Instructions regarding War Diaries and Intelligence Summaries are contained in F. S. Regs., Part II. and the Staff Manual respectively. Title pages will be prepared in manuscript.

V. 40. Trench Mortar Battery

WAR DIARY
or
INTELLIGENCE SUMMARY.

(*Erase heading not required.*)

October

Army Form C. 2118.

80

Place	Date	Hour	Summary of Events and Information	Remarks and references to Appendices
Gonnelieu.	11/10/17	5.30pm	Fired 7 rounds on Barrack Support. 1 blind, 2 air bursts.	Fired 7.
	12/10/17	2.30pm	[illegible] V.40. Fired 6 on 3 targets. Good results observed.	Fired 6.
	13/10/17	Noon	Fired 6 on Bleak Supt. Sand-bags & timber blown in air.	Fired 6.
	14/10/17	Noon	Fired 7 on new so-called concrete pill-box in R.28 c. Heavy retaliation.	Fired 7.
	15/10/17	12.30	- - 10 on - - - - - - - - - - - - by hostile M.T.M. which is out of range from gun, so must be a new type with quite 12 to 1300x range.	Fired 10
	16/10/17		Wires badly cut all day. Could not get communication with guns to fire.	Fired nil
	17/10/17	11.30	Fired 9 rounds feeling for hostile T.M. Timber &c thrown in air. 4.2 retaliation.	Fired 9.
	18/10/17		Aeroplane shoot on concrete pill-box postponed owing to clouds. Hostile T.M. fired 15 rounds at No. 1 gun. No direct hits	Fired nil
	19/10/17		Hostile T.M. fired 6 at No. 1 gun at 4 p.m. 4.45 pm fired 8 rounds on several targets. 2 air-bursts. Ammunition party caught at gun by 2 hostile [illegible] firing 18 rounds. No direct hits	Fired 8.
	20/10/17	5 a.m.	10 4.2s at gun. 2 only near. At 10.30 fired 7 rounds on dug-outs in Bleak Support from which Hostile T.M.s appeared to come last night. Light T.M. fired 50 rounds along Mersey St.	Fired 12
		4.45pm	Fired 5 rounds on same target as morning. One air-burst	
	21/10/17		About 60 4.2s at No. 1 gun. 2 direct hits & 12 or yards or two away. No damage beyond pit filled with earth. Wires cut & mended in 23 places. 3.45 p.m. fired 6 rounds on usual targets. Only 1 bomb in hand through 20th Div. bomb store not indenting for ammunition. No firing can be done for a few days.	Fired 6
	22/10/17		No ammunition.	Fired nil
	23/10/17		T.O.R. 20th Div. T.M. officers round emplacements, O.P.s &c &c. No ammunition	74
	24/10/17		Handed over to V 20. H.T.M.B. at 5 p.m. returned to Fins.	151
Fins Péronne.	25/10/17		Left Fins for Peronne by Decauville & Lorry. Camped near Flamicourt. D.T.M.O. went ahead to Nord France. Ypres.	
	25/10-31/10/17		Move north to Ypres on 28th cancelled suddenly. Remained at Peronne drilling, football, &c &c.	
			Fired during month 150 (1st to 20th)	

Rowan Reid, Capt R.F.A.
O.C. V.40 T.M.B.

A5834 Wt. W4973/M687 750,000 8/16 D. D. & L. Ltd. Forms/C.2118/13.

1.

Army Form C. 2118.

Instructions regarding War Diaries and Intelligence Summaries are contained in F. S. Regs., Part II. and the Staff Manual respectively. Title pages will be prepared in manuscript.

WAR DIARY
or
~~INTELLIGENCE SUMMARY.~~ X 40 T.M. Battery

(Erase heading not required.)

Place	Date	~~Hour~~	Summary of Events and Information	Remarks and references to Appendices
~~[illegible]~~ LIGNY ST FLOCHEL	1 to 13/10/17		The Battery was on a course of 6" Newton T.M. at the 3rd Army School of Mortars	
	13/10/17.		Battery left the school for "Fins" with 3 - 6" T.M., - for Hd. Qrs at "Fins" - on the way we stayed the night of the 13th at "Achiet-le-Grand" arriving at "Fins" on the night of the 14th.	
FINS	15 & 16/10/17		At Hd Qrs "Fins" - Fatigues, Gun drill etc.	
FINS & GONNELIEU	17 to 23/10/17		The Battery went into forward billets at "Gouzeaucourt" - fatigue work up the line reconstructing 2" positions to take 6" Newton T.M - During this period a detachment was at work at "Gonnelieu" making emplacement in sunken road R.27.d.50.80 we fired 10 rounds from this emplacement on the 22nd inst and 10 rounds on the 23 inst ~~at~~ target German H.T.M. R.28.d.50.75 - Also during this period one officer and one N.C.O. remained at Hd Qrs. Fins for the purpose of instructing "Z" and "Y" Batteries on the 6" T.M.	

A6945 Wt. W11422/M1160 350,000 12/16 D. D. & L. Forms/C./2118/14.

Cont.

Cont from 1.

2.

WAR DIARY

or

~~INTELLIGENCE SUMMARY.~~

(Erase heading not required.)

Army Form C. 2118.

Instructions regarding War Diaries and Intelligence Summaries are contained in F. S. Regs., Part II. and the Staff Manual respectively. Title pages will be prepared in manuscript.

Place	Date	~~Hour~~	Summary of Events and Information	Remarks and references to Appendices
FINS	24/10/17		Handed over Guns and Beds to X 20 T.M.B. and the Battery returned to 'Fins' the same night	
	25/10/17		Battery left 'Fins' for "Peronne"	
PERONNE	26 to 31/10/17		At 'Peronne' – drill, sports etc.	

J Chard [illegible]
LT. R.F.A.
for O.C. X 40 T.M.B.

A6945 Wt. W11422/M1160 350,000 12/16 D. D. & L. Forms/C./2118/14.

Instructions regarding War Diaries and Intelligence Summaries are contained in F. S. Regs., Part II. and the Staff Manual respectively. Title pages will be prepared in manuscript.

WAR DIARY
~~or~~
~~INTELLIGENCE SUMMARY~~
(Erase heading not required.)

Y40 Trench Mortar Battery — Army Form C. 2118.

October, 1917.

Place	Date	Hour	Summary of Events and Information	Remarks and references to Appendices
FINS	1st	–	Headquarters and Rest Billets of the Battery remained at FINS, the Battery being at work in	
VILLERS PLOUICH	1st	–	Here the construction of reserve positions was rapidly proceeded with. Temporary emplacements were also constructed in the front line for offensive purposes, to the left of the RIBECOURT road. Advanced Headquarters was made in the village of VILLERS PLOUICH, consisting of officers' quarters, signal dugout, and ammunition store.	
do.	20th	6.30 pm	The reserve guns near the support line on the right of the RIBECOURT road were brought into action. Communication was established by runner (and later by telephone) with the nearest Company Headquarters; the two guns were laid on S.O.S. lines, the detachments being ready to fire at any time on receipt of an S.O.S. message from the Company Commander.	
do.	22nd	11.30 pm	A steady bombardment of the enemy's positions on and around the RIBECOURT road was undertaken. The programme was to fire steadily with two guns from the temporary positions in the front line, with a silencer attachment. Unfortunately one gun went out of action shortly after fire was opened, but the other gun continued to fire between 11.30 and 1 a.m., between 1.45 and 2.45 a.m., and between 3.30 and 4.30 a.m. Excellent bursts were obtained	

2353 Wt. W2544/1454 700,000 5/15 D. D. & L. A.D.S.S./Forms/C. 2118.

P.T.O.

Instructions regarding War Diaries and Intelligence Summaries are contained in F. S. Regs., Part II. and the Staff Manual respectively. Title pages will be prepared in manuscript.

WAR DIARY (continued) October, 1917.
or
INTELLIGENCE SUMMARY. Y40 T.M.B.
(Erase heading not required.)

Army Form C. 2118.

Place	Date	Hour	Summary of Events and Information	Remarks and references to Appendices
			in the enemy's wire and front line.	
FINS and VILLERS PLOUICH	24th	–	The whole of the positions and quarters were handed over to Y20 Trench Mortar Battery, as on this date the 20th Divisional Artillery took over from the 40th D.A.	
FINS	25th	8 a.m.	The Battery moved in lorries to FLAMICOURT, near PERONNE.	
FLAMICOURT.	25th	–	The Battery remained resting till the end of the month. Orders were at first given to entrain on the morning of the 29th to proceed north. These orders were immediately cancelled, and the Battery remained here. On the 31st, orders were issued to proceed next morning to NURLU.	
			Mark Stanford Lieut. O.C. Y40 T.M.B.	

Z 40 Trench Mortar Battery

Instructions regarding War Diaries and Intelligence Summaries are contained in F. S. Regs., Part II. and the Staff Manual respectively. Title pages will be prepared in manuscript.

WAR DIARY
or
INTELLIGENCE SUMMARY.
(Erase heading not required.)

October

Army Form C. 2118.

Place	Date	Hour	Summary of Events and Information	Remarks and references to Appendices
Gonnelieu	1 to 6th		Battery working on defensive emplacements	
"	6th	9-30pm	Fired in conjunction with Artillery in a 1 min Concentration on enemy front line at R28a 25.15	8 rds
"	7-19		Battery working on defensive emplacements	
"	20		One 6" Newton T M placed in forward position R27d 50.80 to silence enemy medium T M firing from R28d 70.50	
"	20	3-30pm	Fired on Enemy T M and silenced it from forward position	10 rds
"	21-23		Battery working on defensive emplacements	
"	23	4pm	Fired on Enemy T M from forward position	10 rds
	24th		Battery relieved by Z 20 T M Battery	
Peronne	25th-31st		Battery in Rest Billets.	

J H Benningfield
Lieut RFA
for OC Z 40 T M B

A5834 Wt. W4973/M687 750,000 8/16 D. D. & L. Ltd. Forms/C.2118/13.

Instructions regarding War Diaries and Intelligence Summaries are contained in F. S. Regs., Part II. and the Staff Manual respectively. Title Pages will be prepared in manuscript.

D.T.M.O

WAR DIARY
or
INTELLIGENCE SUMMARY
(Erase heading not required.)

40th DIVISION.

Army Form C. 2118

Vol 17

Place	Date	Hour	Summary of Events and Information	Remarks and references to Appendices
	November 1917			
GOUZEAUCOURT AREA	1st to 19th		All Trench Mortar Batteries engaged in carrying, loading + unloading 18pdr + 4.5 Ammunt at forward dumps.	
	20th to 30th		All Batteries attached to DAC for work + move. At NURLU on 20-21st, HAPLINCOURT 22nd + TRESCAULT to 30th. (less X/40 18th - 23rd)	
	24th to 30th		DTMO with 2 Offrs + 30 OR proceeded to K 10 d 8.8 SW of GRAINCOURT to put into action + fire a captured German 5.9" How Battery. Three guns were got into action + successfully fired. Targets were INCHY-EN-ARTOIS, QUARRY WOOD and all ground in between. Guns were fired on all SOS calls + by 30th over 200 rounds had been fired. About 50-100 complete rounds remained, there being several hundred shells left without charges. Guns still in action on 30th.	
	18th - 23rd		X/40 TMB were lent to 55th Division for concentration of wire-cutting for an attack. This Battery took part in bombardment + returned to 40th Division on 23rd inst.	

Oscar P Taylor Capt.
DTMO 40th Division

1875 Wt. W593/826 1,000,000 4/15 J.B.C. & A. A.D.S.S./Forms/C. 2118.

NOVR. 1917.

Instructions regarding War Diaries and Intelligence Summaries are contained in F. S. Regs., Part II. and the Staff Manual respectively. Title pages will be prepared in manuscript.

WAR DIARY
or
INTELLIGENCE SUMMARY.
(Erase heading not required.)

Army Form C. 2118.

V40 Trench Mortar Battery.

Place	Date	Hour	Summary of Events and Information	Remarks and references to Appendices
PERONNE	1		Left for NURLU by Decauville – camped in tents.	
NURLU	2-4		Fatigues day & night loading 18 pdr. & 4.5" How ammunition at TRAINTON in train – taking to rear of WELSH RIDGE & unloading.	
			Reconnoitred HIGHLAND RIDGE & ARGYL RIDGE east of VILLERS PLOUICH – BEAUCAMP for twelve 6" Newton Mortars.	
	5-7		Fatigues as above. Handed over above T.M. positions to 6th Divl. T.M's.	
	8		Moved to Sunken Road N. of GOUZEAUCOURT.	
	9-18		Fatigues – Work in billets. Twenty men attd. to the D.A.C.	
	19		Attd. to various Sections of the D.A.C.	
	20		Should have moved to Haplincourt, but move cancelled after "Standing to" all night.	
	21		Moved to HAPLINCOURT.	
	22		" " TRESCAULT.	
	24		Capt. O. R. Taylor, M.C., Capt. N. Reid, R.F.A., Lt. Hammond, R.F.A., together with 27 other ranks of V40, 2 of X40, 4 of Y40, & 1 of Z40, moved to a German 5.9 Howitzer position near GRAINCOURT, to fire captured Guns.	

A5834 Wt. W4973/M687 750,000 8/16 D. D. & L. Ltd. Forms/C.2118/13.

Instructions regarding War Diaries and Intelligence Summaries are contained in F. S. Regs., Part II. and the Staff Manual respectively. Title pages will be prepared in manuscript.

WAR DIARY
or
INTELLIGENCE SUMMARY.
(Erase heading not required.)

Army Form C. 2118.

Place	Date	Hour	Summary of Events and Information	Remarks and references to Appendices
			Beds had to be taken up, moved round, & bolted down again, pits dug away & altered before guns could be fired. There were four Guns, of which one had been partially destroyed by British fire. All guns 1893 pattern – no dial sights, nor range indicators found.	
	25		Recovered a range indicator & got No. 2 Gun in action – fired 2 rds.	
	26		Work on Gun pits – altering beds & buffers which were clamped to bed. Buffers filled with Mobiloil obtained from a Tank Dump. Fired 5 rds. on Batteries in INCHY-EN-ARTOIS & QUARRY WOOD and communications.	
	27		Work as above – fired 7.	
	28		Fired 30 on INCHY-EN-ARTOIS.	
	29		" 22 " "	
	30		3 Guns in action – fired 65 assisting in repelling German counter-attack from BOURLON WOOD to MOEUVRES. Fairly heavy 77cm. shelling of Battery. Casualties to Infantry around position. No. of rds. of 5·9" fired 25–30 = 129.	

[signature] for Capt, R.F.A.,
Cmdg. X40 Heavy T.M. Battery.

A5834 Wt. W4973/M687 750,000 8/16 D. D. & L. Ltd. Forms/C.2118/13.

Instructions regarding War Diaries and Intelligence Summaries are contained in F. S. Regs., Part II, and the Staff Manual respectively. Title pages will be prepared in manuscript.

WAR DIARY
or
INTELLIGENCE SUMMARY.
(Erase heading not required.)

Army Form C. 2118.

X. 40 Trench Mortar Battery.

Place	Date	Hour	Summary of Events and Information	Remarks and references to Appendices
	1917 Nov.			
NURLU	1		The Battery moved from FLAMICOURT, PERONNE, and went into camp at NURLU.	
do	1st–8th		The whole Battery was employed in taking ammunition to forward R.A. positions in preparation for the Advance.	
GOUZEAUCOURT	8th		The Battery moved into a sunken road west of GOUZEAUCOURT	
do	8th–18th		and to the 18th the ammunition fatigue was continued	
do	18th		5 men from Y.40, 4 men from Z.40, and 1 man from V.40 were attached to the Battery to raise the personnel to 2 Officers and 24 O.R. at which strength the Battery went by lorry to ST. EMILIE and was there attached to the 55th Division.	
ST. EMILIE	19th		In accordance with orders issued the Battery moved out at 3.30 a.m. to take up positions on the reverse slope of the ridge in front of SART FARM, as No 3 Battery in the T.M. concentration. Beds were laid and guns were ready by 1 p.m.	
SART FARM	19th–20th		from 4 p.m. to 5.30 a.m. on the 19th all were employed in carrying ammunition to the guns, and all preparation	

2

Instructions regarding War Diaries and Intelligence Summaries are contained in F. S. Regs., Part II, and the Staff Manual respectively. Title pages will be prepared in manuscript.

WAR DIARY
or
INTELLIGENCE SUMMARY.
(Erase heading not required.)

Army Form C. 2118.

X. 40. Trench Mortar Battery.

Place	Date	Hour	Summary of Events and Information	Remarks and references to Appendices
	1917 Nov			
SART FARM	20th		were made to open fire at ZERO – 6.20 a.m. – on the 20th Nov.	
do	20th	6.20 am	The four guns (in the open) commenced 26 mins gun fire on wire between the KNOLL and GUILLEMONT FARM during which time about 250 rounds were fired by the Battery. Hostile shelling was totally ignored by the NCOs and men who worked excellently throughout, particularly the No 1s – Sgt Ilett – Corp. Clark – Bdr Lake – and Gnr Winwood.	
		6.46 am	The Battery withdrew with guns on ceasing fire up to which time there were no casualties. As the men were passing a Field Battery (A.181) at the entrance to LEMPIRE an unfortunate premature wounded Gnr J.R. Bosworth (apparently since died of wounds.)	
ST. EMILIE	20th	9.30 am	The Battery returned to ST EMILIE and rested there until	
	21st	3.30 pm	3.30 p.m. on the 21st when they left to relieve a T.M. Battery of the	
TOMBOIS FARM	21st		55th Division at TOMBOIS FARM with orders to fire only on "SOS" lines.	
do	22nd	8 pm	The Battery was relieved by a Battery of the 55th Division and returned to ST EMILIE.	
ST. EMILIE	23rd/25th	9 am	The Battery left ST. EMILIE in two lorries to rejoin the 40th Div. TMs	

A6945 Wt. W11422/M1160 350,000 12/16 D. D. & L. Forms/C./2118/14.

Instructions regarding War Diaries and Intelligence Summaries are contained in F. S. Regs., Part II. and the Staff Manual respectively. Title pages will be prepared in manuscript.

WAR DIARY
or
INTELLIGENCE SUMMARY.
(Erase heading not required.)

Army Form C. 2118.

X.40 T.M Battery

Place	Date	Hour	Summary of Events and Information	Remarks and references to Appendices
	1917 Nov			
TRESCAULT	24th	12.30 am	After travelling by NURLU, HAPLINCOURT, BERTINCOURT, HERMIES, BEAUMETZ, YTRES, and METZ, - TRESCAULT was reached on 24th at 12.30 am the X 40th TMs being attached to 40th DAC for duty	
TRESCAULT	24th to 30th		The Battery did duty with the 40th DAC who were supplying ammunition to the Div Art in action in the neighbourhood of BOURLON WOOD.	

[signature] Lieut.
O.C. X.40 T.M. Battery.

A6945 Wt. W11422/M1160 350,000 12/16 D. D. & L. Forms/C./2118/14.

Instructions regarding War Diaries and Intelligence Summaries are contained in F. S. Regs., Part II. and the Staff Manual respectively. Title pages will be prepared in manuscript.

WAR DIARY
or
~~INTELLIGENCE SUMMARY.~~
(Erase heading not required.)

Army Form C. 2118.

Y40 Trench Mortar Battery

November, 1917.

Place	Date	Hour	Summary of Events and Information	Remarks and references to Appendices
FLAMICOURT, PERONNE	1·11·17	–	Orders for the move to the YPRES area having been cancelled, the Battery moved back into camp at NURLU	
NURLU	2·11·17	–	The Battery was employed on ammunition fatigues; i.e. taking 18·pdr. and 4·5" ammunition by Light Railway to prospective battery positions near GOUZEAUCOURT.	
do.	8·11·17	–	In order to be nearer to the positions where fatigues were being carried on, a move was made to dugouts in a sunken road in rear of GOUZEAUCOURT.	
GOUZEAUCOURT.	9·11·17	–	Fatigues were continued as above described, the ammunition being taken to positions in readiness for the attack of the 20th.	
do.	18·11·17	–	The fatigues having been concluded, the Battery moved back to NURLU.	
NURLU	20·11·17	–	For facility in moving, the Battery was attached to the 40th D.A.C., the men being used as duty men. During the night the whole D.A.C. stood by in readiness to move.	
do.	21·11·17	–	Move was made with the D.A.C. to HAPLINCOURT.	
HAPLINCOURT	22·11·17	–	Move was made with the D.A.C. to TRESCAULT.	
TRESCAULT	23·11·17	–	The Division being in the line, and attacking BOURLON WOOD, the battery was engaged once more in taking ammunition forward, and continued to the end of the month.	

Mark Stanford Lieut,
O.C. Y40 T.M.B.

30·11·1917

2353 Wt. W2544/1454 700,000 5/15 D. D. & L. A.D.S.S./Forms/C. 2118.

NOVEMBER 1917

Instructions regarding War Diaries and Intelligence Summaries are contained in F. S. Regs., Part II. and the Staff Manual respectively. Title pages will be prepared in manuscript.

WAR DIARY
or
INTELLIGENCE SUMMARY.
(Erase heading not required.)

Z 40 Trench Mortar Battery

Army Form C. 2118.

Place	Date	Hour	Summary of Events and Information	Remarks and references to Appendices
PERONNE	1		Left for NURLU by Decauville camped in tents	
	2-4		Fatigues loading 18 pdr & H.S ammunition at Railton on to Decauville and offloading at Fifteen Ravine near Villers Pluich.	
	5-7		Fatigues as above. Handed over positions reconnoitred near Beaucamp, Highland Ridge & Argyl Ridge to 6th Division TM'S	
	8		Moved to Sunken Road N of GOUZEAUCOURT	
	9-18		Fatigues, work on billets.	
	19		Attached to various sections of the DAC	
	20-21		Moved to Haplincourt	
	22		" " Lurcault	
	24-30		Worked with sections of the DAC	

J Benningfield
Lieut RFA
for OC Z/40 TM Battery

A6945 Wt. W11422/M1160 350,000 12/16 D. D. & L. Forms/C./2118/14.

Instructions regarding War Diaries and Intelligence Summaries are contained in F. S. Regs., Part II, and the Staff Manual respectively. Title pages will be prepared in manuscript.

WAR DIARY
or
INTELLIGENCE SUMMARY.
(Erase heading not required.)

Army Form C. 2118.

D.T.M.O., 40TH DIVISION. No. 1 Date DECR, 1917.

Vol 18

Place	Date	Hour	Summary of Events and Information	Remarks and references to Appendices
TRESCAULT NEUVILLE BERTINCOURT HAMLINCOURT	1 to 12		All T.M. Batteries (V.X.Y.Z.) of the Divn. were attached to the D.A.C. for duty.	
ST. LEGER	12	7p.m.	Arr. at billets of 16th T.M's, whom we eventually relieved on the 17th.	
"	13 to 16		Fatigues in billets - parades, etc.	
"	17 to 31		Batteries relieved corresponding Batteries of the 16th Divn. in the line N. of BULLECOURT, and were in action to the end of the month - detachments doing 4 days in the line & 4 days on rest at H.Q. (& soon) to end of month. From the time of relieving the 16th Divn. our (40th Div. T.M's) H.Q. were at ST. LEGER.	

Oscar Baylis
Capt., R.L.,
D.T.M.O., 40 Div.

A7092 Wt. W128 9/M1293 750,000. 1/17. D. D & L., Ltd. Forms/C2118/14.

Instructions regarding War Diaries and Intelligence Summaries are contained in F. S. Regs., Part II. and the Staff Manual respectively. Title pages will be prepared in manuscript.

WAR DIARY of V.40 T.M.B.
or
~~INTELLIGENCE SUMMARY.~~
(*Erase heading not required.*)

Army Form C. 2118.

Place	Date	~~Hour~~	Summary of Events and Information	Remarks and references to Appendices
TRESCAULT.	Dec. 1st to Dec. 11th.		} attached to Divisional Ammunition Column.	
ST. LEGER	Dec 12th.		Battery moved to ST. LEGER & occupied billets adjacent to those of V.16. T.M.B.	
ditto	Dec 12th to Dec 19th.		Assisting V.16 in the working of their trench mortars.	
ditto	Dec 20th		Detachment of V.40 relieved detachment of V.16 in the line N. of BULLECOURT & all T.M stores of V.16 handed over to V.40. One Mk II H.T.M. taken over in action & three Mk I. H.T.Ms, these latter being out of range of the German lines.	
ditto	Dec. 22nd		The battery took over the billets of V.16, who moved out of ST. LEGER.	
ditto	Dec 20th to Dec 31st.		No firing was done during this period owing to the breaking of the Mk II Sub-bed. This necessitated the dismantling of the T.M. & the dismantling of the sub-bed. The damaged parts of the sub-bed could not be immediately replaced & consequently the T.M. remained out of action.	

31-12-17.

[illegible signature]
2/Lt. R.F.A.
for O.C. V.40 T.M.B.

A5834 Wt. W4973/M687 750,000 8/16 D. D. & L. Ltd. Forms/C.2118/13.

X.40. T.M Battery

Army Form C. 2118.

WAR DIARY
or
INTELLIGENCE SUMMARY.
(Erase heading not required.)

Instructions regarding War Diaries and Intelligence Summaries are contained in F. S. Regs., Part II. and the Staff Manual respectively. Title pages will be prepared in manuscript.

Place	Date	Hour	Summary of Events and Information	Remarks and references to Appendices
	December			
TRESCAULT } NEUVILLE } BERTINCOURT } HAMLINECOURT }	1st	to 12th	Attached to 40th D.A.C for duty	
St LEGER.	12th	7.0pm	Arrived at billets of 16th Div: TMs	
	12–16		Fatigues in billets	
STRAY. RES. N. of BULLECOURT	17th		Relieved X Bty of the 16th Div. Took over 5 – 6" TMs only 3 of which were in action	
	18th		Ammunition recesses deepened, straightened and divided	
	19th		Fired 11 rounds on AEROPLANE EARTHWORKS and Zero lines adjusted	
	20th		Fired 10 rounds on do. ~~20~~ 10 on MATCH ALLEY, 20 on VULCAN ALLEY	
	21st		New recess started.	
	22nd		Fired 2 rds on AEROPLANE EARTHWORKS. 2" Amm IC & cleared to BULL DUMP	
	23rd	8.a.m	Fired 10 do	
	24th	9.30am	Fired 30 do ~~Two~~ 6 guns ordered out.	
	25th – 26th		Work continued on moving out two guns	

A6945 Wt. W11422/M1160 350,000 12/16 D. D. & L. Forms/C./2118/14.

Instructions regarding War Diaries and Intelligence Summaries are contained in F. S. Regs., Part II. and the Staff Manual respectively. Title pages will be prepared in manuscript.

WAR DIARY
or
INTELLIGENCE SUMMARY.
(Erase heading not required.)

Army Form C. 2118.

Place	Date	Hour	Summary of Events and Information	Remarks and references to Appendices
	December			
STRAY. RES.	27th		Work on removing sub bed continued, laying with [illegible] [illegible] + [illegible] billets, removing 2" Ams.	
	28th		Fired 29 rounds on AEROPLANE EARTHWORKS + Sunken Road [illegible]	
	29th		Fired 30 rounds on AEROPLANE EARTHWORKS, Sunken road in rear + CRUMP ALLEY	
	30th		Looking for better observation, OPs found in HUMP SUPPORT, STAFFORD LANE + KNUCKLE AVENUE.	
	31st		Fired 14 rounds on Junction of MATCH ALLEY and CROISILLES – H. Road	
			and 3 rounds on VULCAN ALLEY	
			[signature] for O/C. [illegible] T.M.B. 31/12/17.	

A6945 Wt. W11422/M1160 350,000 12/16 D. D. & L. Forms/C./2118/14.

Instructions regarding War Diaries and Intelligence Summaries are contained in F. S. Regs., Part II. and the Staff Manual respectively. Title pages will be prepared in manuscript.

WAR DIARY
or
INTELLIGENCE SUMMARY.
(Erase heading not required.)

Y.40 Trench Mortar Battery — Army Form C. 2118.

December 1917

Place	Date	Hour	Summary of Events and Information	Remarks and references to Appendices
Bertincourt	1.12.17 to 12.12.17		Attached to various sections of the DAC & worked for them. The men were not very happy with the DAC as they were not accustomed to the work & clothing was very difficult to get as our QM could not draw anything.	
St Ledger	13.12.17		Arrived at 16th Div TM Headquarters. Arranged accommodation for the battery with Y16 as they were still occupying the billets	
St Ledger	14.12.17 to 16.12.17		The men cleaned up 2" TM's which are still in our possession also some went up the line to look round the sector.	
In the line N of Bullecourt	17.12.17	11 AM	Relieved Y16 in the line. The emplacements were very bad, dirty an ammunition was not looked after properly. Took over 6, 6" Newtons. Two of the guns were only in temporary positions & could not be fired as they were not concealed sufficiently.	
		3.30pm	Fired 3 rds at 2.30 pm on Vulcan (Pill Box). A Bdr was wounded in the head & hands by the flash of the gun. A shell stuck half way down the bore & when forced down went suddenly to the bottom & did not give him time to get away.	3 rds
	18.12.17	4 pm	Fired 18 rds at Fag Alley Enfilade & 22 rds on Bunker Road. Observation very difficult owing to a bad OP and communication with guns was bad. Two rounds fell short just behind our own line but did no damage.	18 "
	19.12.17		Saw Infantry Battalion about the short rounds. Moving Y36 gun to a new emplacement.	
		9 to 10am	Went round our front line via Minerva Lane and found a good OP for our right portion of Zone.	
		3 to 4pm	Went round left part of Zone front line. No observation posts suitable. Found a good OP in Burg Support for left portion of Zone. This is a very good OP for the Trenches round Fontaine lez Croisilles	

A7092. Wt W128 9/M1293 750,000. 1/17. D. D & L., Ltd. Forms/C2118/14.

Instructions regarding War Diaries and Intelligence Summaries are contained in F. S. Regs., Part II. and the Staff Manual respectively. Title pages will be prepared in manuscript.

WAR DIARY
or
INTELLIGENCE SUMMARY.
(*Erase heading not required.*)

Army Form C. 2118.

Y40 Trench Mortar Battery

December 1917

Place	Date	Hour	Summary of Events and Information	Remarks and references to Appendices
In the line N of Bullecourt	20.12.17		Worked on Y36 ~~gun~~ new emplacement also tried to lay wire to OP (Bug Sup). Wire very scarce. Removed Y46 bed to new position. No firing	21
	21.12.17		Wired up OP (Bug Sup) & continued it as far towards Fag Alley OP as possible. No firing.	
	22.12.17		Busy putting Y46 in action & wiring. No firing	
	23.12.17		Wiring to Post 34 completed & Y46 in action. No firing	
	24.12.17		Fired 25 rds with Y46 at Fag Alley & Sunken Rd from Bullecourt to Fontaine. Granatenwerfer suspected there. Observation very difficult	25
	25.12.17		Fired 10 rds with Y46 & Sunken Rd & Fag Alley. One short round in Bug Sup no damage	10
	26.12.17		Fired 3 rds at Fag Alley with Y26 registration of guns	3
	27.12.17		Worked on Y36 new position. Took Heavy TM officer round front line to look for OP.	
	28.12.17		Wire to OP cut & communication established with guns too late to fire.	
	29.12.17		Fired 26 rds & Fag Alley & Sunken Rd (Bullecourt to Fontaine) searching for Granatenwerfer with Y46 gun	26
	30.12.17		Fired 17 rds with Y46 Fag Alley.	17
	31.12.17		Y36 in action. Fired 8 rds registration. Observation good. Bed jumped badly so had to cease firing	102 rds

J G Benningfield
Lieut RFA
O/C Y40 TMB

A7092 Wt. W 125 9/M1293 750,000. 1/17. D. D. & L., Ltd. Forms/C2118/14.

Z 40 Trench Mortar Battery.

Instructions regarding War Diaries and Intelligence Summaries are contained in F. S. Regs., Part II. and the Staff Manual respectively. Title pages will be prepared in manuscript.

WAR DIARY
or
~~INTELLIGENCE SUMMARY~~.
(Erase heading not required.)

I

Army Form C. 2118.

Place	Date	Hour	Summary of Events and Information	Remarks and references to Appendices
NEUVILLE TRESCAULT HAMLINCOURT	1/2/17 to 11/2/17		The battery was attached to the 40th D.A.C. The men were split up among the various sections [struck out] Such things as may usually be obtained at the Q.M. stores were impossible to obtain for them during the period and most finished in rags and with very bad boots. This method of moving the batteries causes much discontent but it seems to be unavoidable.	
ST LEGER	12/2/17 to 16/2/17		The battery was in rest at St Leger re-equipping and working on their billets and stables.	
	17/2/17		Relief of Z 16 by this battery Four guns were taken over [6" Newtons]. The pits and dugouts were poorly built, small and dirty. Fired 23 on sunken road* from FONTAINE to BULLECOURT.	* henceforth referred to as Target A
	18/2/17		Fired 44 on sunken road and KANDY TRENCH† Shifting gun from STRAY SUPPORT to LINCOLN SUPPORT. [Z 20] This gun is being put in a converted heavy trench mortar position.	† Target B.

A7092 Wt W1128 9/M1293 750,000 1/17. D. D & L., Ltd. Forms/C2118/14.

Instructions regarding War Diaries and Intelligence Summaries are contained in F. S. Regs., Part II. and the Staff Manual respectively. Title pages will be prepared in manuscript.

WAR DIARY
or
~~INTELLIGENCE SUMMARY~~.
(Erase heading not required.)

11

Army Form C. 2118.

Place	Date	Hour	Summary of Events and Information	Remarks and references to Appendices
ST. LEGER	19/2/17 20/2/17		No firing these two days owing to heavy ground mists. Work was done each day on Z. 20 emplacement	
	21/2/17		Fired 2 rounds on Target A from Z. 16 in LINCOLN SUPPORT. This gun is in an open position and below trench level and will be moved to CHERRY LANE [Z. 4] as soon as a thaw makes digging and revetting possible.	
	22/2/17 23/2/17		Fired 12 rounds on Target A from Z. 16. Work on ammunition recesses at all guns	
	24/2/17		Fired 8 rounds on Target B from Z. 26. Observation very bad and impossible to register.	
	25/2/17 26/2/17 27/2/17		Fired 19 rounds } on " 13 rounds } on Target B from Z. 26. " 12 rounds } on Most of the time was spent in wiring up the guns to headquarters and to suitable O.P's	
	28/2/17		Fired 25 rounds from Z. 36 on Sunken road in neighbourhood of COPSE TRENCH. Carrying party brought up bombs to Z. 20 and removed heavy trench mortar bombs from this position.	

A7092. Wt. W128 9/M1293 750,000. 1/17. D. D & L., Ltd. Forms/C2118/14.

Instructions regarding War Diaries and Intelligence Summaries are contained in F. S. Regs., Part II. and the Staff Manual respectively. Title pages will be prepared in manuscript.

WAR DIARY
or
~~INTELLIGENCE SUMMARY.~~

(Erase heading not required.)

111

Army Form C. 2118.

Place	Date	Hour	Summary of Events and Information	Remarks and references to Appendices
ST LEGER	29/12/17		Z.20 in action. Fired 18 rounds on sunken road near Target B. In the afternoon Z.26 fired 12 rounds on Target B. Carrying parties morning to 20 & afternoon to 26 & 36	
	30/12/17		Z.26 fired 24 rounds on target B. Telephone communication very bad — wires broken in several places — no firing in the morning owing to this.	
	31/12/17		Z.16 fired 30 rounds on target A and to the left of this point. One burst in the sunken road caused flames to shoot up This gun will be moved to CHERRY ROW in a few days now. A few shorts still occur and no satisfactory explanation can yet be found.	
			R.J. Hammond [illegible] O.C. Z.6th T.M. Bty 1/1/18	

A7092 Wt. W128 9/M1293 750,000. 1/17. D. D & L., Ltd. Forms/C2118/14.

Instructions regarding War Diaries and Intelligence Summaries are contained in F. S. Regs., Part II. and the Staff Manual respectively. Title pages will be prepared in manuscript.

WAR DIARY
or
INTELLIGENCE SUMMARY.
(Erase heading not required.)

JANUARY - 1918.

Army Form C. 2118.

Place	Date	Hour	Summary of Events and Information	Remarks and references to Appendices
ST. LEGER, and N. of BULLECOURT.	1 to 31		During the whole of the month the Headquarters, and rest billets of 40th Divl Trench Mortar Batteries, have been at ST. LEGER. All the Batteries (V. X Y. Z) have been in action N. OF BULLECOURT throughout the month, - V Bty. having one Mk. III (long range) Heavy T.M. in action, X Bty. having five 6" Newton T.M's. in action, Y Bty. six 6" Newton T.M's. and Z Bty. five 6" Newton T.M's. in action. Since the 21st V Bty. have not been able to fire owing to a round which burst about a foot or two outside the bore wrecking the emplacement. The Medium Batteries have fired daily as far as possible (av. 30 to 200 rds. daily) on trench junctions, T.M. positions, occupied dugouts, etc. The men of V Bty. not in the line with their own Battery, consequent upon only one of V Battery's guns being in	

A7092. Wt. W128 9/M1293 750,000. 1/17. D. D. & L., Ltd. Forms/C2118/14.

Instructions regarding War Diaries and Intelligence [illegible]ies are contained in F. S. Regs., Part II. [illegible] the Staff Manual respectively. Title pages will be prepared in manuscript.

WAR DIARY
or
INTELLIGENCE SUMMARY.
(Erase heading not required.)

Army Form C. 2118.

Place	Date	Hour	Summary of Events and Information	Remarks and references to Appendices
ST. WEGER and CROISILLES.	1 to 31		action, have been assisting the men of X. Y. & Z Batteries in building emplacements. Detachments have done 4 days in the line and 4 at St. Leger, and so on the whole of the month. The detachments when at ST. WEGER have been employed on constructing Reserve positions at CROISILLES.	
			Total 6" fired 1421 Total 9.45" 10	
			Casualties 2 O.R. wounded.	

Oscar Baylis
CAPTAIN.
D.T.M.O. 40TH DIVISION.

V. 40. Trench Mortar Battery.

Instructions regarding War Diaries and Intelligence Summaries are contained in F. S. Regs., Part II. and the Staff Manual respectively. Title pages will be prepared in manuscript.

WAR DIARY
or
INTELLIGENCE SUMMARY.
(Erase heading not required.)

January 1918.

Army Form C. 2118.

Place	Date	Hour	Summary of Events and Information	Remarks and references to Appendices
St Leger.	1/1/18.		The only gun in action is a long range MarK III. at U.13.c. 50-15. There are also 3. MK.I. positions in Lincoln Reserve & Stay Support, but these are now out of range owing to our having captured the enemy front line & Tunnel Trench. The MK.III. is temporally out of action owing to the sub-bed having broken. All men are occupied working for 6" positions & digging dug-out at the gun.	
	2/1/18 to 20/1/18.		Work as usual for positions &c. necessary portions of sub-bed have been borrowed again from the 3rd Division T.M's. Gun in action & 10 rounds fired on U 9 c. 1-2. - junction of trenches. All bursts good. not too accurate for line.	Fired 10.
	21/1/18.		First round fired burst about a foot or two outside the gun completely wrecking the emplacement, & injuring carriage of gun. No casualties. Decided to alter MK.I. emplacement at U.13.d. 35-40. to suit a MK.III. instead of rebuilding present one. Work commenced with assistance of 229 Coy. R.E's.	
	25/1/18		A site also selected in Valley support at U.21.c. 2-3. Tunneling R.E's. & 24 of our men already at work on the dug-out &c.	
	26/1/18 to 31/1/18.		Work continued on both emplacements.	

Norman Reid. Capt. R.F.A.
O.C. V. 40. T.M.B.

A5834 Wt. W4973/M687 750,000 8/16 D. D. & L. Ltd. Forms/C.2118/13.

Instructions regarding War Diaries and Intelligence Summaries are contained in F. S. Regs., Part II. and the Staff Manual respectively. Title pages will be prepared in manuscript.

WAR DIARY
or
INTELLIGENCE SUMMARY.
(Erase heading not required.)

Army Form C. 2118.

X 40 T.M. BTY.

JANUARY - 1918.

Place	Date	Hour	Summary of Events and Information	Remarks and references to Appendices
ST. LEGER	1 to 31		During the whole of the month, the Headquarters and rest billets of the Battery were in ST. LEGER.	
N. of BULLECOURT, ST. LEGER, and CROISILLES	1 to 31		The Battery has been in action (*5 guns) the whole of the month - detachments doing 4 days in the line and 4 days in ST. LEGER, and so on throughout the month. As far as possible, we have fired daily (15 to 25 rds) on targets such as trench junctions, occupied dugouts, trench mortars, etc. When not firing, all guns were laid on their S.O.S. lines. Each time the detachments came out of the line to ST. LEGER, they were employed on building Reserve positions at CROISILLES.	
			[illegible] Capt [illegible] for O/C X 40 T.M.B.	

A7092. Wt. W128 9/M1293. 750,000. 1/17. D. D. & L., Ltd. Forms/C2118/14.

Instructions regarding War Diaries and Intelligence Summaries are contained in F. S. Regs., Part II. and the Staff Manual respectively. Title pages will be prepared in manuscript.

WAR DIARY
or
~~INTELLIGENCE SUMMARY~~
(Erase heading not required.)

Y40 Trench Mortar Battery. Army Form C. 2118.

January, 1918.

Place	Date	Hour	Summary of Events and Information	Remarks and references to Appendices
ST. LÉGER. and CROISILLES.	1st	-	The Headquarters and rest billets of the Battery were in St. Léger during the month, while it was in action east of Croisilles with six guns, advanced headquarters being situated on the left of the Croisilles – Hendecourt road. The Battery covered the sector from the southern edge of Fontaine-les-Croisilles to the Croisilles – Hendecourt road.	
			Firing was carried out daily as far as possible on such targets as Trench Junctions, occupied dugouts, granatenwerfer, trench mortars, &c. All guns when not firing were laid on selected S.O.S. targets; in each case a point on the sunken Fontaine – Bullecourt road, which, being in No Man's Land, would form an obvious rallying-point for an enemy attack.	
	5th	11.30am	A ten-minute concentration was fired in conjunction with all the other Trench Mortar Batteries on the Divisional Front (34th Division). Field Artillery Batteries also took part. The targets chosen were principally the enemy trenches in Fontaine and the front line to the south of it.	
	6th		Ordinary daily firing was continued from the 6th to the 14th, between 20 and 30 rounds daily being fired at vulnerable points. All fire was carefully observed, but difficulty was experienced in maintaining communication, as the wires in the front trench system were frequently cut. A hard frost lasted throughout this period.	
	15th	-	The thaw now set in, and was accompanied by rain. This caused works of all kind to collapse; the trenches became impassable and the gun pits fell in. Consequently for eight days no firing could be done, and the men of the Battery were fully employed in digging out the pits and the trenches leading to them. It was not until the 23rd that the first gun was got into action once more.	

[P.T.O.

A5834 Wt. W4973/M687 750,000 8/16 D. D. & L. Ltd. Forms/C.2118/13.

Instructions regarding War Diaries and Intelligence Summaries are contained in F. S. Regs., Part II. and the Staff Manual respectively. Title pages will be prepared in manuscript.

WAR DIARY
or
~~INTELLIGENCE SUMMARY.~~

(Erase heading not required.)

Y40 Trench Mortar Battery — Army Form C. 2118.

January, 1918 (continued).

Place	Date	Hour	Summary of Events and Information	Remarks and references to Appendices
ST. LEGER and CROISILLES.	23rd	–	Daily firing was resumed, the weather having improved. Bregun was in action on this day. Work was also commenced on reserve positions in the "Intermediate Line" (immediately in front of Croisilles) and the first site chosen was just on the edge of Croisilles, on the Fontaine road.	
	25th to 31st	3pm	All guns were got into action by this time, and normal conditions prevailed till the end of the month. A Light Railway line was repaired and began to be utilised for ammunition supply. Work on Reserve position proceeded steadily.	

Mark Stanford Lieut.
O.C. Y40 Trench Mortar Battery.

A5834 Wt. W4973/M687 750,000 8/16 D. D. & L. Ltd. Forms/C.2118/13.

Z.40 Trench Mortar Battery.

Instructions regarding War Diaries and Intelligence Summaries are contained in F. S. Regs., Part II. and the Staff Manual respectively. Title pages will be prepared in manuscript.

WAR DIARY
or
~~INTELLIGENCE SUMMARY.~~

(Erase heading not required.)

Army Form C. 2118.

Place	Date	Hour	Summary of Events and Information	Remarks and references to Appendices
CROISILLES	1.1.18		Fired 43 rounds on KANDY TRENCH and OLDENBURG LANE. This cold weather is seriously affecting the charges and a constant loss of range is very marked. Two rounds fell abnormally short but did no damage to our own trenches	
	2.1.18		16 rounds were fired in the afternoon from the open pit in LINCOLN SUPPORT. Some hits on the sunken FONTAINE-BULLECOURT Road were observed. This road is now only occupied by the enemy where it is crossed by CEYLON TR. It is therefore proposed to dismantle this pit and to place the gun to cover more important targets by FONTAINE. 54 rounds were also fired on KANDY TR. and its environs notably the tunnel just north of this trench. One round fell noticeably short. Some retaliation fell round our support line.	
	3.1.18		This afternoon 60 rounds were fired on targets near KANDY TR. Several hits on OLDENBURG LANE were observed. Two of our rounds fell short in our wire. Telephone wire has been laid to an O.P. in HUMBER SUPPORT and from here to 36. All guns are now in communication with the O.P.	
	4.1.18		Fired 20 rounds on junction of KANDY & PRINCE TR.s Our stock of bombs is now very small.	

A7092. Wt. W128 9/M1293 750,000. 1/17. D. D & L., Ltd. Forms/C2118/14.

Fried 193

II

Instructions regarding War Diaries and Intelligence Summaries are contained in F. S. Regs., Part II. and the Staff Manual respectively. Title pages will be prepared in manuscript.

WAR DIARY
or
INTELLIGENCE ~~SUMMARY~~.

(Erase heading not required.)

Army Form C. 2118

Place	Date	Hour	Summary of Events and Information	Remarks and references to Appendices
CROISILLES	5.1.18		Today we fired all guns simultaneously on selected targets at U8c 40-80, U8a 25-65, U8d 20-95, U8d 60-70	
			For this purpose 20 rounds were taken to the open pit in LINCOLN. This pit has been definitely abandoned now however and will be dismantled and the gun put in a new position at CHERRY LANE.	
	6.1.18		Fired 4 rounds on KARDI to check ranges for night and S.O.S. lines	
	7.1.18		Fired 20 rounds on PRINCE TRENCH. The gun has been dismounted and work has been started on the bed. This is very difficult to remove and probably the present bed will be broken.	
	8.1.18		No firing owing to mists and to shortage of bombs. The telephone wire has extended from HUMBER SUPPORT to a point half way down MOLE LANE.	
	9.1.18		10 rounds fired on KARDI and 15 rounds on COPSE TRENCH. The shooting on COPSE was particularly accurate. One round of the first ten fell short but was harmless. No fatigue party causing bomb shortage again.	

A7092: Wt W123 9/M1293 750,000. 1/17. D. D & L., Ltd. Forms/C2118/14.

III.

Instructions regarding War Diaries and Intelligence Summaries are contained in F. S. Regs., Part II. and the Staff Manual respectively. Title pages will be prepared in manuscript.

WAR DIARY

or

~~INTELLIGENCE SUMMARY.~~

(Erase heading not required.)

Army Form C. 2118.

Place	Date	Hour	Summary of Events and Information	Remarks and references to Appendices
CROISILLES	10.1.18		No firing. A new bomb store has been constructed at the position near Nellie Avenue+ and two recesses have been begun at Z.26 position in LINCOLN near SAP LANE.	+Z.20
	11.1.18		No firing. The piece and bed have been shifted to the CHERRY LANE* position and a new sub-bed has been brought up to headquarters. About forty 2" bombs have been removed from the dugout at this position & a 3" Stokes gun placed here has been shifted to MOLE LANE.	*Z.4
	12.1.18		Work continued on Z.4. The sub-bed is now in position but the emplacement has not been revetted nor has a recess been made for the firing member. Fired 20 on COPSE TRENCH from Z.26	
	13.1.18		Fired 16 on HARDY TRENCH from Z.20. One round fell short and the tail became detached in flight.	
	14.1.18		Fired 9 on COPSE TRENCH from position in BURG SUPPORT near APPLE LANE ϕ Z.4 position ready for action (temporarily)	ϕZ.36
	15.1.18		Officer and men all day at Z.4 position (9am–3pm) waiting for an aeroplane	

A7092 Wt W1128 9/M1293 750,000. 1/17. D. D & L., Ltd. Forms/C2118/14.

IV

Instructions regarding War Diaries and Intelligence Summaries are contained in F. S. Regs., Part II. and the Staff Manual respectively. Title pages will be prepared in manuscript.

WAR DIARY
or
~~INTELLIGENCE~~ ~~SUMMARY~~.
(Erase heading not required.)

Army Form C. 2118.

Place	Date	Hour	Summary of Events and Information	Remarks and references to Appendices
CROISILLES	15.1.18 (cont)		shoot which did not take place owing to breakdown of communication from wireless station. The day was thus wasted.	
	16.1.18		The thaw set in today and the trenches completely collapsed. Very little firing will be possible for a few days.	
	17.1.18		Fired 7 rounds from Z.4 on COPSE TRENCH. The work of digging out all the other guns and revetting as far as possible has been begun. It was impossible to guard against the collapse of the trenches during the frost owing to the hardness of the ground, the shortage of men and the necessity of maintaining a vigorous fire policy.	
	18.1.18		Z.36 fired 8 rounds on COPSE TRENCH. At the eighth round the timbers in rear of the bed broke causing a short round and putting the gun out of action. Work of reconstruction continuing.	
	19.1.18		Z.20 is now clear of mud the the passage to LINCOLN has been dug out and partially revetted. Z.4 has been dug out and connected by wire to the MOLE LANE O.P.	
	20.1.18		Z.4 fired 8 rounds checking line for aeroplane shoot.	
	21.1.18		Z.4 fired 35 rounds on hostile T.M. in OLDENBURG LANE with aeroplane observation. Z.20 fired 5 rounds retaliation for shelling of LUMP LANE	14 2523

A7092 Wt W128 9/M1293 750,000. 1/17. D. D & L., Ltd. Forms/C2118/14.

I

Instructions regarding War Diaries and Intelligence Summaries are contained in F. S. Regs., Part II. and the Staff Manual respectively. Title pages will be prepared in manuscript.

WAR DIARY
or
~~INTELLIGENCE SUMMARY.~~
(Erase heading not required.)

Army Form C. 2118.

Place	Date	Hour	Summary of Events and Information	Remarks and references to Appendices
CROISILLES	22.1.18		wire laid to Dump Support from Hqrs. This O.P. will be used for all guns until it is possible to keep a wire in repair. At present the trenches make this impossible. Z. 20 fired 18 on KANDY. Wire cut in afternoon & repaired after dark.	
	23.1.18		Z. 20 fired 20 on Tunnel near KANDY. The gun at 26 has been dismantled and the sub-bed removed owing to the breaking of two angle irons. The pit has been revetted and the trench is being revetted from the gun pit to the ammunition recess.	
	24.1.18		Z. 20 fired 20 rounds on PRINCE TRENCH. Bombs were today pushed up by decauville trucks from RIFLE DUMP to BARKER AVE & LINCOLN with great success. It is proposed to make a forward dump here and to carry bombs from here to all guns provided that ARGYLE AVENUE is dugout.	
	25.1.18		No firing owing to mist. The bed at 20 was taken up and replaced as it had sunk towards the rear. The sub-bed has been put in 26 and this emplacement will be finished tomorrow.	
	26.1.18 } 27.1.18 }		No firing. Mist still very thick. All positions are now in telephonic communication with Hqrs & with O.Ps in Hole Lane, Hamber Support & Dump Support. 20 & 26 have been revetted and 4 will be revetted tomorrow.	
	28.1.18		Fired 26 on KANDY, QUACK & COPSE Trenches. Telephone communication excellent.	

A7092 Wt W128 9/M1293 750,000. 1/17. D. D & L., Ltd. Forms/C2118/14.

Instructions regarding War Diaries and Intelligence Summaries are contained in F. S. Regs., Part II. and the Staff Manual respectively. Title pages will be prepared in manuscript.

XI

WAR DIARY
or
~~INTELLIGENCE SUMMARY.~~
(Erase heading not required.)

Army Form C. 2118.

Place	Date	Hour	Summary of Events and Information	Remarks and references to Appendices
CRMBILLES (?)	29/1/18		Fired 15 on OUNCE TRENCH. at least five direct hits. Communication excellent. Work on 4 and on reserve positions carried out today. The bedding 26 has been relaid 8° more left, hitting OUNCE TRENCH at 8° Right.	
	30/1/18 31/1/18		Fired 18 on OUNCE TRENCH & KARDY (?) TRENCH. Work of revetting pits and making up establishment of bombs continued.	
			R J Hammond Lt RFA OC Z/40 TM Bty	

A7092. Wt W128 9/M1293 750,000 1/17. D. D & L., Ltd. Forms/C2118/14.

Z. 40 Trench Mortar Battery.

Instructions regarding War Diaries and Intelligence Summaries are contained in F. S. Regs., Part II. and the Staff Manual respectively. Title pages will be prepared in manuscript.

WAR DIARY
or
~~INTELLIGENCE SUMMARY.~~

(*Erase heading not required.*)

Army Form C. 2118.

Place	Date	Hour	Summary of Events and Information	Rds	Remarks and references to Appendices
CROISILLES	1/1/18		No firing today owing to misty weather. Partial headcover has now been made at 26* position. This is only intended to keep the pit dry and affords protection from only the smallest splinters.		*26 position is near the junction of LINCOLN & SPRAT Trenches
	2/1/18		Fired 30; 15 from 26, 15 from 20† on PUNCH TRENCH. Several direct hits were obtained with 26, but the shooting of 20 was poor and erratic. Fire was on working carrying party. The sub bed broken at 26 has been brought to the head quarters at 5th DEVER. The first reserve position is ready for the sub bed and the ammunition recess has been started.	50	†20 position at junction of LINCOLN & NELLIE Trenches
	3/1/18		Fired 40, 20 from 20 & 20 from 36° on [illegible] CROW Trenches. There is still some [illegible] to be done at 36 but all guns are now in action. Relief by half battery today. From today positions are numbered as follows: 20 becomes 31, 26 becomes 32, 36 becomes 33 & [illegible] becomes 34.	40	°36 position in [illegible] [illegible] [illegible]
	4/1/18		Fired 20 from 31 gun on [illegible] TRENCHES. Work continued on 34° and 33.	30	° [illegible] [illegible] [illegible] support
	5/1/18		Fired 30 from 34 on FONTAINE & the trenches protecting this village. I was able to use fourth charge and with this charge obtained very consistent shooting. Work was continued as usual.	30	
	6/1/18		Fired 31 from 34. This gun is firing rather erratically. An alternative position has been chosen about 20 away and as soon as this can be put in action the back of the pit will be cut away & revetted anew and the bed & sub bed taken up and relaid.	31	
	7/1/18		Fired 40 from 31 & 34. From 34 we took on a new target north west of FONTAINE obtaining 3 direct hits & causing an explosion.	40	
				211	

A5834 Wt. W4973/M687 750,000 8/16 D. D. & L. Ltd. Forms/C.2118/13.

Instructions regarding War Diaries and Intelligence Summaries are contained in F. S. Regs., Part II. and the Staff Manual respectively. Title pages will be prepared in manuscript.

WAR DIARY
or
~~INTELLIGENCE SUMMARY.~~
(Erase heading not required.)

Army Form C. 2118.

Place	Date	Hour	Summary of Events and Information	Remarks and references to Appendices
[illegible]	8/2/18		Fired 42 rounds S.O.S at 6.45 a.m. from 31 & 32. Fired 20 from 34 on U1d 80.80. A new O.P. at U1b 20.20 has been connected by telephone line with 34.	211 rds 62
	9/2/18		Fired 32 on S.O.S targets and on Rotten Trench where a lot of Boches were seen.	32
	10/2/18		Fired 48 on usual targets drawing slight retaliation. 33 is almost ready to fire now.	48
	11/2/18		Fired 45 on usual targets but the wind made the shooting very erratic. The infantry fatigue party is now scarcely large enough to keep us supplied.	45
	12/2/18		Fired nil. Detachment working on two forward emplacements.	
	13/2/18		Fired nil " " " "	
	14/2/18		Fired nil " " " "	
	15/2/18		Fired 55 rds on Jct Kandy Tr & Ounce Tr, MG post U8a 90.90 shooting good several direct hits on trench	55
	16/2/18		Fired 46 rds on Tunnel U8a 30.75, U1d 95.60 MG, & Dug Outs U2c 50.70 many direct hits timber sent up	46
	17/2/18		Fired nil men working on No 33 gun tunnelling a shaft through & making an amm recess	
	18/2/18		Fired 30 rds with No 34 gun at TM U8a 90.90 Copse Tr U8b 05.80 & Junct Copse & Ounce Tr	30
	19/2/18		Fired nil	
	20/2/18		Fired 41 rds on MG U8a 20.70 Dug Outs U8a 95.85 & Copse Tr shooting very good timber & sandbags sent up.	40
	21/2/18		Fired 30 rds with No 24 gun on Copse & Ceylon Tr direct hits obtained	30
	22/2/18		Fired 60 rds with 33 & 34 same targets as above also MG post in Kandy Tr	60
	23/2/18		Fired 30 " with 34 targets as above. Gun shooting very erratically on account of bad sub bed	30
	24/2/18		Fired 40 rds at Rotten Trench a lot of Huns were seen here on Sentry duty & were soon dispersed	40
	25/2/18		Fired 43 " with 33 at Ceylon & Copse MG U8a 53.00 silenced the MG	43
	26/2/18		Fired 50 rds SOS with 31 & 32 men worked very well. SOS was all wind. Fired 50 " with 33 & 34 at Ceylon Copse Ounce Trs also Rotten Trench good shooting	100
	27/2/18		Fired 45 rds with 34 on MG posts U8a 53.00 & U8a 5.3	45
	28/2/18		Fired nil	917

Casualties for mth:- 1 man wounded.

J. Benningfield Lt RFA
for OC Z40 TMB

A5834 Wt. W4973/M687 750,000 8/16 D. D. & L. Ltd. Forms/C.2118/13.

Instructions regarding War Diaries and Intelligence Summaries are contained in F. S. Regs., Part II. and the Staff Manual respectively. Title pages will be prepared in manuscript.

WAR DIARY
or
INTELLIGENCE SUMMARY.
(Erase heading not required.)

D.T.M.O. 40TH DIVISION. Feby. 1918.

Army Form C. 2118.

Vol. 20

Place	Date	Hour	Summary of Events and Information	Remarks and references to Appendices
ST. LEGER " " N. OF BULLE-COURT.			During the whole of the month the Headquarters and rest billets of each Battery (V. X. Y. and Z40) have been in ST. LEGER. Up to the 23rd of the month, V Bty. were employed on various fatigues for the Medium (X. Y. Z.) Batteries. After the 23rd V Bty. were in action (one Gun - 9.45" MK III) and to the end of the month they fired 38 rds. Detachments of the Medium Batteries have been doing 4 days in the line just N. of BULLECOURT, and 4 days at ST. LEGER, and so on right throughout the month. As far as possible, the Medium Batteries have fired each day on to suspected Trench Mortars, Machine Guns, occupied dugouts, posts, etc. Whilst at ST. LEGER the men have been employed on camp fatigues, physical training, etc. Total fired by all Batteries during the month: V Bty... 38 rds. 9.45" MK. III. X. Y. Z.:- 2061 rds. 6". Casualties for the month:- 1 N.C.O. & 3 men wounded.	

[signature] CAPTAIN. D.T.M.O. 40TH DIVISION.

A7092. Wt. W128 9/M1293 750,000. 1/17. D. D. & L., Ltd. Forms/C2118/14.

V 40. Trench Mortar Battery

February

WAR DIARY
or
INTELLIGENCE SUMMARY.
(Erase heading not required.)

Army Form C. 2118.

Instructions regarding War Diaries and Intelligence Summaries are contained in F. S. Regs., Part II. and the Staff Manual respectively. Title pages will be prepared in manuscript.

Place	Date	Hour	Summary of Events and Information	Remarks and references to Appendices
St. Leger.	1/2/18 to 22/2/18		Personnel of Battery employed in building a large dug-out in Valley support U 21.c. 00-15 altering an old Mark I gun pit in STRAY RESERVE. U. 13. d 3-4 so as to suit a Mark III. Also altering line of fire about 30° more left. The dug-out is also being doubled in size. The old bed in wrecked emplacement at U. 13. c. 5-15 had to be dug out from under the wreckage of baulks, elephant shelters, etc.	
	23/2/18.		Gun in action by nightfall.	
	24/2/18.	11-30 am.	Fired 12 rounds on U 9 c. 1-1 & Battalion H.Q at U. 9. a 4-1. Gun as usual shooting very badly. Almost impossible to register it. One direct hit.	Fired. 12
	25/2/18.	10 p.m.	Weather too bad for shooting & observation. 10 p.m. S.O.S. went up & 10 rounds were fired on S.O.S. lines	Fired. 10
	26/2/18.	10-30 am	Fired 10 rounds on U 8. b 5-3. & U. 9. a 4-1. 3 direct hits observed	Fired. 10
	27/2/18.	12 noon.	Fired remaining 6 rounds on working party at U. 15 a. 8-3. No more can be fired at present because all MK I bombs are supplied from A.R.P and the punch used for making holes in vanes (which spoils the bombs) has broken.	Fired. 6
	28/2/18.		Impossible to fire, on account of A.R.P sending MK I. Changes for a MK. III gun	

Casualties for mth:- 1 man wounded.

Fired during mth:- 38 rds.

A5834 Wt. W4973/M687 750,000 8/16 D. D. & L. Ltd. Forms/C.2118/13.

V. 40 (HEAVY) TRENCH MORTAR BATTERY. No. .... Date 1/3/18

Norman Reid
Capt. R.F.A.
O.C. V. 40. T.M.B

X. 40. Trench Mortar Battery.

Instructions regarding War Diaries and Intelligence Summaries are contained in F. S. Regs., Par. II. and the Staff Manual respectively. Title pages will be prepared in manuscript.

WAR DIARY
or
INTELLIGENCE SUMMARY.
(Erase heading not required.)

Army Form C. 2118.

Place	Date	Hour	Summary of Events and Information	Remarks and references to Appendices
	1918 Feb			
N. of BULLECOURT	1.		Ammunition recesses improved in VALLEY SUPPORT and STRAY	
	2		Observation almost impossible. Fired 5 rds on New Work near MATCH ALLEY	
	3		Lieut T S Ward RFA to hospital	
	4 }		Work continued in enlarging ammunition recesses	
	5 }			
	6		15 rounds fired on new work near MATCH ALLEY	
	7		Work started on new Ammunition Recess at No 3 Gun KNUCKLE AVENUE	
	8.		24 rounds fired on "SOS" 6" TM Ammn Dump started in ECOUST	
	9		Post 5 in U 20 b selected as O.P. Wire laid	
	10		Work continued on new Ammn Recess	
	11		13 rounds fired on DOG TRENCH from VALLEY SUPPORT	
	12-17th		General work in sector: chiefly carrying of ammunn and No 3 Emplacement	
	18th		Preparations made in expectation of hostile attack on the 19th which did not come off	
	19th		Work completed on No 3 Emplacement	
	20		25 rounds fired on sunken road in U 15 C from No 3.	

A6945 Wt. W11422/M1160 350,000 12/16 D. D. & L. Forms/C./2118/14.

X 40 Trench Mortar Battery

Instructions regarding War Diaries and Intelligence Summaries are contained in F. S. Regs., Part II, and the Staff Manual respectively. Title pages will be prepared in manuscript.

WAR DIARY
or
INTELLIGENCE SUMMARY.
(Erase heading not required.)

Army Form C. 2118.

Place	Date	Hour	Summary of Events and Information	Remarks and references to Appendices
	1918 Feb			
N of BULLECOURT	21		36 rounds fired on sunken road in U.15.c and MATCH ALLEY	
			Night firing scheme introduced	
	22		Improvements made at No 3 position	
		1.30 pm	10 rounds fired on MATCH ALLEY	
		10 pm	10 rounds on sunken road in U.15.c	
	23		Work started on No 2 position in VALLEY SUPPORT	
		Night	20 rounds fired on junction of MATCH ALLEY and COPSE TRENCH	
	24		General work on emplacements.	
	25	9 pm	20 rounds fired on MATCH ALLEY	
	26	10.15 pm	15 rounds fired on T head in U.21.b	
		11 pm	15 rounds fired on suspected TM in U.15.a	
	27	7 am	5 rounds fired on sunken road in U.15.c	
		4 pm	6 rounds fired on suspected TM in U.15.a	
	28	8 am	9 rounds on the same target. Preparations made for shoot with Aeroplane observation.	
		11.15 pm	25 rounds fired on COPSE TRENCH in U.15.a - TRIDENT ALLEY + COPSE TR in U.15c	

A6945 Wt. W11422/M1160 350,000 12/16 D. D. & L. Forms/C./2118/14.

Fired during mth: - 253 rds. - Casualties: 1 OR to Hosp, Sick. 1 man wounded.

[illegible] O.C. X 40 T.M.B.

Instructions regarding War Diaries and Intelligence Summaries are contained in F. S. Regs., Part II. and the Staff Manual respectively. Title pages will be prepared in manuscript.

WAR DIARY

~~INTELLIGENCE SUMMARY~~.

(Erase heading not required.)

Y40 Trench Mortar Battery, Army Form C. 2118.

February, 1918.

Place	Date	Hour	Summary of Events and Information	Remarks and references to Appendices
ST. LEGER.	1st	-	Headquarters and rest billets of the Battery were located here throughout the month.	
CROISILLES.	1st	-	The Battery remained in action as shown in last month's diary. Advanced Headquarters were situated on the CROISILLES – HENDECOURT. road, and the gun positions were on the left of this road. At the beginning of the month four guns were in action, about six hundred yards in rear of the front line. Work was proceeding, however, on advanced positions in front of the Support Line, and also on Reserve Positions (the first Reserve position was made just outside CROISILLES on the FONTAINE road. Firing was carried out almost every day on such targets as offered themselves; many trench junctions were fired at, and also machine gun emplacements, trench mortar emplacements, suspected granatenwerfer and sniper's posts, and occupied dugouts. Routine work as above was carried out during the month, the only outstanding events being as follows.	
do.	22nd	-	The Reserve Position on the CROISILLES – FONTAINE road was completed ready for use. Work was then commenced on a new position just outside ~~on~~ CROISILLES on the HÉNINEL road, this being some 600 yards in rear of the other.	
FONTAINE ~~do~~	25th ~~24th~~	9.30pm.	The enemy attempted to raid on of our posts south-west of the village,	

Instructions regarding War Diaries and Intelligence Summaries are contained in F. S. Regs., Part II. and the Staff Manual respectively. Title pages will be prepared in manuscript.

WAR DIARY
or
INTELLIGENCE SUMMARY.
(Erase heading not required.)

Y40 T.M.B.

Army Form C. 2118.

February, 1918 (continued).

Place	Date	Hour	Summary of Events and Information	Remarks and references to Appendices
			and in response to the S.O.S. signals sent up by the infantry, the Battery opened fire, and fired 50 rounds on to the FONTAINE-BULLECOURT road, in accordance with the pre-arranged plan.	
CROISILLES.	28th.	5pm.	The forward position was completed, and a gun was mounted here. Ammunition had been carried up and the gun was prepared for firing the following day.	
			Altogether 891 rounds were fired during the month. Casualties:- 1 man wounded.	
			M. Stanford Lieut. O.C. Y40 T.M.B.	

Instructions regarding War Diaries and Intelligence Summaries are contained in F. S. Regs., Part II. and the Staff Manual respectively. Title pages will be prepared in manuscript.

WAR DIARY
or
INTELLIGENCE SUMMARY.
(Erase heading not required.)

D.T.M.O. 40TH DIVISION. MARCH - 1918.

Vol 21

Army Form C. 2118.

Place	Date	Hour	Summary of Events and Information	Remarks and references to Appendices
ST. LEGER N of BULLE-COURT.	1 to 4		Batteries in action N. of BULLECOURT - Rest billets being at ST. LEGER.	
SOUASTRE	5 to 7		Left for SOUASTRE - going there on rest, re-fitting, etc.	
BOYELLES SOUASTRE	8		X Bty moved to BOYELLES in reserve in case of hostile attack. Y Bty remaining at SOUASTRE until 11th	
BOYELLES.	9 to		X Bty doing gun drill - marching drill, etc, at BOYELLES From the 12th to the 20th Y Bty. ~~were~~ ~~were~~ in reserve at	
BOIRY-ST-MARTIN	20		BOIRY-ST-MARTIN.	
BUCQUOY. BEAUMETZ. BOISLEUX-AU-MONT. MONCHY-AU-BOIS.	21 to 27		Consequent upon the enemy's great attack on the 21st, the Batteries had to retire to several places - BUCQUOY - BEAUMETZ - BOISLEUX-AU-MONT - MONCHY-AU-BOIS.	
COULLEMONT.	27		Batteries arrived at COULLEMONT to refit.	

[signature]

D.T.M.O. 40TH DIVISION

A7092 Wt W128 9/M1293 750,000. 1/17. D. D & L., Ltd. Forms/C2118/14.

X. 40. Trench Mortar Battery.

Instructions regarding War Diaries and Intelligence Summaries are contained in F. S. Regs., Part II. and the Staff Manual respectively. Title pages will be prepared in manuscript.

WAR DIARY
or
INTELLIGENCE SUMMARY.
(*Erase heading not required.*)

March.

Army Form C. 2118.

Place	Date	Hour	Summary of Events and Information	Remarks and references to Appendices
St. Leger.	1/3/18 to 3/3/18.		In action between Fontaine les Croisilles & Bullecourt. (5 guns). Firing daily & building new & alternative emplacements.	
	3/3/18.		Handed over to X/34. T.M.B.	
	4/3/18.		Left for Souastre for Divisional Rest.	
Souastre.	5/3/18 to 7/3/18		Souastre. Drilling &c. Inspection by Corps Commander.	
	8/3/18.		Left for Boyelles to be in reserve in case of hostile attack.	
Boyelles.	9/3/18 to 20/3/18		Guns supplied (10) beds, sub. beds &c. Gun drill, marching drill &c. New men & men from V. 40. T.M.B. trained in 6" Newtons.	
	21/3/18		Hun attack on 50 mile front. Slight progress near Boyelles.	
	22/3/18.		Awaiting orders. Shelled by shrapnel & 6" H.V. gun.	
	23/3/18 to 24/3/18		Enemy advance. When our front line was ridge in front of Boyelles, Guns, Ordnance, Kits &c. were got away in various passing lorries, Decauville train &c. &	X. 40 TRENCH MORTAR BATTERY. No. ... Date 31/3/18.
Bucquoy.			collected again at Boileux-au-Mont & Bucquoy. Moved to Bucquoy.	
Monchy-au-Bois	26/3/18		Left Bucquoy for Monchy-au-Bois. Lorries commandeered to move guns to Beaumetz	
Beaumetz	27/3/18		Left for Coullemont 28th at Coullemont.	
	29/3/18		Officers & 40 O.R. go to Field Batteries temporarily to assist & were so employed to end of month.	

Norman Reid Capt RFA.
O.C. X.40. T.M.B.

Y/40. Trench Mortar Battery

Instructions regarding War Diaries and Intelligence Summaries are contained in F. S. Regs., Part II. and the Staff Manual respectively. Title pages will be prepared in manuscript.

WAR DIARY
or
~~INTELLIGENCE~~ SUMMARY.
(Erase heading not required.)

March 1918.

Army Form C. 2118.

Place	Date	Hour	Summary of Events and Information	Remarks and references to Appendices
ST. LEGER	1.3.18 – 4.3.18		Battery in action east of CROISILLES.	
	4.3.18		Relief of battery by 34th Division Trench Mortars.	
SOUASTRE	5.3.18 – 11.3.18		Battery in rest at SOUASTRE refitting and reorganising.	
BOIRY-ST-MARTIN	12.3.18		The battery moved into VI th Corps reserve at BOIRY ST MARTIN	
	13th – 21.3.18		Battery in reserve.	
BUCQUOY	22.3.18		The battery withdrew according to plan to position in BUCQUOY.	
	24.3.18		The battery provided personnel to man ammunition refilling point at GOMIECOURT. Nearly all the kit was lost here.	
MONCHY.	25.3.18		The battery moved to MONCHY-AU-BOIS.	
	26.3.18		The battery moved surplus artillery kit to DOULLENS and in the evening retired to BRAUMETZ.	
COUILLEMONT	27.3.18		The battery arrived at COUILLEMONT to refit.	
	30.3.18 & 31.3.18		The battery moved forward to assist the divisional artillery who were tired out.	

R J Hammond
Capt RFA
OC Y/40 TM Bty.

2353 Wt. W2544/1454 700,000 5/15 D. D. & L. A.D.S.S./Forms/C. 2118.

X. 40. Trench Mortar Battery

WAR DIARY
or
INTELLIGENCE SUMMARY.
(Erase heading not required.)

April 1918.

40 DTM Bty

Army Form C. 2118.

Instructions regarding War Diaries and Intelligence Summaries are contained in F. S. Regs., Part II. and the Staff Manual respectively. Title pages will be prepared in manuscript.

95/22

Place	Date	Hour	Summary of Events and Information	Remarks and references to Appendices
Gomiecourt	1/4/18.		Moved to Simencourt. Handed 6 six inch T.M's to T.M's Guards Div:	
Simencourt	2/4/18.		Sent 1 Officer & 20 men to 178 Bgde. R.F.A. to be attached to Batteries.	
"	7/4/18.		Moved to Gouy.	
Gouy	8/4/18.		20 men sent to 181 Bgde. R.F.A. for 2 days to dig gun pits.	
"	9/4/18.		1 Off. & 20 O.R. return from 178 Bgde. R.F.A.	
"	10/4/18		Moved to Rebreuviette. Drill &c. everyday	
Rebreuviette.	16/4/18.		" " Berles-au-Bois.	
Berles-au-Bois	20/4/18.		Drew 6 six inch T.M's from Ordnance. Sent 10 men to 178 Bgde. R.F.A.	
"	26/4/18.		Transferred 1 officer & 10 O.R. to Y 40. T.M.B. on latter's departure. Men return from 178 Bgde.	
"	27/4/18		Sent 12 O.R. to A.P.P. & 12 to 178 Bgde. R.F.A. for work	
"	28/29/30		3 Officers & 16 O.R. (mostly employed) remain at Berles-au-Bois.	

Norman Reid Capt. R.F.A.
O.C. X 40. T.M.B.
30.4.18

A6945 Wt. W11422/M1160 350,000 12/16 D. D. & L. Forms/C./2118/14.

Instructions regarding War Diaries and Intelligence Summaries are contained in F. S. Regs., Part II. and the Staff Manual respectively. Title pages will be prepared in manuscript.

WAR DIARY
or
~~INTELLIGENCE SUMMARY.~~

(Erase heading not required.)

Y40 Trench Mortar Battery

Army Form C. 2118.

April, 1918.

Place	Date	Hour	Summary of Events and Information	Remarks and references to Appendices
SIMENCOURT	1st	—	The Battery was brought up from COULLEMONT when the remainder of the 40th Divisional Artillery went into action. It remained here until the 5th, when it was compelled to move, as it was out of the VI Corps area.	
GOUY-en-ARTOIS	5th	—	The Battery remained here until the withdrawal of the Divisional Artillery was contemplated, when it moved in anticipation of that relief.	
REBREUVIETTE	11th	—	The Battery stayed here, together with the 40th D.A.C., until it was decided that the Artillery should remain in the line. Consequently the Battery moved forward again.	
BERLES-au-BOIS	16th	—	Men were once more provided to assist the Field Batteries while the Headquarters of the Battery remained here. Preparations were made to put the Battery into action in support of the Guards Division, but on the 24th sudden orders were received that a move would be made under secret orders, by this Battery and the D.T.M.O.	
SAULTY	26th	9 a.m.	The Battery entrained at the railhead with orders to report at Abbeville.	
ABBEVILLE	27th	2 a.m.	Having arrived in the small hours of the morning, it was found that no orders were awaiting the Battery. The whole day was therefore spent in seeking instructions, which were eventually obtained from VI Corps. These were to entrain again for Valheureux, near Candas, and report to the Reserve Army School of Mortars. The Battery entrained once more at	

2353 Wt. W2544/1454 700,000 5/15 D. D. & L. A.D.S.S./Forms/C. 2118.

Instructions regarding War Diaries and Intelligence Summaries are contained in F. S. Regs., Part II. and the Staff Manual respectively. Title pages will be prepared in manuscript.

WAR DIARY
or
INTELLIGENCE SUMMARY.
(Erase heading not required.)

Y40 Trench Mortar Battery — Army Form C. 2118.

April 1918 (contd.)

Place	Date	Hour	Summary of Events and Information	Remarks and references to Appendices
			10 pm on the 28th.	
VALHEUREUX near CANDAS	29th	11 am	The Battery reported at the Reserve Army School of Mortars, and commenced a further Course of Instruction in conjunction with a Battery of the 52nd Division. This division having just arrived from Egypt, its Trench Mortar units were being formed at the School. This Battery was now transferred to the 52nd Division, and became Y52 Trench	
—	30.4.18	—	Mortar Battery.	

J Mark Stanford Lieut.
O.C. Y40 T.M.B.

Y/40 TRENCH MORTAR BATTERY.
No. April 1918
Date 30.4.18.

2353 Wt. W2544/1454 700,000 5/15 D. D. & L. A.D.S.S./Forms/C. 2118.

Instructions regarding War Diaries and Intelligence Summaries are contained in F. S. Regs., Part II. and the Staff Manual respectively. Title pages will be prepared in manuscript.

July

WAR DIARY
or
INTELLIGENCE SUMMARY.
(Erase heading not required.)

Army Form C. 2118.

40 DTM Bty

Vol 5

Place	Date	Hour	Summary of Events and Information	Remarks and references to Appendices
7	1st to 25th		X/40 & Y/40 Medium Trench Mortar Batteries reforming at Barly	
	5th		2/Lt Wm. Brown A/178 Brigade RFA posted to Y/40 M.T.M. Bty, on reformation	
	9th		Lieut F P Enright 10th S.W.B's att 115 LTM Bty posted to X/40 MTM Bty on reformation	
	17th		X/40 & Y/40 Medium Trench Mortar Batteries inspected by BRIG GEN C.E. PALMER CMG DSO RA CRA 40th DIVN Royal Artillery, at BARLY.	
	20th		4 officers and 39 other ranks proceeded on 6" Trench Mortar Course at 4th Army Trench Mortar School.	
	26th		a/D.T.M.O. Capt J G Beningfield RFA relieved 3rd Canadian T.M. Batteries in FISCHEUX SECTOR. X/40 T.M.B. HQ. Shelled by the enemy.	
	27th		Lt F.P. Enright made a tour of inspection of all reserve guns.	
	28th		Lt F.P. Enright visited (X/Y) Forward Gun, same being taken out of action and taken to Rear HQ Wailly	
	31st		Remaining personnel of X/40 and Y/40 M.T.M Batteries left BARLY and proceeded to HQ in action at WAILLY under orders of CRA 40th DIVN R.A	

Rowland Reid Capt RFA
D.T.M.O.
40 RA

D. D. & L., London, E.C.
(20360) Wt W5300/P713 750,000 3/18 E. 888 Forms/C2118/16

40th DIVNL TRENCH
MORTAR BATTERIES

Instructions regarding War Diaries and Intelligence Summaries are contained in F. S. Regs., Part II. and the Staff Manual respectively. Title pages will be prepared in manuscript.

WAR DIARY
~~or~~
~~INTELLIGENCE SUMMARY.~~
(Erase heading not required.)

FOR AUGUST 1918

Army Form C. 2118.

VR 23

Place	Date	Hour	Summary of Events and Information	Remarks and references to Appendices
	Aug 1st		Half personnel and officers away on a course at 4th Army School of Mortars. Remainder in action with one forward gun at M 35 d 45·88 S of MERCATEL and six Reserve guns covering PURPLE DEFENCE line near FICHEUX	
	Aug 1st		Half personnel returned from school of mortars, other half departed for 2 weeks course at 4th Army School of Mortars.	
	Aug 2nd to 14th		Forward gun inactive owing to lack of targets and lack of personnel and Officers. Reserve positions improved and altered.	
	Aug 15th		Another offensive mobile gun placed in action at M 35 d 55·51. Fired on hostile T.M's, posts etc. Fired 14 rounds	
	Aug 16th		In accordance with Army Order, Six more Reserve emplacements with one hundred rounds at each, commenced in PURPLE system of defence. Fired on various targets, Retaliation, Fired 36 Rounds.	
	Aug 17th		Fired Nil, Observation for shooting very bad.	
	Aug 18th		Fired 18 Rounds	
	Aug 19th		Fired Nil, Work continuing on Reserve positions with limited labour available	
	Aug 20th		Another Mobile T.M. placed in action at M 29 d 74·76 in order to shoot on DOG SAP, MYRTLE SAP etc. Mobile bed at M 35 d 55.51 broke in half and was replaced by sub. bed at M 32 d 42·90 Fired 16 Rounds	

D. D. & L., London E.C.
(10340) Wt W3300/P713 750,000 3/18 E 688 Forms/C2118/16.

40th Div Trench Mortar Batteries

WAR DIARY ~~or INTELLIGENCE SUMMARY.~~

For August 1918

Army Form C. 2118.

Instructions regarding War Diaries and Intelligence Summaries are contained in F. S. Regs., Part II. and the Staff Manual respectively. Title pages will be prepared in manuscript.

(Erase heading not required.)

Place	Date	Hour	Summary of Events and Information	Remarks and references to Appendices
	Aug 21st		Fired 11 Rounds	
	Aug 22nd		Another Mobile T M placed in action at S 25 d 83.22 to shoot near BOIRY BECQUERELLE for attack on 23rd. Fired in support of attack during night of 22nd/23rd Fired 29 Rounds.	
	Aug 23rd		Attack on HENIN TRENCH etc. All T.M's now out of range. Mobile T.M's could have been taken forward in support of advance, or captured light T.M's could have been used, but transport for ammunition was not available. Mobile Trench Mortars are of no use unless ammunition is made mobile.	
	Aug 24th 31st		Guns withdrawn to WAILLY - and in Reserve. Personnel assisting D.A.C. On 26th 2 officers and 50 other ranks returned from 4th Army Trench Mortar School.	
			Total number of rounds of ammunition fired during month 124	

Rowan Reid Capt RFA
D.T.M.O
40 RA

31/8/1918

D. D. & L., London E.C. (10340) W1 W3300/P713 750,000 3/18 E 688 Forms/C2118/16

X/Y/40. Trench Mortar Batteries. R.F.A.

Instructions regarding War Diaries and Intelligence Summaries are contained in F. S. Regs., Part II. and the Staff Manual respectively. Title pages will be prepared in manuscript.

WAR DIARY
or
INTELLIGENCE SUMMARY.
(Erase heading not required.)

~~October~~ September 1918. 40 D T M Bty

Army Form C. 2118.

Place	Date	Hour	Summary of Events and Information	Remarks and references to Appendices
WAILLY	1.9.18 to 11.9.18		All T.M. personnel attached to the D.A.C. to assist in supply of ammunition to the Batteries	
Quéant	11.9.18 to 25.9.18		4. 77 m.m. German Field Guns which had been overhauled by I.O.M. were obtained & put in action at D.11.d.9-5. near INCHY. (Sheet 57.C. N.E.) No firing was done by day except registration. During the night concentrations of Yellow Cross Gas were put down on various parts of BOURLON Wood and vicinity. Over 3000 rounds were fired. One gunner was wounded. During the night of 25th 26th, the guns were withdrawn.	Fired 3000 rounds. Yellow Cross Gas.
	27.9.18.		4. Officers & 50. O.R. proceeded about zero hour to canal crossings at E. 20.d.8-5. & under machine gun & Trench Mortar Fire, cleared the barbed wire, filled in trenches & made a crossing over the canal for the Batteries. 2. Officers (2/Lt. F.L. Gubbin & 2/Lt. W.J. Outland. R.F.A.) were wounded, & 1. man killed. & 1 wounded. D.T.M.O. was with attacking Brigade ready to give assistance of T.M's when necessary. Meanwhile Capt. J.L. Bruingfield R.F.A. with 4. German Mobile Light Trench Mortars & over 200 rounds of ammunition on G.S. wagons, crossed canal & picked up officers & men working there & proceeded to E.27.b.6-7. Near there 1. T.M. was got into action & in conjunction with 2 Tanks firing 6 Pdrs. fired a few rounds on enemy M.G's which were holding out about E.28.d.45-30. The T.M's were then taken up through Graincourt to ANNEUX & got into action on the edge of the village firing on enemy line ~~at~~ F26.	until T.M's got into action. He then formed them for remainder of operation
	28.9.18.		The attack being resumed at dawn the T.M's were withdrawn from ANNEUX. & proceeded up Bapaume - Cambrai Road. through FONTAINE. NOTRE-DAME. to La FOLIE. WOOD near CANAL de. L'ESCAUT. & got into action against MARCOING. LINE. (on both sides of the canal) which was	

(A7092). Wt. W12839/M1293. 750,000. 1/17. D. D. & L., Ltd. Forms/C.2118/14.

2

X Y/40. T.M. Batteries. R.F.A.

Instructions regarding War Diaries and Intelligence Summaries are contained in F. S. Regs., Part II. and the Staff Manual respectively. Title pages will be prepared in manuscript.

WAR DIARY
or
INTELLIGENCE SUMMARY.
(Erase heading not required.)

September

Army Form C. 2118.

Place	Date	Hour	Summary of Events and Information	Remarks and references to Appendices
FONTAINE-NOTRE-DAME.	28.9.18.		holding up our infantry by machine gun fire	
			That night all ammunition having been expended & all ranks being exhausted. Personnel were withdrawn for 24 hours. During operations 27/28. 226 rounds were fired against enemy strong points which were holding up the advance.	226 rounds of L.T.M. fired
			Casualties during 28th: 1. man Killed, & 3 wounded. Several animals were wounded.	
	30.9.18.		Personnel. (apart from guards on stores & Rit at ECOUST & QUÉANT) proceeded to FONTAINE-NOTRE-DAME. to get into action in PROVILLE.	
			Only 4 officers are left including the D.T.M.O.	

D.T.M.O.,
40TH DIVISION.
No. ....
Date 2.10.18

Norman Reid. Capt. RFA.
D.T.M.O.

(A7092). Wt. W12839/M1293. 750,000. 1/17. D. D. & L., Ltd. Forms/C.2118/14.

40th Division Trench Mortars. R.F.A.

WAR DIARY
or
INTELLIGENCE SUMMARY.

(Erase heading not required.)

October 1918.

Army Form C. 2118.

Vol 25

Instructions regarding War Diaries and Intelligence Summaries are contained in F. S. Regs., Part II. and the Staff Manual respectively. Title pages will be prepared in manuscript.

Place	Date	Hour	Summary of Events and Information	Remarks and references to Appendices
PROVILLE.	1.10.18.		In action against hostile M.G. posts with 4 Heavy light T.M's.	Fired
	2.10.18.		Fired 126 rounds against machine guns.	126
	3.10.18		" 162 " " "	162
	4.10.18		" 174 " " "	174
	5.10.18		" 246 " " " 1 gun destroyed by hostile fire.	246
	6.10.18		" 192 " " " 1 gun destroyed by premature. 1 man wounded.	192.
	7.10.18		" 100 " " "	100
			At midday 2 guns & ammunition were brought out of action & taken to ROMILLY, ready to go forward on 8th	
NIERGNIES.	8.10.18.		advanced from ROMILLY with three light T.M's in support of 63rd Division. T.M's were got into action on our posts at NIERGNIES against hostile M.G. posts on main Road & Cemetery.	
			Some 7.7.c.m. guns were also turned round & fired over open sights at those posts at a range of under 800x	
			Fired 160. Light T.M. (1 gun destroyed by enemy fire). 90 rounds of 7.7.c.m.	160 + 90.
			1 man killed & 3 wounded.	
AWOINGT.	9.10.18		2 long 7.7.c.m. were fired with streamline shell against roads, batteries etc. Fired 358. rounds.	358.
			3 men killed 2 wounded (1 very slight) & 2 officers (very slight)	
CAMBRAI. (RUE DE L'ARDRE)	10.10.18. 11.10.18		AVESNES, RIEUX etc. were reconnoitred with a view to finding & firing hostile guns & trench mortars. None of these were found.	
"	12.10.18.		Handed over to D.T.M.O. 61st Div.	
	13.10.18		Moved to PROVILLE.	
PROVILLE.	14.10.18		at. "	
"	15.10.18		with 6 lorries left for MORCHIES picking up stores etc. dumped at QUEANT & ECOUST.	

D. D. & L., London E.C.
(10340) Wt W5300/P713 750,000 3/18 E 658 Forms/C2118/16

2.

40th Div: Trench Mortars. R.F.A.

WAR DIARY
or
INTELLIGENCE SUMMARY.
(Erase heading not required.)

October 1918.

Army Form C. 2118.

Instructions regarding War Diaries and Intelligence Summaries are contained in F. S. Regs., Part II. and the Staff Manual respectively. Title pages will be prepared in manuscript.

Place	Date	Hour	Summary of Events and Information	Remarks and references to Appendices
MERCHIES.	16.10.18.		Lorries with 2 Off: & 30 O.R. proceeded by road to LAMOTTE. (FORÊT DE NIEPPE) 1 Officer & 50 O.R by train from BAPAUME.	
LAMOTTE.	17.10.18.		at LA MOTTE.	
ARMENTIERES	18.10.18.		Lorries & march to ARMENTIERES. Division at Rest.	
"	19.10.18 to 25.10.18		Training at ARMENTIÈRES.	
LANNOY.	26.10.18.		H.G.S. wagons for stores & personnel marched to LANNOY. S.E. of ROUBAIX	
	27.10.18		–	
"	28.10.18		PECQ & WARCOINGTC reconnoitred. Only Targets visible or Ruined are Belgian Civilians.	
"	29.10.18		Decided to put mobile 6" section in.	
	30.10.18		4 6" mobile T.M's obtained.	
	31.10.18			

Fired during month. Enemy Light T.M. 1160. rounds

" 77 c.m. 448. "

Total 1608 "

Norman Reid
Capt. R.F.A.
D.T.M.O.

D. D. & L., London E.C.
(10344) Wt W5300/P713 750,000 3/18 E 688 Forms/C2118/16

40th Div. Trench Mortars R.F.A.

Instructions regarding War Diaries and Intelligence Summaries are contained in F. S. Regs., Part II. and the Staff Manual respectively. Title pages will be prepared in manuscript.

WAR DIARY
or
~~INTELLIGENCE SUMMARY.~~
(Erase heading not required.)

November 1918.

Army Form C. 2118.

VR 26

Place	Date	Hour	Summary of Events and Information	Remarks and references to Appendices
LANNOY.	1/11/18. to 6/11/18.		Training. No targets to fire at. Only Belgian civilians.	
WARCOING and PECQ.	7.11.18. 8.11.18 9.11.18		3 guns in action in WARCOING & 1 in PECQ. Firing on Enemy M.G's } Fired 50 rounds. A L.G.S. & 4 forepart of L.G.S. 32 mules & 16 Drivers received }	
	10.11.18.		Enemy retired.	
WARCOING.	11 to 14 11.18.		at Warcoing training &c.	
WAMBRECHIES.	14.11.18		Moved to Wambrechies	
	15 to 30. 11.18.		Training. guards &c.	

Norman Reid. Capt. RFA.
D.T.M.O

Dec. 1st 1918.

D. D. & L., London E.C.
(10340) Wt W5300/P713 750,000 3/18 E 688 Forms/C2118/16.

December. 1918.

40. DIV. Trench Mortars. R.F.A.

WAR DIARY

or

~~INTELLIGENCE SUMMARY.~~

(Erase heading not required.)

Army Form C. 2118.

Instructions regarding War Diaries and Intelligence Summaries are contained in F. S. Regs., Part II. and the Staff Manual respectively. Title pages will be prepared in manuscript.

VIII 27

Place	Date	Hour	Summary of Events and Information	Remarks and references to Appendices
WAMBRECHIES	1/12/18 to 31/12/18.		In Billets training for ceremonial parades. recreational training. Guards on R.E. Dumps &c. A few Coal miners demobilized.	

Norman Reid Capt RFA.
D.T.M.O.

D.T.M.O.,
40th DIVISION.
No. ....
Date 31.12.18.

D. D. & L., London E.C. (10340) Wt W5300/P713 750,000 3/18 E 688 Forms/C2118/16.

Army Form C. 2118.

Instructions regarding War Diaries and Intelligence Summaries are contained in F. S. Regs., Part II. and the Staff Manual respectively. Title pages will be prepared in manuscript.

WAR DIARY
or
INTELLIGENCE SUMMARY.
(Erase heading not required.)

40th Medium Trench Mortar Batteries
40 Divisional Artillery

Place	Date	Hour	Summary of Events and Information	Remarks and references to Appendices
WAMBRECHIES	1.1.19		Usual Parades, Physical Training & Games Demobilization continued Strength Officers 3 OR's 96	
	to			
	31.1.19		Ditto Strength Officers 3 OR's 78	
			8/2/19 J Benningfield Capt RGA for DTMO 40 Div Arty	

D. D. & L., London E.C. (10340) Wt W5300/P713 750,000 3/18 E 688 Forms/C2118/16.

www.ingramcontent.com/pod-product-compliance
Lightning Source LLC
Chambersburg PA
CBHW080843010526
44114CB00017B/2361
* 9 7 8 1 4 7 4 5 1 9 3 9 7 *